AGNOTOLOGY

AGNOTOLOGY

The Making and Unmaking of Ignorance

Edited by Robert N. Proctor
and Londa Schiebinger

Stanford University Press
Stanford, California

Stanford University Press
Stanford, California

Printed in the United States of America on acid-free, archival-quality paper

Library of Congress Cataloging-in-Publication Data

Agnotology : the making and unmaking of ignorance / edited by Robert N. Proctor and Londa Schiebinger.
    p. cm.
  Includes bibliographical references and index.
  ISBN 978-0-8047-5652-5 (cloth : alk. paper) — ISBN 978-0-8047-5901-4 (pbk. : alk. paper)
    1. Ignorance (Theory of knowledge)—Social aspects—Congresses. 2. Secrecy—Congresses. I. Proctor, Robert, 1954– II. Schiebinger, Londa L.
  BD221.A36 2008
  001—dc22   2007049811

Portions of the following chapters have been previously published as indicated: CHAPTER 2: Peter Galison, "Removing Knowledge," *Critical Inquiry* 31 (2004): 229–243. © 2004, The University of Chicago. Reprinted by permission of The University of Chicago Press. CHAPTER 4: D. Michaels and C. Monforton, "Manufacturing Uncertainty: Contested Science and the Protection of the Public's Health and Environment, *American Journal of Public Health* 95 (2005): S39–S48. © 2005 American Public Health Association. CHAPTER 5: Nancy Tuana, "Coming to Understand: Orgasm and the Epistemology of Ignorance," *Hypatia: A Journal of Feminist Philosophy* 19 (2004): 194–232. © 2004 by Hypatia, Inc. Reprinted by permission of Indiana University Press. CHAPTER 6: Londa Schiebinger, *Plants and Empire: Colonial Bioprospecting in the Atlantic World.* © 2004 by Londa Schiebinger. Reprinted by permission of Harvard University Press. CHAPTER 7: Adrienne Mayor, *Fossil Legends of the First Americans.* © 2005 by Princeton University Press. Reprinted by permission of Princeton University Press. CHAPTER 10: Charles W. Mills, "White Ignorance," pp. 13–38 in *Race and Epistemologies of Ignorance*, Shannon Sullivan and Nancy Tuana, eds. © 2007 State University of New York Press. Reprinted by permission of State University of New York Press.

Designed by Bruce Lundquist
Typeset at Stanford University Press in 10/15 Sabon

Contents

Preface

WE LIVE IN AN AGE OF IGNORANCE, and it is important to understand how this came to be and why. Our goal here is to explore how ignorance is produced or maintained in diverse settings, through mechanisms such as deliberate or inadvertent neglect, secrecy and suppression, document destruction, unquestioned tradition, and myriad forms of inherent (or avoidable) culturopolitical selectivity. Agnotology is the study of ignorance making, the lost and forgotten. One focus is on knowledge that could have been but wasn't, or should be but isn't, but we shall also see that not all ignorance is bad.

Our primary purpose here is to promote the study of ignorance, by developing tools for understanding how and why various forms of knowing have "not come to be," or disappeared, or have been delayed or long neglected, for better or for worse, at various points in history. Swimming as we do in oceans of ignorance, examples could be multiplied ad infinitum. Contributors to this volume probe the secrecy maintained by military classification, the "doubt" peddled by manufacturers of carcinogens ("doubt is our product"), the denialist claims of environmental troglodytes, the nontransfer of technologies (such as birth control) from colonial outposts to imperial centers, the role of disciplinarity and media "balance routines" on agnogenesis, and certain aspects of racial and sexual ignorance. The idea is that a great deal of attention has been given to epistemology (the study of how we know) when "how or why we don't know" is often just as important, usually far more scandalous, and remarkably undertheorized.

This volume emerged from workshops held at Pennsylvania State University in 2003 and at Stanford University in 2005, the goal of which was to come to grips with how ignorance has been understood, created, and ignored, linking these ideas also to allied creations of secrecy, uncertainty, confusion, silence, absence, and impotence—especially as these pertain to scientific activities. For financial support, we owe a debt of gratitude to the National Science Foundation—and at Penn State, to the Science, Medicine, and Technology in Culture initiative, the Institute for Arts and Humanities, the Rock Ethics Institute, and the departments of History, English, and Anthropology. At Stanford we are also grateful to the History & Philosophy of Science, the Suppes Center, the Humanities Center, Modern Thought and Literature, and the Stanford Center for Biomedical Ethics. We are also thankful for administrative help provided by Rosemary Rogers, Michelle Cale, and Jeanette Jenkins.

We are hoping this volume will be taken as opening a door to a broader realm of inquiry. We invite others to step through this door, and to explore the many other realms of ignorance that saturate and define our world.

AGNOTOLOGY

CHAPTER I

Agnotology

A Missing Term to Describe the Cultural
Production of Ignorance (and Its Study)

ROBERT N. PROCTOR

We are often unaware of the scope and structure of our ignorance. Ignorance
is not just a blank space on a person's mental map. It has contours and coher-
ence, and for all I know rules of operation as well. So as a corollary to writing
about what we know, maybe we should add getting familiar with our ignorance.
Thomas Pynchon, 1984

Doubt is our product.
Brown & Williamson Tobacco Company, internal memo, 1969

PHILOSOPHERS LOVE TO TALK ABOUT KNOWLEDGE. A whole field
is devoted to reflection on the topic, with product tie-ins to professor-
ships and weighty conferences. *Epistemology* is serious business, taught
in academies the world over: there is "moral" and "social" epistemology,
epistemology of the sacred, the closet, and the family. There is a Compu-
tational Epistemology Laboratory at the University of Waterloo, and a
Center for Epistemology at the Free University in Amsterdam. A Google
search turns up separate websites for "constructivist," "feminist," and
"evolutionary" epistemology, of course, but also "libidinal," "android,"
"Quaker," "Internet," and (my favorite) "erotometaphysical" epistemology. Harvard offers a course in the field (without the erotometaphysical
part), which (if we are to believe its website) explores the epistemic status
of weighty claims like "the standard meter is 1 meter long" and "I am not
a brain in a vat."[1] We seem to know a lot about knowledge.[2]

What is remarkable, though, is how little we know about ignorance.[3]
There is not even a well-known word for its study (though our hope is to

change that), no fancy conferences or polished websites. This is particularly remarkable, given (a) how much ignorance there is, (b) how many kinds there are, and (c) how consequential ignorance is in our lives.

The point of this volume is to argue that there is much, in fact, to know. Ignorance has many friends and enemies, and figures big in everything from trade association propaganda to military operations to slogans chanted at children. Lawyers think a lot about it, since it often surfaces in consumer product liability and tort litigation, where the question is often "Who knew what, and when?" Ignorance has many interesting surrogates and overlaps in myriad ways with—as it is generated by—*secrecy*, *stupidity*, *apathy*, *censorship*, *disinformation*, *faith*, and *forgetfulness*, all of which are science-twitched. Ignorance hides in the shadows of philosophy and is frowned upon in sociology, but it also pops up in a great deal of popular rhetoric: it's no excuse, it's what can't hurt you, it's bliss. Ignorance has a history and a complex political and sexual geography, and does a lot of other odd and arresting work that bears exploring.

And deploring—though we don't see inquiry in this area as necessarily having the goal of *rectification*. Ignorance is most commonly seen (or trivialized) in this way, as something in need of correction, a kind of natural absence or void where knowledge has not yet spread. As educators, of course, we are committed to spreading knowledge. But ignorance is more than a void—and not even always a bad thing. No one needs or wants to know everything all the time; and surely all of us know things we would rather others not know. A founding principle of liberal states is that omniscience can be dangerous, and that some things should be kept private. Rights to privacy are essentially a form of sanctioned ignorance: liberal governments are (supposed to be) barred from knowing everything; inquisitors must have warrants. Juries are also supposed to be kept ignorant, since knowledge can be a form of bias. There is virtuous ignorance, in the form of resistance to (or limits placed on) dangerous knowledge.[4]

The causes of ignorance are multiple and diverse. Not many people know that the biggest building in the world is a semi-secret facility built to produce explosive uranium-235, using enormous magnets, near a nondescript town in southern Ohio (Piketon); but that is for reasons that are different from why we don't know much about the origin of life, or anything at all about time before the Big Bang circa 14 billion years ago. And there are many different ways not to know. Ignorance can be the flipside of memory, what we don't know because we have forgotten, parts of which can be restored by historical inquiries but most of which is forever lost. (And we often cannot say which.) Ignorance can be made or unmade, and science can be complicit in either process.

THE PURPOSE OF THE PRESENT VOLUME is programmatic, to begin a discussion of ignorance as more than the "not yet known" or the steadily retreating frontier. We need to think about the conscious, unconscious, and structural production of ignorance, its diverse causes and conformations, whether brought about by neglect, forgetfulness, myopia, extinction, secrecy, or suppression. The point is to question the *naturalness* of ignorance, its causes and its distribution. Why have so few Americans heard about the *Nakba*? Why did epidemiologists miss the high levels of pellagra among early-twentieth-century African Americans?[5] How did World War I-era research into the reproductive effects of alcohol become "scientifically uninteresting"?[6] Why have today's geneticists developed a "collective amnesia" about Francis Galton?[7] Why do "we" (many men and surely fewer women) know so little about the clitoris (see Nancy Tuana, this volume), or laws of nature classified for national security, or indigenous abortifacients (see Londa Schiebinger, this volume), or the countless Xs or Ys or Zs that we cannot even name, given how low they fly under the radar?

Now, certain kinds of exploration require that we make distinctions; that is a reasonable first step into understanding. "Cutting up" and "dividing into parts" is implicit in the etymology of *scientia*, which derives from the proto-Indo-European *skein*, via the Latin *seco* and *scindo* (to cut), from which we get *scissors* and *schism*, *scat* and *skin*. There must be as many kinds of ignorance as of knowledge—perhaps more, given how scant is our knowledge compared to the vastness of our ignorance. And though distinctions such as these are somewhat arbitrary, I shall make three to begin the discussion: ignorance as *native state* (or resource), ignorance as *lost realm* (or selective choice), and ignorance as a deliberately engineered and *strategic ploy* (or active construct). There are of course other ways to divide this pie, and several of the contributors to this volume provide alternative taxonomies.

IGNORANCE AS NATIVE STATE

This may be the most common way that scientists think about our topic: ignorance is like Kansas, a great place to be from. Knowledge grows out of ignorance, as a flower from honest soil, but the direction of movement is pretty much one way. Here, though, ignorance can also be a *prompt* for knowledge, insofar as we are constantly striving to destroy it—fact by fact. Ignorance has both an ontogeny and a phylogeny: babies start out ignorant and slowly come to know the world; hominids have become sapient over millions of years from the happy accident of upright posture and not knowing what to do with our idle hands. (I personally favor the theory that bipedalism enabled us to "put things in quotes" with our newly freed fingers.)

Ignorance in this sense of a primitive or native state is something to be fought or overcome; we hope and plan for it to disappear over time, as knowledge triumphs over foolish superstition. Ignorance is not necessarily evil—it can be innocent (as knowledge can be sin). But it seems to be something we are all supposed to want to grow out of, to put behind us, in the process of generating (or acquiring) knowledge. Johannes Kepler in the sixteenth century had a rather brutal way of putting it: ignorance was "the mother who must die for science to be born."[8]

And foolish ignorance abounds. Jay Leno makes good sport interviewing people who don't know whether the Earth has one or two moons, or what day of the week Good Friday lands on. More serious is the fact that 52 percent of all Americans answer "yes" when asked whether "the earliest humans lived at the same time as the dinosaurs."[9] Science educators (and all thinking people) worry about the fact that about half of all Americans believe the Earth is only 6,000 years old, among them several former and living presidents. Ronald Reagan once proclaimed in a televised speech that America was great "because it has never known slavery"; ignorance seems to know no bounds.

Ignorance in this sense of "native" or "originary" state implies a kind of deficit, caused by the naiveté of youth or the faults of improper education—or the simple fact that here is a place where *knowledge has not yet penetrated*. Ignorance is compared to innocence or, in the secular variant, knowledge in its infancy, with ontogeny more or less recapitulating phylogeny.[10] Scientists often cherish this kind of ignorance, using it as a prompt to inquiry. There is the familiar grant application version: we know this and that but not yet this other thing—so fund me please! Fill this gaping hole (which also happens to be my pocketbook)! Less cynical renditions are familiar from the history of philosophy: Socrates taught that the truly wise are those who realize how little they know; knowledge of one's ignorance is a precondition for enlightenment. The modern twist has ignorance as something to be escaped but also as a kind of rejuvenating force, since it is only by asking the right questions—by knowing wherein fruitful (that is, eradicable) ignorance lies—that we can ever come to knowledge.[11] Creative intellects are ignorance experts: they know where it can be found, and how to make it go away.

Modernity gives this a greater sense of urgency, insofar as ignorance becomes a kind of *vacuum* or hollow space into which knowledge is pulled. Science rushes in to fill the void, or rushes out to greet the world, if we recall the birthing metaphor of Kepler. Psychoanalytics aside, we could give various names to this theory of ignorance. I have called it *native ignorance*, because the notion is of a kind of *infantile absence* by virtue of primitivity, a dearth or cavity that is rectified (filled) by growth or birth—though other metaphors are used. Light floods the darkness, keys are found to unlock locks, ignorance is washed away, teaching uplifts out of ignorance, which is thereby destroyed or chased, and so forth.[12]

Ignorance here is seen as a *resource*, or at least a spur or challenge or prompt: ignorance is needed to keep the wheels of science turning. New ignorance must forever be rustled up to feed the insatiable appetite of science. The world's stock of ignorance is not being depleted, however, since (by wondrous fortune and hydra-like) two new questions arise for every one answered. Some veils of ignorance are pushed aside but others always pop up, saving us from the end of inquiry. This regenerative power of ignorance makes the scientific enterprise sustainable. The nightmare would be if we were somehow to run out of ignorance, idling the engines of knowledge production. We need ignorance to fuel our knowledge engines. Science is sustainable because ignorance proliferates, a triumph not foreseen by early champions of modernity. Bacon and Descartes both envisioned a time in the not so distant future—perhaps within their own lifetimes—when all scientific problems would be solved—but later Moderns knew a good thing when they saw it, and how to keep it going.

A vast literature exists on how to escape from ignorance, including the recognition that learning often implies a process of "unlearning" (try any of the 542,000 Google hits for this term). But there is also the appreciation that the *distribution of ignorance is unequal,* hence the digital divide, remedialisms of various sorts, and so forth. Technologies can cause the proliferation of ignorance: "the public seems to be awakening to the fact that in the midst of the 'information' explosion, there has been an 'ignorance' explosion as well."[13] Media analyst Sut Jhally in 1991 made headlines when he found that people were misinformed about the Gulf War in direct proportion to how much TV they had watched on the topic.[14] Radio was early on criticized as a vehicle for propaganda (spreading ignorance, as was often said), and Walter Benjamin discussed the quaint idea from the 1920s that film could lead to a kind of dictatorship of the imagination, via an enforced railroading of the eye (versus the freedom purportedly allowed by static graphic arts).[15] The Internet has certainly fostered the spread of fictions along with facts—as when South Africa's president Thabo Mbeki "during a late-night Internet surfing session" happened on, and became convinced by, a website challenging the view that HIV was the cause of AIDS.[16] The president's views were later used to justify a slowdown in efforts to combat exposure to the virus.

Our interest here, though, is less in remediation than in what Nancy Tuana has called the "liberatory moment"—which brings us to a more subtle form of agnotology.

IGNORANCE AS LOST REALM, OR
SELECTIVE CHOICE (OR PASSIVE CONSTRUCT)

This second variant recognizes that ignorance, like knowledge, has a political geography, prompting us to ask: Who knows not? And why not? Where is there ignorance and why? Like knowledge or wealth or poverty, ignorance has a face, a house, and a price: it is encouraged here and discouraged there from ten thousand accidents (and deliberations) of social fortune. It is less like a vacuum than a solid or shifting body—which travels through time and occupies space, runs roughshod over people or things, and often leaves a shadow. Who at Hiroshima did not know to leave the city that day, and turned into a shadow on the asphalt?

Part of the idea is that inquiry is always selective. We look *here* rather than *there*; we have the predator's fovea (versus the indiscriminate watchfulness of prey), and the decision to focus on *this* is therefore invariably a choice to ignore *that*. Ignorance is a product of inattention, and since we cannot study all things, some by necessity—almost all, in fact—must be left out. "A way of seeing is also a way of not seeing—a focus upon object A involves a neglect of object B."[17] And the world is very big—much bigger than the world of Descartes and Bacon, with their hopes for an imminent finish to the project of science. A key question, then, is: how should we regard the "missing matter," knowledge not yet known? Is science more like the progressive illumination of a well-defined box, or does darkness grow as fast as the light?

Both images are common. Selectivity is often conceived as transient, evanescent, a kind of "noise" in the system or scatter about the line, with bias slowly being rectified. Science is like mowing your lawn: you can choose any place to start, but things end up looking pretty much the same. I was recently faced with a succinct (albeit unpleasant) version of this in a peer review of a grant proposal of mine to the National Science Foundation. This rather disgruntled hooded "peer" was unhappy with my request for funds to study the history of paleoanthropology, given my failure to recognize, as he or she put it, that science was biased "*only in the past, but not in the present.*" In this undialogic context I did not have the opportunity to respond to this wonderfully self-refuting chestnut, which soured as soon as it was uttered; I couldn't point out that errors often do languish, projects go unfunded, opportunities are lost, the dead do not spring back to life, and justice does not always prevail—even in science. This is a different sense of selectivity: that knowledge switched onto one track cannot always return to areas passed over; we don't always have the opportunity to correct old errors.[18] Research lost is not just research delayed; it can also be forever marked or never recovered.

Londa Schiebinger describes a clear instance of agnotology of this sort in her essay for this volume. The background here is that for three or four centuries following the first transits of the Atlantic and circumnavigations of Africa, European monarchs and trading companies sent out ships in search of fame or fortune, conquering and colonizing but also capturing knowledge and wealth from far-flung territories. Not all knowledge gained in the peripheries flowed back to the center, however. The passage was unequal in that only certain *kinds* of goods were imported, while others were ignored. Abortifacients in particular were excluded: African and European women knew many different ways to prevent childbirth, but these were judged irrelevant to the kind of knowledge/extraction projects favored by the colonizing Europeans. The potato was fine, as was quinine from the bark of the *Cinchona* tree (for malaria), but not the means by which (white) women might have prevented conception or caused abortion. European governments were trying to grow their populations and conquer new territories, for which they needed quinine but not the peacock flower (the abortifacient described by Sibylla Maria Merian in 1710). Methods of contraception or abortion were low on the list of priorities, and the plants used for such purposes by the indigenes were simply ignored.

It may well be that no *decision* was ever made to ignore or destroy such knowledge. It is not hard to imagine an "overdetermined" mix of deliberate and inadvertent neglect, though the boundary between these two is not always clear. The mechanisms involved in producing or maintaining ignorance can change over time, and once things are made unknown—by suppression or by apathy—they can often remain unknown without further effort. Once lost or destroyed, a document or a species or a culture does not spring back to life. Diego de Landa must have known this when he burned the Mayan royal libraries at Mani on the Yucatán in 1562, defending this act of cultural vandalism with the argument that such codices contained only "superstitions and lies of the devil." This bridges into our next form of agnogenesis: the deliberate production of ignorance in the form of strategies to deceive.

IGNORANCE AS STRATEGIC PLOY, OR ACTIVE CONSTRUCT

The focus here is on ignorance—or doubt or uncertainty—as something that is made, maintained, and manipulated by means of certain arts and sciences. The idea is one that easily lends itself to paranoia: namely, that certain people don't want you to know certain things, or will actively work to organize doubt or uncertainty or misinformation to help maintain (your) ignorance.

They know, and may or may not want you to know they know, but you are not to be privy to the secret. This is an idea insufficiently explored by philosophers, that ignorance should not be viewed as a simple omission or gap, but rather as an active production. Ignorance can be an actively engineered part of a deliberate plan. I'll begin with trade secrets, moving from there in the next three sections to tobacco agnotology, military secrecy, and the example of ignorance making (or maintenance) as moral resistance.

There have always been lots of reasons to keep things secret—for love, for war, for business, for every conceivable human desire or enterprise.[19] Thought itself, of course, is secret until expressed in perishable verbal form, or in the more durable medium of print or some other enduring mode of capture. Secrets are as old as human thought and perhaps older still, judging from the fantastic variety of animal techniques of deception, ranging from insect camouflage to predators stashing their prey to the myriad disguises of herbivores. Recall how the white underbellies of deer and most other ungulates help turn these animals into non-objects by canceling shadows.

Science and trade are often said to be (or forced) open, but secrecy plays an important role in both realms—think of peer review, or the jealous guarding of discoveries until publication. Science and industry are increasingly interwoven, with R&D pursued under cloaks of privacy to maintain some business advantage. Science even in the best of circumstances is "open" only under highly ritualized constraints. The point of confidential peer review, for example, is to guarantee objectivity—here a kind of balanced fairness—to allow one's peers to criticize without fear of recrimination. Blinded review comes at a cost, however, since it means that an author—the recipient of criticism in this instance—cannot "consider the source." Reviewers can also act without taking responsibility for their opinions, except insofar as an editor or grant officer takes this into account.[20] A similar weakness plagues Wikipedia-style publishing, though preservation of page histories makes it at least theoretically possible to minimize vandalism (the bigger problem here is the perpetual "balance of terror" produced on controversial topics such as intelligent design).

Scientific secrecy long predates peer review. Alchemy and astrology were often advertised as occult sciences, in the sense of harnessing dark powers but also of being practiced in the dark, hidden from view.[21] The two senses were intertwined, since the principles sought were supposed to lie behind or beyond ordinary kinds of knowledge that flourished in the light. Much of early modern science was also guild-like, insofar as "secrets of the trade" were taken for granted. Trade secrets were guarded to control access to a particular kind of technique, resource, ritual, or market. Much of the rhetoric of the so-called Scientific Revolution was directed toward eliminating secrecy, to open up practices to inspection—whence the omnipresent rhetorics of "light," "clarification," and eventually "enlightenment." Alchemy done in the light became chemistry.

Trade secrets are still a vital part of manufacturing,[22] however, and it is probably not far from the mark to say that older forms of secrecy have simply been replaced by newer ones. A great deal of modern chemistry is tied up with industrial production, making it hard to speak of an open exchange of ideas. Three or four people are supposed to know the formula for Coca-Cola, locked in a vault in Atlanta; the same is true for the spices used in Kentucky Fried Chicken (in Louisville) and many other celebrated consumables.[23] Publication is one way of claiming intellectual property, but ideas are also often shared "openly" only within some restricted social space. Military technologies are an obvious example, but there is a great deal of private speech inside law firms, hospitals, governments, and every other kind of institution, for whom knowledge is not just power but *danger*—which is why institutional amnesia may be as valued as institutional memory. Within academia, scholars will often keep certain ideas secret or limit their circulation to avoid improper use; and it is only after publication that circulation becomes difficult to control. Information flows are also limited for legal or PR purposes, or for reasons of national security. The apparent free flow of ideas celebrated in academia is actually circumscribed by the things that make it onto the public table; I taught at Pennsylvania State University for almost a dozen years before I stumbled onto a department called "Undersea Warfare," which is also about how long it took for me to learn that Penn State was the official university of the United States Marine Corps. I don't know how many of my former colleagues were aware of either of these closely held facts.

But there are other ways ignorance is crafted, and one of the most dramatic examples stems from the black arts of tobacco manufacturers.

Tobacco Industry Agnotology

One of my favorite examples of *agnogenesis* is the tobacco industry's efforts to manufacture doubt about the hazards of smoking. It was primarily in this context (along with military secrecy) that I first began exploring this idea of manufactured ignorance,[24] the question again being "Why don't we know what we don't know?" The none-too-complex answer in many instances was "because steps have been taken to keep you in the dark!" We rule you, if we can fool you. No one has done this more effectively than the tobacco mongers, the masters of fomenting ignorance to combat knowledge. Health fears are assuaged by reassurances in the form of "reasonable doubt"—a state of mind with both PR and legal value. The logic is simple, but it also has some devious twists and turns. I'll deal here only with the U.S. case, though the duplicity project is now being franchised globally to buttress the continued sale of 5.7 trillion cigarettes per annum, enough to circle the Earth some 13,000 times.

Marketing has always involved a certain persuasion bordering on deception, insofar as laundry soap is pretty much the same throughout the world. The tobacco industry early on recognized health concerns as market impediments, which is why L&M Filters were offered as "just what the doctor ordered," Camels were said to be smoked by "more doctors," and so forth. The industry was barred from making such claims in the 1950s and moved to more subtle inducements, associating smoking with youth, vigor, and beauty, and later freedom, risk, and rebellion. For a time in the 1980s, when health infringements centered around secondhand smoke, we were told that smoking was a form of free speech. The industry likes to have it both ways: smoking is patriotic yet rebellious, risky yet safe, calming yet exciting, and so forth.

Marketing tools of a novel sort were introduced in the early 1950s, following the explosion of evidence that cigarettes were killing tens of thousands every year. Responding to this evidence, the industry launched a multimillion dollar campaign to reassure consumers that the hazard had not yet been "proven." Through press releases, advertisements, and well-funded industry research fronts, epidemiology was denounced as "mere statistics," animal experiments were said not to reflect the human condition, and lung pathologies revealed at autopsy were derided as anecdotes without "sound science" as backing. Cigarette manufacturers often invoked the laboratory as the site where the "controversy" would be resolved, knowing that it was difficult to mimic human smoking harms using animal models. Small animals just don't contract cancer from breathing smoke; it takes twenty or thirty or more years for human smokers to develop cancer, and rats don't live that long. And even when cancers were successfully produced in mice (by painting tobacco tars on their shaven backs), the industry admitted only the presence of "mouse carcinogens" in smoke. Cigarette apologists worked in a conveniently tight logical circle: no evidence was good enough, no experiment close enough to the human condition. True proof was hard to have short of experimenting on humans—but do you really want us to experiment on humans? What are you, some kind of Nazi?

We don't yet know what evil genius came up with the scheme to associate the continued manufacture of cigarettes with prudence, using the call for "more research" to slow the threat of regulation, but it must rank as one of the greatest triumphs of American corporate connivance.[25] The idea was that people would continue to smoke so long as they could be reassured that "no one really knows" the true cause of cancer. The strategy was to question all assertions to the contrary, all efforts to "close" the controversy, as if closure itself were a mark of dogma, the enemy of inquiry. The point was to keep the question of health harms open, for decades if possible. Cancer after all was a complex disease with multiple causes, all of which would have to be explored without rushing to any kind of judgment. We owed as much to those poor souls suffering from this terrible scourge, we had to keep an open mind, leaving the question of causation open. Do you want to close down research? Can't you keep an open mind?

Establishing and maintaining "the tobacco controversy" was a key element in the industry's PR strategy from the beginnings of the modern conspiracy in the 1950s. Controversy was like hope, something you (they) wanted to keep alive. Interminable controversy had an immediate value in keeping smokers smoking and legislators pliable. It eventually also had a legal value, insofar as the industry could claim it had never *denied* the hazards, but had only called for further evidence. The idea of "no proof" becomes one of the two main pillars of the industry's defense against law-suits, the other being *common knowledge*: everyone has always known

about the dangers, so smokers have only themselves to blame for whatever illnesses they may contract. *Universal awareness* was matched with
open controversy: everyone *knew* that cigarettes are harmful, but no one
had ever *proven* it.[26]

The strategy is a clever one, though it does require that we adopt a
rather broad rift between popular and scientific knowledge. In court, the
industry's experts do some fancy dancing to make this work, pointing
to historical examples of "folk" wisdom predating scientific knowledge,
with more "cautious" confirmations coming only later. Folk healers use an
herb to effect a cure, but it takes some time for doctors to accept this and
grasp how it works. So while *popular* belief may recognize that tobacco
is hazardous, the *science* has been much harder to nail down. In court,
the industry's experts like to emphasize the continuance of "legitimate
scientific doubt" long past even the Surgeon General's report of 1964.
Kenneth Ludmerer, a St. Louis medical historian and frequent witness
for the industry, recently claimed under cross-examination that there was
"room for responsible disagreement" with the hazards consensus even
after the Surgeon General's report. Indeed, he says, "There's always room
for disagreement."[27]

A crucial issue in many lawsuits is whether the industry acted respon-
sibly in denying any proof of a hazard. "Common knowledge" and "open
controversy" come to the rescue, the hoped-for point being that since everyone has always known that cigarettes are dangerous, the manufacturers
can't be faulted for failing to warn. The establishment of controversy in
the scientific community is also crucial, though, because it gives cigarette
makers yet another excuse for negligence in failing to warn. Why did the
industry not warn smokers of a hazard? Because the issue had not been
settled! No proof was forthcoming—so the industry maintained, duplici-
tously[28]—so we cannot say it acted irresponsibly.[29]

The tobacco industry was rarely innocent in any of these respects,
since its goal at many points was to *generate* ignorance—or sometimes
false knowledge—concerning tobacco's impact on health. The industry
was trebly active in this sphere, feigning its *own* ignorance of hazards,
while simultaneously affirming the *absence of definite proof* in the scientific community, while also doing all it could to *manufacture ignorance*

on the part of the smoking public. This last-mentioned goal was achieved by many different means, including release of duplicitous press releases, publication of "nobody knows the answers" white papers, and funding decoy or red-herring research to distract from genuine hazards (which also functioned as "alibi research" in subsequent litigation). Common knowledge was really only a legal arguing point—the reality desired by the industry was common ignorance (to keep people smoking). "Smoke-screen" is an appropriate epithet, but we could also talk about disestablishing facts, via several key strategies.

One was simply to conceal whatever hazards the industry knew about, but another was to fund research that would *seem* to be addressing tobacco and health, while really doing nothing of the sort. The chief instrument for this was the Tobacco Industry Research Council (TIRC), established in 1954 with great fanfare in full-page ads published in 448 of the nation's leading newspapers. The TIRC (later renamed the Council for Tobacco Research) eventually funded hundreds of millions of dollars of research, very little of which had anything to do with smoking. Little of it ever addressed the question supposedly in doubt: whether and to what extent cigarettes are bad for your health. The political value of research of this kind (mostly basic biochemistry) was the *fact of its being funded*—which allowed the industry to say it was "studying the problem." Industry researchers knew from the beginning what they were supposed to find (and not find): per instructions from the Tobacco Institute, the TIRC was supposed to manifest confidence that "we do not now know what causes lung cancer or any other kind of cancer."[30] Press releases and publications from the industry beat this drum pretty hard. In lawyerly fashion, health implications were thought of as "charges" to be refuted rather than as topics to be honestly investigated.

Yet another strategy was to publicize alternatives to the "cigarette theory." A key instrument in this was the already-mentioned Tobacco Institute, which metastasized from the TIRC in 1958 to serve as the lobbying and propaganda arm of the industry. For decades, the Tobacco Institute trumpeted the "no proof" position of the industry, usually in response to new confirmations of one or another tobacco hazard. The institute also published a monthly newsletter, the *Tobacco and Health Report*, drawing attention to whatever could be used to distract from tobacco hazards. The magazine was sent to hundreds of thousands of physicians, plus thousands of other opinion makers from industry, government, and journalism, the purpose being to highlight every possible cause of cancer except for tobacco. Typical for 1963 and 1964 were articles with titles such as "Rare Fungus Infection Mimics Lung Cancer," "Viral Infections Blamed in Bronchitis Outbreaks," "English Surgeon Links Urbanization to Lung Cancer," "Nicotine Effect Is Like Exercise," "Lung Cancer Rare in Bald Men," "28 Reasons for Doubting Cigarette-Cancer Link," and "No One Yet Knows the Answers." The magazine blamed bird keeping (feather mites), genetics, viruses, air pollution, and every other possible cause of the lung cancer epidemic—except tobacco.

Throughout this period, the goal of the industry was to comfort by virtue of allying itself with science. One remarkable organ for this purpose was *Science Fortnightly*, an ambitious popular science magazine published by the Lorillard Tobacco Company from 1963 to 1965, mailed free of charge every two weeks to 1.4 million people. This was one of the best popular science publications of the decade, treating new archaeological finds, theories of the origins of the Earth, sociological questions about the role of blacks and women in science, and dozens of other hot topics. The point was to introduce a breath of fresh air to science reporting, including also in every issue a couple of large and serious ads for Kent's micronite filter, "made of a pure, dust-free, completely harmless material that is so safe that it is actually used to help filter the air in operating rooms of leading hospitals." That semi-secret "harmless material" for a time at least in the 1950s was crocidolite asbestos.

Cigarette makers were successful for a time in keeping many people in the dark about the magnitude of certain hazards. A Harris Poll of adults in 1966 found that not even half of those questioned regarded smoking as a "major" cause of lung cancer.[31] Surveys conducted that same year for the U.S. Public Health Service found that only 46 percent of those polled answered "yes" when asked: "Is there any way at all to prevent a person from getting lung cancer?" Twenty percent of those answered "yes" in response to the same question about emphysema and chronic bronchitis.[32] Thirteen- and fourteen-year-olds were not polled, but it would be surprising if their awareness was any higher. Even today, how many people know that smoking is a major cause of blindness, bladder cancer, and cancers of the pancreas? Or (possibly) cancers of the human breast?[33] We need better measures of this and other kinds of ignorance—*agnometric indicators* that will tell us how many people don't know X, Y, or Z.

A new element in the tobacco story over the past twenty years or so has been the industry's hiring of historians to tell the tobacco story in a way that jurors might find sympathetic. Historians are employed to point out that correlation does not imply causation, that history is messy, that we must be careful in judging the past, that good history may even require our *not* judging the past, and so forth.[34] Historians are most often brought into tobacco trials to testify to what is known as "state of the art" and "common knowledge"—basically the science of the times, and what people knew about the hazard. As of 2005 at least thirty-six academic historians had testified under oath for the industry—whereas only three had testified against (myself, Louis Kyriakoudes, and Allan Brandt).[35] The industry's goal has been to control the *history* of tobacco just as earlier they'd controlled the *science* of tobacco. A typical instrument in this was Philip Morris's "Project Cosmic," an effort launched in 1987 to create "an extensive network of scientists and historians from all over the world" to write the history of drug use.[36] David Musto of Yale, David Harley of Oxford, John Burnham of Ohio State, and a number of others were approached to write articles for the industry to "see to it that the beneficial effects of nicotine are more widely understood."[37] Musto's work was considered particularly useful for presenting "a moderate view of substance use in the media."[38] Hundreds of thousands of dollars were paid to Cosmic research directors; Musto alone received nearly $500,000.[39] Grantees published on the history of tobacco without ever acknowledging the industry's support. David Harley, for example, published an article on "The Beginnings of the Tobacco Controversy" in the *Bulletin of the History of Medicine*, thanking a certain Daniel Ennis for "encouraging my interest in this topic."[40] Nowhere does he mention that Ennis's "encouragement" took the form of large piles of cash from Philip Morris.

There is an interesting sense in which the most common definitions of expertise in recent tobacco trials are biased in favor of the defense. Biased, because in restricting their focus to the "state of the art," a historian might fail to recognize the "state of the deception." If there is a diversity of views on tobacco as a cause of cancer, what fraction of that diversity has been created by the industry itself? Similar problems confront our grappling with the extent to which tobacco harms were "common knowledge." We need to know what people knew, but also what they didn't know (and why not). "Common ignorance" must be explored and understood as much as common knowledge.

Big Tobacco wants us to believe that there are really only two kinds of knowledge in question: popular and scientific. Ignored is the role of the industry itself in creating ignorance: via advertising, duplicitous press releases, funding of decoy research, establishment of scientific front organizations, manipulation of legislative agendas,[41] organization of "friendly research" for publication in popular magazines, and myriad additional projects from the dark arts of agnotology. Tremendous amounts of money have been thrown into this effort, which the industry's own lawyers have (privately) characterized as a form of "studied ignorance."[42] The industry eventually recognized itself as a manufacturer of two separate, but codependent products: cigarettes and *doubt*. As Tobacco Institute VP Fred Panzer put it in a 1971 memo, the industry's goal was to create "doubt about the health charge without actually denying it."[43] Brown & Williamson officials had earlier confessed (internally) that "doubt is our product,"[44] and in the 1980s Philip Morris responded to the "threat" of environmental tobacco smoke (ETS) by formulating as their number one "strategy objective": "to maintain doubt on the scientific front about ETS."[45]

There is no central tenet in tobacco industry agnotology, however; their philosophy is opportunistic, and always subordinate to the goal of selling cigarettes and winning lawsuits, usually via stalling tactics known in the business as "sand in the gears."[46] Cigaretteers will jump from being Popperian to constructivist as it suits them; they love to argue that no number of experiments can verify a theory, but they also know how to hammer away at the language of a claim until it falls to pieces. (Recall the Academy for Tobacco Studies' scientist in *Thank You for Smoking* who could "disprove gravity.") And on the question of demonstrating harms, the industry's standards for proof are so high that nothing in this world could satisfy them. "More research" is always needed, a "benefit of the doubt" is always granted, as if cigarettes were on trial and innocent until proven guilty. The industry loves this form of the "null hypothesis": they start by assuming "no harm done," and then fail in their feeble efforts at falsification. Similar strategies have been used by other industries to disprove hazards of lead, asbestos, and the like; and petrochemical and neoconservative doubters of global warming have learned a lesson or two from the tobacco doubt mongers (as Naomi Oreskes shows in her contribution to this volume).[47]

Military Secrecy

Tobacco duplicity is notorious, but deliberate ignorance also comes from numerous other sources, such as military classification. Estimates are that a quarter of the world's technical personnel have some kind of military clearance; there are secret scientific facts, secret scientific methods, secret scientific societies, secret scientific journals, and (probably) secret laws of nature. Military men don't always want to keep secrets from themselves, so firewalls are established to allow a community of cognoscenti with "clearance" to meet in private to discuss classified matters. The National Security Agency, for example, maintains an Internet firewalled from the outside world, as do some of our larger private corporations. The Manhattan Project in World War II (to make an atomic bomb) set the stage for much of America's postwar secret research; the project diverted much of the country's scientific talent and the name itself was a deception, as was Britain's comparable "Tube Alloys Project." Nuclear technologies have been clothed in secrecy from quite early on: the very existence of plutonium, for example, was classified for several years after its discovery, and words like "radiation" and "radioisotope" were not supposed to be bandied about. Neither word was mentioned in the first 200 articles written on the atom bomb.[48]

Atomic secrecy was also the rationale for entire scientific disciplines going underground, with code names devised for sensitive topics. The field of "Health Physics," for example, has its origins in the need to explore the novel hazards of atomic radiation, with the name being deliberately kept vague to disguise the fact that projects were underway to explore health and safety in the nuclear workplace.

The whole point of secrecy in this realm is to hide, to feint, to distract, to deny access, and to monopolize information. Global positioning system locations are tweaked to keep "sensitive" locations (for example, the White House) unknowable—and so untargetable—and entire cities have been erased from maps or never drawn in. The National Security Agency is larger and more secretive even than the Central Intelligence Agency (NSA = "No Such Agency")[49] and the National Reconnaissance Office is more shadowy still, and even better funded. Most secret would be those offices and operations "we" in the outside world know nothing about. Classified research in the United States is hidden in the so-called Black Budget, which currently exceeds the amounts funded for education and many other social services. In November of 2005, Mary Margaret Graham, deputy director of National Intelligence at the CIA, revealed the total U.S. intelligence budget to be $44 billion per annum.[50]

The impact of military secrecy on science has been profound, affecting nearly every branch of knowledge. An interesting case concerns the seafloor stripes discovered during World War II. These large, linear, magnetic anomalies are caused by a combination of seafloor spreading and periodic reversals in the Earth's magnetic field. They were also useful in locating enemy German (and later Russian) submarines, assisting in the scanning for underwater metallic objects. Seafloor stripes were important in the acceptance of continental drift, but their locations and even their existence were classified until the 1950s. Had these been openly available to the scientific community, the theory of continental drift could have been accepted years before it was. Secrecy in this instance produced ignorance in the form of delayed knowledge.[51]

There are other examples of military agnogenesis. Military-sponsored research in the 1940s led to early predictions of global warming and the melting of the polar ice caps; the guardians of military secrecy kept this quiet, however, and the topic was not widely and openly discussed.[52] Climate science has suffered new kinds of agnotology in recent years, as Bush administration strategists have tried to keep the question of anthropogenic global warming "open."[53] As with tobacco industry apologetics, calls for "more research" on climate change have served as an effective stalling tactic: the strong evidence of warming is denied, using the pretence of a quest for rigor as a trick to delay action. Calls for precision can play out as prevarication.

Military research has more often generated ignorance by passive agnogenesis: we have many examples where military funding has pushed certain areas, leaving others to languish. Carbon-14 research, for example, was heavily supported by the military as part of nuclear isotope research (Libby's work), whereas oxygen isotope analysis languished underfunded. Science responds to funding opportunities, which means that ignorance can be maintained or created in certain areas simply by "defunding." When Ronald Reagan took office in 1980, federal funding for solar energy research was zeroed out. Semiconductor studies that could have advanced knowledge in this realm were transferred to areas such as the "hardening" of silicon chips to resist the neutron flux from an atomic blast. Solar technology "know-how" suffered from this loss of funding; ignorance here resulted from a decision to emphasize fossil fuels over renewable energy sources.

VIRTUOUS IGNORANCE? "NOT KNOWING" AS RESISTANCE OR MORAL CAUTION

The prospect sounds anathema: how could anyone want to hold back the progress of science? Knowledge is the light; why bathe in the dark? Once past the bluster, however, there are obviously many things "we" don't want to know—and many more we'd rather have others not know about us. I've mentioned the "right to privacy," but there are other realms where "less is more" when it comes to knowledge, including scientific knowledge.

We know this from popular sayings, as in the notion that it is not always easy to put some genies "back in the bottle." Knowledge escapes, that we'd rather have confined or relegated to history. This would include many technologies and bodies of skill: if not those surrounding plutonium or uranium, then perhaps the know-how involved in torture, or the manufacture of neutron bombs, or some of our more horrific bioweapons. People can work to undo rotten knowledge; that is one goal of education, but it is also the principal rationale for military classification, in that powers that be don't want dangerous knowledge falling into the wrong hands.

Universities routinely bar many kinds of research—research with strings attached, for example, or research that involves certain kinds of risks for human or animal subjects, or research of a sort intended solely for profit, and so forth. Many universities bar research that is classified for military purposes, along with research seen to involve certain kinds of conflict of interest. UCSF's Energy Institute won't take money from oil and gas interests, for example, and many universities have been struggling over whether to allow projects funded by the tobacco industry. Rationales for such restrictions differ in each instance, but one overarching theory is that certain kinds of research will produce knowledge that could be biased or undesirable.

Scientific journals often have other kinds of restrictions. There are the familiar restrictions of disciplinarity and rhetoric, but projects receiving funding from certain sources are sometimes barred, as are research objects of illegitimate provenance (notably in archaeology). The entire notion of "research ethics" presumes that ignorance in certain situations is preferable to knowledge by improper means. The American Medical Association in 1996 recommended that scientific journals refuse to publish research funded by the tobacco industry,[54] and there are calls now for history journals to do the same—given the covert industry support for such publications.[55] Historians haven't yet had much experience limiting research from such sources, and few professional journals require disclosure of potential conflicts of interest. That could change, as historians realize that their research can be "bought" as easily as any other kind. Disclosures and even "transparency" are double-edged swords, however, as shown by the tobacco industry's work to draft and organize passage of the Data Access Act of 1998 and the Data Quality Act of 2000. The new laws allow the industry to obtain the raw data of anyone publishing any kind of scientific or medical study using federal funds; the industry pushed for legislation of this sort to allow it to reanalyze and reinterpret (that is, look for flaws in) research suggesting a tobacco hazard of one sort or another.[56] Philip Morris employed Multinational Business Services and other front organizations to push through these laws—over objections from both the National Academy of Sciences and the American Association for the Advancement of Science. The bottom line: the seemingly noble goal of transparency can be an instrument in the service of organized duplicity.

One key principle of research ethics—as of ethics more generally—is that not all things are worth knowing at any cost. Many kinds of scientific experiments are barred, either legally or less formally, which amounts to a tolerance for ignorance in realms where the costs of gaining knowledge are judged to be too high. An interesting example of deliberate refusal of knowledge is the agreement by most journals of archaeology not to publish artifacts without an explicit and acceptable "provenance" demonstrating that the object in question was obtained either legally in recent years, or illegally prior to some agreed-on cutoff point. Estimates are that as many as half of all artifacts in museum collections have been obtained illegally—though legal standards have changed considerably in this realm over time. The logic for the policy is that unrestricted publication will encourage looting, since publication is part of the process by which artifacts obtain value (via both certification and publicity). Different archaeological traditions regard this question of how to treat lootings very differently. "Contextualists" (aka "dirt archaeologists," who study sites laid out in square meters) tend to take the hard line, arguing that artifacts without proper provenance should not be published. (Some even imply they should be destroyed, in the same way that Daniel Arap Moi burned all that ivory.) Linguistic archaeologists—decoders—tend to be more tolerant, pointing out that all evidence available must be taken into account if translations (of Mayan stelae, for example) are to be possible. These different epistemic traditions have different attitudes toward looting: "dirt" archaeologists tend to value context, the first victim of looting, whereas philologists tend to value comparative analysis of series of "great artifacts," which often requires access to artifacts in private collections. The two traditions have different understandings of the costs of certain kinds of knowledge and ignorance.

If knowledge is power (which it sometimes is but not always), then to dismantle certain kinds of power may require the reintroduction of bodies of ignorance—hence impotence—in that realm. History is full of such undoings, the deliberate abandonment of skills to improve some way of life. And we're not just talking Amish virtues: who now knows all the techniques slave owners once possessed of how to control slaves? That is lost knowledge, as it should be, save perhaps for museums. Who could lament the loss of knowledge of all the world's ways to torture, the cognitive equivalent of smallpox stocks? Refusals of technology are often of this sort. We often hear that you can't turn the clock back, an idea as absurd as the notion that thieves cannot be brought to justice. It is not only for foolishness that technologies have been avoided, refused, or abandoned.

In Ireland, the eel fishermen of Lough Neagh no longer fish with power-driven nets; a decision was made in the 1960s to restrict all fishing in the lake to hand-drawn nets, to sustain the diminishing stocks. Leaf blowers are being banned in many communities, and many of us look forward to the day when doctored monocrop lawns will be seen as pathology. The Japanese lived for more than a hundred years without the gun. Protests against novel technologies are often lumped under the ridiculous rubric of "luddism," a term too often forgotten to have sprung from moral complaints with good reasons. Iain Boal in his forthcoming *Long Theft* shows how the breaking of looms in the early decades of the nineteenth century gave rise to the modern industrial strike (for better working conditions); protests against technologies and knowledge practices are rarely the result of people fearing modernity in the abstract.

There are many other reasons people might not want to have all knowledge omnipresent all the time. Not everyone wants to know what kinds of genetic diseases they (or their children) may be harboring in their genomes. Archaeologists deliberately don't publish the location of certain excavation sites, fearing looting (botanists do the same for new cactus finds), and some ethnographers are publishing knowledge of certain biopharmaceuticals in "indigenous" languages to give locals an edge against the multinationals. Access to all kinds of information is limited—ignorance is deliberately created—for more reasons than the moon has craters.

The lesson is one that should have been applied in all of the recent hysteria over the myriad vulnerabilities of Americans to terrorist attack. The nightly news for months was full of exposés of how this or that bridge or granary could be bombed or poisoned, in a gargantuan paranoid proclamation of national victimhood. "News" about potential threats and "security gaps" arguably did more to give people worries (and ideas) than to encourage any truer sense (and reality) of safety; there is such a thing as dangerous knowledge, things we don't need to know. Total Information Awareness is not for everyone.

SOME QUESTIONS

There are lots of ways to think about ignorance—as tragedy, as crime, as provocation, as strategy, as stimulus, as excess or deprivation, as handicap, as defense mechanism or obstruction, as opportunity, as guarantor of judicial neutrality, as pernicious evil, as wondrous innocence, as inequity or relief, as the best defense of the weak or the common excuse of the powerful, and so forth. There are surely as many ways to think about ignorance as of knowledge, with the sociology just as intricate in both instances. There are lots of different kinds of ignorance, and lots of different reasons to expose it, undo it, deplore it, or seek it.

Here some questions for further reflection: What other kinds of work does ignorance do? How else is it created, via what other kinds of inattention, disinterest, calculation, resistance, tradition, or distraction? And when does knowledge create ignorance? Wes Jackson has called the modern university "an engine of distraction"; how does pursuit of certain kinds of knowledge produce such "distractions"? Is ivory tower reclusion required for certain kinds of knowledge production? How do disinterests and apathies come into being, and what patterns of competence or disability are thereby brought into being?

We tend to think of ignorance as something negative, but when can it become a virtue? Or an imperative? The philosopher John Rawls has championed a "veil of ignorance" as a kind of ethical method: we are supposed to imagine ourselves not knowing where we ourselves will figure in an ethical situation; ignorance of how we personally might gain is supposed to guarantee a kind of neutrality and therefore balance in judging such situations. We find something similar in the courtroom, where jurors are supposed to be ignorant of the particulars of the crime they are evaluating—versus prior to the seventeenth century, when jurors were supposed to know as much as possible about the case in question. (Jurors were only later clearly separated from witnesses, the theory being that ignorance will prevent bias.) Knowledge here is interestingly attached to bias, ignorance to balance.

And how important is the genesis of ignorance for modern corporations? Many companies cultivate ignorance as a kind of insurance policy: if what you don't know can't hurt you, sometimes it is safer not to know. Document retention policies of many companies were revised in the wake of the Master Settlement Agreement (1998), which forced tens of millions of previously secret tobacco industry documents onto the Internet. The traditional corporate lawyers' trick of flooding a plaintiff with documents (aka "dumping") backfired with the rise of the Internet and search engines, leading information holders to recognize the dangers of a long paper trail. In the new millennium, many companies have adopted email deletion policies to avoid leaving such trails (paper or electronic), the theory again being that what you don't know can't hurt you. (Though failure to keep accurate records has itself been used in certain lawsuits, alleging destruction of documents.)

And what about in medicine, or the science of public health? Richard Peto has argued that ignorance of a certain type is essential for progress in the science of epidemiology. No one needed to know anything about the biochemistry of cancer to realize that cigarettes were causing the disease; it was crucial to "black box" the things we didn't know, rather than waiting paralyzed until knowledge had come in on every front.[57] The tobacco industry has spread confusion on this point, pretending that every last fact must be known about a disease before we can say what causes it. John Snow's removing the handle from the water pump at Charing Cross is the contrary lesson—warts and all: sometimes we know enough to act, despite oceans of ignorance. Ignorance must be productive or virtuous (not the same thing) in many other contexts—what are they? The history of discovery is littered with fertile mistakes—think of Columbus, emboldened to cross the Atlantic by virtue of an overly conservative estimate for the size of the globe. What other examples are there of fertile ignorance?

And when does ignorance beget confidence, arrogance, or timidity? Charles Darwin once wrote that "ignorance more frequently begets confidence than does knowledge: it is those who know little, and not those who know much, who so positively assert that this or that problem will never be solved by science."[58] Darwin implies that knowledge leads us to a kind of productive humility—but how often is this true? His point is not the Socratic one, that "the more you know the more you realize how little you know," but rather that the more you know, the more you realize that science can go forward, trouncing ignorance. George Gaylord Simpson has taken a different tack, claiming that our capacity for ignorance is central to what it means to be human: "Man is among many other things, the mistaken animal, the foolish animal. Other species doubtless have much more limited ideas about the world, but what ideas they do have are much less likely to be wrong and are never foolish. White cats do not denigrate black, and dogs do not ask Baal, Jehovah, or other Semitic gods to perform miracles for them."[59] To be human is to be ignorant, apparently.

Crucial also is: ignorance for whom? and against whom? Ignorance has a history and is always unevenly distributed; the geography of ignorance has mountains and valleys. Who is ignorant and why, and to what extent? How can we develop better agnometric indicators? What keeps ignorance in one place, while it evaporates in some other? And which among our myriad ignorances will be tolerated or combated?

Many of these same questions can be asked about knowledge since, like ignorance, it occupies space and takes us down one path rather than another. Knowledge, too, has a face, a house, and a price—there are people attached, institutions setting limits, and costs in the form of monies or opportunities lost. Decisions of what kind of knowledge "we" want to support are also decisions about what kinds of ignorance should remain in place.

SUMMARIZING, THEN: it is our hope that readers will be convinced that there are a lot of good reasons to explore ignorance. There is surely quite a lot of it, as much as we are willing to let our arrogance acknowledge. Agnotology could be a challenge to hubris, if there is modesty in learning how deeply ignorant we are. Think of the countless different ways it is generated: by ingesting lead or by watching TV, or by fatigue or fear or isolation or poverty or any of the other myriad experiences that deaden human life. Think of ignorance generated by failures of the body, or failures to fund education, or free access to bogus information, or practices and policies that enlarge secrecy or prevarication or compartmentalization. People have extracted very different things from different kinds of unknowns, and will no doubt continue to mix suspect with admirable reasons for letting those flourish or disappear.

POSTSCRIPT ON THE COINING OF
THE TERM "AGNOTOLOGY"

Some time into this project I learned that there already was a word that has been used to designate the study of ignorance, albeit with a quite different slant from how we shall be using the term. Apart from being obscure and somewhat inharmonious, *agnoiology* has often been taken to mean "the doctrine of things of which we are necessarily ignorant" in some profound metaphysical sense. My hope for devising a new term was to suggest the opposite, namely, the historicity and artifactuality of non-knowing and the non-known—and the potential fruitfulness of studying such things. In 1992, I posed this challenge to the linguist Iain Boal, and it was he who came up with the term *agnotology*, in the spring of that year.

Coinage for science terms in Anglophonia is conventionally from the Greek, so that is where he started. Ignorance in Greek really has two forms: *agnoia*, meaning "want of perception or knowledge," and *agnosia*, meaning a state of ignorance or not knowing, both from *gnosis* (with a long *o* or omega) meaning "knowledge," with the privative (negating) *a*-prefix. (We didn't look for a harmonious negation of *episteme*.) Alternative designations for the study of ignorance could have been *agnosiology*, or *agnarology* (using the Latin compounding rule), or even *agnoskology*, designating more properly a study of the unwillingness or inability to learn, from *gignosko* (with both *o*'s as omegas), the first-person singular present indicative active form of the verb meaning "to know."

Iain crafted *agnotology* from among these possible options, using *gno* as the root (meaning "to know"), *a* as the negating prefix, a *t* added as the marker of the participial (yielding *gnot*), and *-ology* as the denominative suffix. We chose *-ology* largely on phonaesthemic grounds, with the *logos*-derived suffix lying roughly in the midrange of the hubris continuum, avoiding alternatives such as the more archaic *agnonomy*, the vivid yet micro-tainted *agnoscopy* (with its tilt to molecular coproscopy), the Latin-Greek mongrel *ignorology*, the Anglo-Saxon romantic yet overly quaint "ignorance-lore" (Lorraine Daston's tongue-in-cheek suggestion), the hyperempirical *ig-* or *agnotometry* (or *-metrics*), and the self-marginalizing "ignorance science" or "ignorance studies," with its taint for those who scoff that "if there's *science* in the title, it isn't one."

We had originally spelled our new term with two *a*'s (*agnatology*) to avoid having people elongating and accenting the second *o* (as in agnostic or ignoble), recognizing also that vowels are essentially fillers in written language, following Voltaire's famous maxim that etymology is "a science in which the consonants count for very little, and the vowels for even less." (Try replacing all vowels in a text with the letter *a*, *e*, or *i*; and of course there are many languages that drop them altogether, such as Hebrew.) Protests over this second *a* came from a number of quarters, among these a few biologists who insinuated that we were infringing on the study of jawless ("agnathic") fish. More serious was the objection that *agnate* was already a word, meaning "relative" (from *ad gnatus*). In the spirit of scholarly harmony we decided to rechristen our neologism *agnotology*, recognizing that while the meanings of words lie only in their use, their use can also depend on how and for what ends they are created.

SOME FAMOUS QUOTATIONS ABOUT IGNORANCE

Real knowledge is to know the extent of one's ignorance.
Confucius (551 BC–479 BC)

The loss which is unknown is no loss at all.
Publilius Syrus, *Maxims* (c. 100 BC)

To know that we know what we know, and to know that we do not know what we do not know, that is true knowledge.
Nicolaus Copernicus (1473–1543)

Ignorance of certain subjects is a great part of wisdom.
Hugo De Groot (1583–1645)

Ignorance is preferable to error; and he is less remote from the truth who believes nothing, than he who believes what is wrong.
Thomas Jefferson, *Notes on the State of Virginia* (1785)

All you need in this life is ignorance and confidence; then success is sure.
Mark Twain, December 2, 1887

Education is a progressive discovery of our own ignorance.
Will Durant (1885–1981)

Ignorance is strength.
George Orwell, *1984*

Theology is the effort to explain the unknow-
able in terms of the not worth knowing.
H. L. Mencken (1880–1956)

Ignorance is king, many would not prosper by its abdication.
Walter M. Miller, *A Canticle for Leibowitz* (1959)

It's innocence when it charms us, ignorance when it doesn't.
Mignon McLaughlin, *The Neurotic's Notebook* (1960)

Our knowledge can only be finite, while our ig-
norance must necessarily be infinite.
Karl Popper, *Conjectures and Refutations* (1963)

Reports that say that something hasn't happened are always interesting
to me, because as we know, there are known knowns; there are things
we know we know. We also know there are known unknowns; that is
to say we know there are some things we do not know. But there are
also unknown unknowns—the ones we don't know we don't know.
And if one looks throughout the history of our country and other free
countries, it is the latter category that tend to be the difficult ones.
Donald H. Rumsfeld, Department of Defense news briefing,
February 12, 2002

NOTES

1. The reference is to Harvard's Philosophy 253.

2. A Google search of December 2001 yielded 145,000 hits for "epistemology," including objectivist, subjectivist, virtue, analytic, genetic, affective, iceberg, and Chicana feminist. For the gamut, see http://pantheon.yale.edu/~kd47/e-page.htm.

3. Two solid exceptions: Peter Wehling, "Weshalb weiss die Wissenschaft nicht, was sie nicht weiss? Forschungsperspektiven einer Soziologie des wissenschaftlichen Nichtwissens," http://www.sciencepolicystudies.de/wehling%20Expertise.pdf; and Michael Smithson, "Toward a Social Theory of Ignorance," *Journal for the Theory of Social Behavior* 15 (1985): 151–172. An earlier discussion in the functionalist mood can be found in W. E. Moore and M. M. Tumin, "Some Social Functions of Ignorance," *American Sociological Review* 14 (1949): 787–795.

4. The philosopher Paula Driver argues that one version of modesty consists in being ignorant of one's actual merits. Charity can similarly consist in not noticing—or failing to be aware of—the faults of others; see her *Uneasy Virtue* (Cambridge, UK: Cambridge University Press, 2001).

5. Harry Marks, "Misunderstanding Pellagra: Gender, Race and Political Economy in Early-20th-Century Epidemiology," History of Science Colloquium, Welch Medical Library, *JHMI* (2001).

6. Fetal alcohol syndrome was discovered circa 1900 and then forgotten with the discrediting of its eugenics scaffolding; see Philip J. Pauly, "How Did the Effects of Alcohol on Reproduction Become Scientifically Uninteresting?" *Journal of the History of Biology* 29 (1996): 1–28.

7. David Reich, "Building Superman," review of Nicholas Gillham, *A Life of Sir Francis Galton* (New York: Oxford University Press, 2001), in the *New York Times Book Review*, February 10, 2002: 16.

8. "So long as the mother, Ignorance, lives, it is not safe for Science, the offspring, to divulge the hidden cause of things" (Kepler, 1571–1630).

9. Malcolm Ritter, "Americans Show They Don't Know Much about Science," *AP*, June 16, 2002 (based on an NSF-funded survey).

10. August Comte makes this explicit in his *Cours de philosophie positive* (1830–1842); see *Auguste Comte and Positivism, the Essential Writings*, ed. Gertrud Lenzer (New York: Harper and Row, 1975), 73, 94, 465–474, and 84.

11. This is Robert K. Merton's idea of "specified ignorance"; see his "Three Fragments from a Sociologist's Notebooks: Establishing the Phenomenon, Specified Ignorance, and Strategic Research Materials," *Annual Review of Sociology* 13 (1987): 1–28. Merton's point is really only that questions not asked are questions not answered, and that scientists need to make what they don't know explicit as "a first step toward supplanting that ignorance with knowledge" (10).

12. R. Duncan and M. Weston-Smith, *The Encyclopaedia of Medical Ignorance: Exploring the Frontiers of Medical Knowledge* (Oxford: Pergamon, 1984).

13. Smithson, "Toward a Social Theory of Ignorance," 153.

14. Sut Jhally, Justin Lewis, and Michael Morgan, "The Gulf War: A Study of the Media, Public Opinion, and Public Knowledge" (Research Report. Centre for the Study of Communication, Doc. #P-8, February 1991).

15. Walter Benjamin, "The Work of Art in the Age of Mechanical Reproduction" (1935), in his *Illuminations*, ed. Hannah Arendt (New York: Schocken, 1969), 238.

16. David Dickson, "Weaving a Social Web," *Nature* 414 (2001): 587.

17. Kenneth Burke, *Permanence and Change* (New York: New Republic, 1935), 70. The idea of selective bias has fallen on hard times in recent sociology of science. All science is said to be selective, so it becomes only trivially true to say that any particular pattern of inquiry is selective, since it cannot have been otherwise. The so-called Strong Programme in the sociology of knowledge also tended to regard the social construction of ignorance (or error) as "easy" or "trivial" by comparison with the social construction of truth.

18. Ian Hacking, *The Social Construction of What?* (Cambridge, MA: Harvard University Press, 2000).

19. Sissela Bok, *Secrets: On the Ethics of Concealment and Revelation* (New York: Random House, 1990).

20. Mario Biagoli, "From Book Censorship to Academic Peer Review," *Emergences* 12 (2002): 11–45.

21. William R. Newman and Anthony Grafton, eds., *Secrets of Nature: Astrology and Alchemy in Early Modern Europe* (Cambridge, MA: MIT Press, 2001).

22. W. R. Van Meter in his "Putting False Faces on Formulas" (*Food Industries*, October 1941, 41–42) advised food chemists to disguise valuable formulas "so that workmen do not get wise to it and competitors cannot steal it. The idea is to use arbitrary units of measurement and adopt coined names for ingredients" (41).

23. William Poundstone, *Big Secrets: The Uncensored Truth about All Sorts of Stuff You Are Never Supposed to Know* (New York: William Morrow, 1985).

24. See my *Cancer Wars: How Politics Shapes What We Know and Don't Know about Cancer* (New York: Basic Books, 1995), esp. p. 8n and Chapter 5 on "Doubt Is Our Product."

25. The PR firm of Hill and Knowlton is often blamed, but Paul Hahn, president of the American Tobacco Co., was surely involved; see my forthcoming *Golden Holocaust*. Compare also my *Cancer Wars*, Chapter 5; Gerald Markowitz and David Rosner, "Expert Panels and Medical Uncertainty," *American Journal of Industrial Medicine* 19 (1991): 131–134; and Allan M. Brandt, *The Cigarette Century* (New York: Basic Books, 2007), 159–207.

26. See my "Everyone Knew but No One Had Proof: Tobacco Industry Use of Medical History Expertise in U.S. Courts, 1990–2002," *Tobacco Control* 15 (2006): iv117–125.

27. Kenneth Ludmerer, testimony in *Boeken v. Philip Morris, Inc., et al.*, Superior Court of California for the County of Los Angeles, Case No. BC 226593, *Transcript of Proceedings*, vol. 31A, 5262.

28. The words "deceive," "misleading," "fraud," and cognates appear 454 times with reference to tobacco industry actions in Judge Gladys Kessler's "Final Opinion" in *USA v. Philip Morris et al.* (August 18, 2006), online at http://www.tobaccolawcenter.org/documents/ FinalOpinion.pdf. The Court here notes that numerous "acts of concealment and deception" were made "intentionally and deliberately" as part of a "multifaceted, sophisticated scheme to defraud." The Court also concludes that "from at least 1953 until at least 2000, each and every one of these Defendants repeatedly, consistently, vigorously—and falsely—denied the existence of any adverse health effects from smoking. Moreover, they mounted a coordinated, well-financed, sophisticated public relations campaign to attack and distort the scientific evidence demonstrating the relationship between smoking and disease, claiming that the link between the two was still an 'open question'" (330–331).

29. The tobacco industry sometimes defends itself by suggesting that the public was never convinced by its "no proof of harm" propaganda. During my expert deposition of

July 2002 for the plaintiffs in *USA v. Philip Morris* I was shown an industry document from the 1970s suggesting that confidence in the industry was low by comparison with medical and public health groups. The industry's inference was essentially: yes, we lied, but nobody believed us. Fraud, it seems, is not fraud if no one believes you.

30. Cited in Jones, Day, Reavis, and Pogue's 450-page "Corporate Activity Project" (1986), available online at http://www.tobacco.org/resources/documents/jonesday1.html, 390. Clarence Cook Little was scientific director of TIRC but "took orders" from the TI on this occasion.

31. Louis Harris, "Most Still Doubt Cigarettes Are Major Cause of Cancer," *Washington Post*, January 2, 1967, Bates 500323778.

32. *Use of Tobacco: Practices, Attitudes, Knowledge, and Beliefs. United States—Fall 1964 and Spring 1966* (U.S. Department of Health, Education, and Welfare: July 1969), 52, 68.

33. California EPA, *Proposed Identification of Environmental Tobacco Smoke as a Toxic Air Contaminant* (Sacramento: California EPA, 2003).

34. See my "Should Medical Historians Be Working for the Tobacco Industry?" *Lancet* 363 (2003): 1174.

35. See my "Everyone Knew but No One Had Proof," iv117–iv125.

36. "Chronology and Development of Project Cosmic" (Philip Morris), 1988, Bates 2023919844–9907; "Project Cosmic," February 18, 1992, Bates 2040573257–3270. Documents with "Bates" numbers (litigation codes) are searchable online at http://legacy.library.ucsf.edu/.

37. "Plans for the Smoking Research Project" (Philip Morris), 1988, Bates 2001260131–0136.

38. "Chronology and Development of Project Cosmic," Bates 2023919844–9847.

39. "Project Cosmic: Budget/Spending Status," February 1991, Bates 2023160927.

40. David Harley, "The Beginnings of the Tobacco Controversy: Puritanism, James I, and the Royal Physicians," *Bulletin of the History of Medicine* 67 (1993): 28. Harley's article conveys this message of a timeless "controversy" that may never be resolved; Musto similarly talked about a pendulum swinging from endorsement to condemnation of drug use, with a periodicity of about seventy years. This latter idea was picked up by a number of science reporters (Gina Kolata, for example), none of whom recognized the thesis as an industry concoction designed to make smoking seem natural and inevitable.

41. Stanton A. Glantz, John Slade, Lisa A. Bero, Peter Hanauer, and Deborah E. Barnes, eds., *The Cigarette Papers* (Berkeley: University of California Press, 1996), 171–200.

42. Jones, Day, Reavis, and Pogue, "Corporate Activity Project," 71.

43. Fred Panzer to Horace R. Kornegay, May 1, 1972, Bates 87657703–7706.

44. Glantz et al., *Cigarette Papers*, 171.

45. Daniel J. Edelman, "INFOTAB ETS-Project: The Overall Plan," March 12, 1987, Bates 2022934011–4024, p. 8.

46. Craig L. Fuller, Senior Vice President, Corporate Affairs, and Kathleen Linehan, Vice President, Government Affairs, "Presentation for the Board of Directors—June 24, 1992," June 24, 1992, Bates 2047916010.

47. See Naomi Oreskes' essay in this volume and George Monbiot, *Heat: How to Stop the Planet from Burning* (London: Allen Lane, 2006); also my *Cancer Wars*, Chapter 5.

48. Carole Gallagher, *American Ground Zero: The Secret Nuclear War* (New York: Doubleday, 1993).

49. James Bamford, *The Puzzle Palace: A Report on America's Most Secret Agency* (Boston: Houghton Mifflin, 1982).

50. Scot Shane, "Official Reveals Budget for U.S. Intelligence," *New York Times*, November 8, 2005.

51. Naomi Oreskes, *The Rejection of Continental Drift: Theory and Method in American Earth Science* (New York: Oxford University Press, 1999).

52. Ronald E. Doel, "Polar Melting When Cold War Was Hot," *San Francisco Examiner*, October 3, 2000, A15.

53. Republican political strategist Frank Luntz prior to the November 2000 presidential election warned party members that the scientific debate on global warming was "closing but not closed," and advised his party to be more aggressive in recruiting sympathetic experts who would encourage the public not to "rush to judgment before all the facts are in." The stakes were clear: "Should the public come to believe that the scientific issues are settled, their views about global warming will change accordingly. Therefore, you need to continue to make the lack of scientific certainty a primary issue." Cited in Heather Boonstra, "Critics Charge Bush Mix of Science and Politics Is Unprecedented and Dangerous," *The Guttmacher Report on Public Policy*, May 2003, 2.

54. "Tobacco-funded Research," AMEDNEWS.COM, July 22, 1996, at http://.ama-assn .org/sci-pubs/amnews/amn_96/summo722.htm [accessed January 2002].

55. See again my "Should Historians Be Working for the Tobacco Industry?"

56. Annamaria Baba, Daniel M. Cook, Thomas O. McGarity, and Lisa A. Bero, "Legislating 'Sound Science': The Role of the Tobacco Industry," *American Journal of Public Health* 95 (2005): S20–27; Rick Weiss, "'Data Quality' Law Is Nemesis of Regulation," *Washington Post*, August 16, 2004, p. A1.

57. Richard Peto, "Ignorance in Cancer Research," in Duncan and Weston-Smith, eds., *The Encyclopaedia of Medical Ignorance*, 129–133.

58. Charles Darwin, *Descent of Man* (1871) (Princeton, NJ: Princeton University Press, 1981), 3.

59. George Gaylord Simpson, *This View of Life* (New York: Harcourt, Brace and World, 1964), viii.

PART I

Secrecy, Selection, and Suppression

CHAPTER 2

Removing Knowledge

The Logic of Modern Censorship

PETER GALISON

YOU MIGHT THINK that the guarded annals of classified information largely consist of that rare document—a small, tightly guarded annex to the vast sum of human writing and learning. True, the number of carefully archived pages written in the open is large. While hard to estimate, one could begin by taking the number of items on the shelves of the Library of Congress, one of the largest libraries in the world: 120 million items carrying about 7.5 billion pages, of which about 5.4 billion pages are in 18 million books.[1]

In fact, the classified universe, as it is sometimes called, is certainly not smaller, and is very probably much larger than this unclassified one. No one has any very good idea how many classified documents there are. No one did before the digital transformation of the late twentieth century, and now—at least after 2001—even the old sampling methods are recognized to be nonsense in an age where documents multiply across secure networks like virtual weeds. So we biblio-owls of Minerva are counting sheets just as the very concept of the classified printed page fades into its evening hours. Undeterred, we might begin with a relatively small subset of the whole classified world, about 1.6 billion pages from documents twenty-five years old or older that qualify as historically valuable. Of these 1.6 billion pages, 1.1 billion have been released over the last twenty years, with most opened since Bill Clinton's April 1995 Executive Order 12958. How many new classified documents have been produced since 1978 or so is much harder to estimate—the cognoscenti disagree by several orders of magnitude—but there isn't an expert alive who thinks the recent haul is anything less than *much* larger than the previous twenty-five post–World War II years.

Some suspect as many as a trillion pages are classified (200 Libraries of Congress). That may be too many. For example, 2001 saw 33 million classification actions; assuming (with the experts) that there are roughly 10 pages per action, that would mean roughly 330 million pages were classified last year (about three times as many pages are now being classified as declassified). So the United States added a net 250 million classified pages in a year. By comparison, the entire system of Harvard libraries—over a hundred of them—added about 220,000 volumes (about 60 million pages, a number not far from the acquisition rate at other comparably massive universal depositories such as the Library of Congress, the British Museum, or the New York Public Library). Contemplate these numbers: about five times as many pages are being added to the classified universe than are being brought to the storehouses of human learning, including all the books and journals on any subject in any language collected in the largest repositories on the planet.[2]

If that were typical—or at any rate the right order of magnitude—then twenty-five years of such actions would yield a very rough figure in the range of 8 billion pages since 1978. The fact that the number has been growing is not to the point—even if it increased linearly from zero in 1978 to its current rate twenty-five years later, that would only divide the total in two, "down" to 4 billion pages. Indeed, however one calculates, the number of classification actions is increasing dramatically both as a result of a boosted defense, intelligence, and weapons lab budget, *and* because we are living in a climate of augmented secrecy. Figured another way, the supervising agency, the Information Security Oversight Office (ISOO), reports a total expenditure in 2001 of $5.5 billion to keep classified documents secure. The Department of Energy costs are now about $0.30 per secure document per year. Estimating by this economic measure, we would figure that about 7.5 billion pages are being kept under wraps, a classified Library of Congress with an acquisition rate five times greater than the great library Thomas Jefferson bequeathed to this country over two centuries ago.

One last set of numbers: there are approximately 500,000 college professors in the United States, including both two- and four-year institutions. Of course, there are others—inventors, industrial scientists, computer programmers—responsible for generating and conveying knowledge, especially technical knowledge. But to fix ideas, 4 *million* people hold clearance in the United States, plus some vast reservoir who did in the past but no longer do. Bottom line? Whether one figures by acquisition rate, by holding size, or by contributors, the classified universe is, as best I can estimate, on the order of five to ten times larger than the open literature that finds its way to our libraries. Our commonsense picture may well be far too sanguine, even inverted. The closed world is not a small strongbox in the corner of our collective house of codified and stored knowledge. It is we in the open world—we who study the world lodged in our libraries, from aardvarks to zymurgy, *we* who are living in a modest information booth facing outward, our unseeing backs to a vast and classified empire we barely know.

One can trace the history of secrecy back to the ancient Babylonians through medieval longbows and fin-de-siècle invisible ink, from tightly guarded formulae for Venetian glassmaking to the hidden pouches of diplomatic couriers. Trade, state, and military secrets are all part of the background to the modern system. But this modern secrecy system has its substantive start not in antiquity, but in the vast infrastructure of World War II. In part, this new secrecy issued from the government, and yet in no small measure it emerged in the hands of scientists themselves as they launched a discipline of self-censorship on matters relating to the nucleus. Out of the $2 billion Manhattan Project and its subsequent evolution into the Atomic Energy Commission (AEC, now the Department of Energy) came one sector of secrecy, with its twin classification categories of Restricted Data and Formerly Restricted Data (FRD), this last for uninteresting historical reasons covering military applications of nuclear weapons rather than their production or design. Alongside nuclear secrecy arose another fundamental category, National Security Information.

At the pinnacle of the National Security Information world is the president, who himself can classify or, more realistically, have his agency heads classify information. These agency heads in turn delegate that power to a relatively small number of others—just over 4,000 for the whole of the United States—who bear the title of *original classifiers*. Only this initiated cadre can transform a document, idea, picture, shape, or device into the modal categories Top Secret, Secret, or Confidential. And of these 4,132 or so original classifiers, only 999 (as of 2001) are authorized to stamp a document into the category Top Secret.[3]

Those few people are the unmoved prime movers of the classified world; it is they who begin the tagging process that winds its way down the chain of derivative classification. For every document that subsequently refers to information in those originally classified gains the highest classification of the documents cited in it. Like the radio tagging of a genetic mutant, the classified information bears its mark through all the subsequent generations of work issuing from it. More numbers: in 2001, there were 260,678 original classifications (acts that designated a body of work classified) and 32,760,209 derivative ones.[4] A cascade of classification.

But there is another way for documents to become classified. Under the Atomic Energy Acts of 1946 and 1954, materials produced about nuclear weapons–related activities are exempt from the blessing hands of the original classifiers. Nuclear weapons knowledge is born secret. No primal act of classification is needed, no moment when it passes out of light into darkness, no justification, no term of expiration to wrap it in the protective blanket of restriction. Nuclear knowledge becomes classified the instant it is written down, even by someone who has no nuclear weapons (Q) clearance. If I think of a new scheme for channeling x-rays from a fission primary to a thermonuclear secondary and write that idea down, I am (senso strictu) forbidden from possessing the page I just created. (Technically, I could be arrested for espionage for reading or even possessing the letters or pictures in my printer, on my screen, or under my pen.) And yet in this world of natal secrecy, there is a subtlety born in the holy matrimony of industry and the weapons laboratories: an isotope-separating technology used to produce special nuclear materials such as U235 or U233. A separation technique—in some sense the heart of nuclear weapons of mass destruction—remains entirely in the open until just that moment when it might demonstrate (as the Federal Register puts it) "reasonable potential for the separation of practical quantities of special nuclear material."[5] At precisely this moment of efficacy it morphs into Restricted Data; as classifier Arvin Quist puts it in a document addressed to his fellow guardians of the faith, the separation technology becomes "classified only when it reaches 'adolescence.'"[6]

In 1995, the National Research Council working with the Department of Energy (DOE) estimated that the DOE's born and adolescent classified documents numbered some 280 million pages—an amount that would take its current complement of reviewers 9,000 years to review—if, against reality, not a line of new material were added.[7] However incomplete it is now, this nine-millennium stack is ten times larger than the previous estimate given a few years earlier. Needless to say, neither the DOE nor any other agency has the budget, the mandate, or the intention of catching up. In the last few years, the rate of classification increased fivefold, with no end in sight. Secret information is accumulating, at a rate that itself is accelerating, far quicker than it is being declassified.

THE CLASSIFIED THEORY OF KNOWLEDGE

With such a vast reservoir of learning under wraps, the DOE must have—if not explicitly then at least implicitly—some sense of what can and cannot be released. What, we may ask, is the theory of interdicting knowledge? Let us begin with a distinction imposed since 1945, segregating subjective from objective secrecy. *Subjective* secrets are said by classifiers to display four key characteristics: compact, transparent, changeable, and perishable. Compact means they can be expressed very briefly; transparent that they are readily understandable ("two of the Abrams tanks are disabled"); changeable means that they typically can be revised ("the 101st Airborne will conduct its first drop at first light"); and they are perishable (normally after some decent interval, for example, once the 101st has landed the fact that they did so has lost its potency). *Objective* secrets are supposed to contrast with each of these qualities separately—they are supposed to be diffuse, technical, determinable, eternal, and long-lasting qua secrets. That is, they may be far from expressible in a few words (a theory of neutron diffusion involves integro-differential equations and takes volumes to express when it is put into useable form); they may not be understandable to anyone without a technical training (no untrained observer simply grasps the details of fluorocarbon chemistry); they are supposed to be determinable insofar as they can be deduced if the right question is posed (the number of neutrons emitted in uranium fission can be found with enough effort and equipment); and finally the objective secret is supposed to be in some sense unchangeable (in the limit case a law of nature but, if not that, then at least as unchangeable as the finely articulated process of preparing equipment against the corrosive effects of uranium hexafluoride). As such, objective secrets are long-lasting secrets.[8]

In important ways, objective secrets pose the more difficult problem, though subjective ones can be quite deadly if exposed (Loose Lips Sink Ships). Particular movements or strengths of troops or materiel seem more straightforward. But to accomplish the goal of secrecy, the blocking of knowledge transmission is an extraordinarily difficult task. And given the resources devoted to it, it is perhaps worth inquiring just what its principles are.

In other words, suppose we ask about the transmission of knowledge not by asking the usual social studies of knowledge question, "How does replication occur?" but instead by probing the staggeringly large effort devoted to impeding the transmission of knowledge. Already before America's entry into World War II, nuclear scientists began a self-imposed ban on publishing matters relating to nuclear fission. The effect was immediate: Nazi scientists spent the war struggling to moderate neutrons (slow them down to the point where they were effective in causing fission) using heavy water (deuterium) rather than the vastly more useful graphite. This self-imposed muzzle continued through the war, issuing in the founding document of modern secrecy, the Atomic Energy Act of 1946. That act released certain parts of the basic chemistry and physics of materials including uranium, thorium, and polonium but kept a lid on the details of a vast amount of technical knowledge, including some basic physics. For example, in 1950 it was permitted to say that the impact of a neutron on $U233$, $U236$, $Pu239$, or $Pu240$ could release a gamma ray but it remained forbidden to say just how likely this reaction was. Only in 1956 would the process technology for producing uranium metal and preparing alloys of uranium and thorium be released. More indirectly, the cost of highly enriched uranium (about $25,000/kg) was only declassified in 1955; presumably the mere quotation of a price conveyed certain information about how it was done (ordinary metallic uranium was running about $40/kg).[9]

Indeed, one of the most classified parts of the fission bomb was the process by which highly enriched metallic $U235$ was produced. It is instructive to follow the sequence of declassification orders from 1946 to 1952 showing the gradual erosion of restriction on electromagnetic separation:

1946: Physics of electrical discharges in a vacuum, experimental data and theory.

1946: "Electrical controls and circuits . . . *omitting reference to classified installations*"

1947: "Experimental and theoretical physics of [electromagnetic separation] *provided they do not reveal production details or processes.*"

1952: "Experimental and theoretical physics and chemistry, engineering designs and operating performance of single electromagnetic process units *without identification as components of the Electromagnetic Production Plant* ("RDD")."[10]

Each step gave more detail, more about the internal wiring and construction of the machinery, until, by the end, the major secret was simply the label of the documents as being for the separation facility at Oak Ridge.

But perhaps the best way to grapple with the secrecy system is to follow the instructions. Suppose you are an original classifier at the Department of Defense. The *Handbook for Writing Security Classification Guidance* is your bible, and it begins by reviewing the various arenas of classified material from weapons, plans, and cryptology to scientific, technological, and economic matters affecting national security. Then you are to ask yourself these questions. First, "Is the information owned by, produced by or for, or under the control of the United States Government?" If yes, then check that the information falls in one of the regulated domains (such as cryptology). If it still looks like a classification candidate, then pose this question: "Can the unauthorized disclosure of the information reasonably be expected to cause damage to the national security?" And if the information is of the destructive type, then the acid test is this:

What is the level of damage ("damage," "serious damage," or "exceptionally grave damage") to the national security expected in the event of an unauthorized disclosure of the information? If the answer to this question is "damage," you have arrived at a decision to classify the information Confidential. If the answer is "serious damage," you have arrived at a decision to classify the information

Secret. If the answer is "exceptionally grave damage," you have arrived at a decision to classify the information Top Secret.[11]

You, the classifier, should then designate the material secret for a period of time less than ten years or, for a variety of reasons, you may want to justify an extension beyond ten years. Just a few of such reasons to carry on with secrecy: revelation of hidden information that might assist in the development of weapons of mass destruction, impair the development of a U.S. weapon system, reveal emergency plans, or violate a treaty.

Next in this antiepistemology you have to do what anyone pursuing a more positive program would: establish the state of the art. This includes, of course, published materials in the United States and abroad but also, and more problematically, known but unpublished material including that possessed by unfriendly countries. By consulting with the intelligence services, you will want to find out what the foreign knowledge is of unpublished materials in the United States. All this is, however, preliminary. Having established what is known, you must identify how classification will add to the "net national advantage," that is, "the values, direct and indirect, accruing or expected to accrue to the United States." Such advantage might derive from the suppression of the fact that the government is interested in a particular effort, or that it has something in its possession. Or the capabilities, performance, vulnerabilities, or uniqueness of an object (or bit of knowledge) that the United States has. The net national advantage might be in guarding surprise or lead time, manufacturing technology, or associations with other data.[12] The real heart of a classification guide is the identification and enunciation of the specific items or elements of information warranting security protection. Regardless of the size or complexity of the subject matter of the guide, or the level at which the classification guide is issued, certain identifiable features of the information create or contribute to actual or expected national security advantage.[13]

Getting at those "special features or critical items of information" and tying them to the net national advantage is the primary task of the classifier. This is where the writer of the guide has to get inside the information being hidden. The questions are subtle. "Are the counter-countermeasures obvious, special, unique, unknown to outsiders or other nations?" Or would knowledge of the counter-countermeasures assist in carrying out new countermeasures? "What," the guide demands, "are the things that really make this effort work?" Here is the analysis of science and technology opened in many of its aspects, all in the service of stopping the flow of science. It puts me in mind of an experimental film I once saw, a black-and-white, 16 mm production, printed in negative, all shot within a single room filled with tripods and lamps. As each light came on, it cast black over its portion of the screen. Here is something similar. Understanding the ways in which things work, are made, deployed, and connected is used to interdict transmission. Your job as a classifier is to locate those critical elements that might lead to vulnerabilities and then to suppress those that can be protected by classification. The guide insists that secrets are not forever. You must answer the question: how long can this particular secret reasonably be expected to be kept?[14]

Epistemology asks how knowledge can be uncovered and secured. Antiepistemology asks how knowledge can be covered and obscured. Classification, the antiepistemology *par excellence*, is the art of nontransmission.

PRESSURES TO DECLASSIFY

With the end of the Cold War in 1989–1990 and the election of President Bill Clinton, the executive branch pressed the agencies to release some of the vast trove of secrets. Secretary of Energy Hazel O'Leary announced on December 7, 1993, that the DOE had begun to "lift the veil of Cold War secrecy" and to make visible some of the hidden data.[15] Increasingly, scientists, scholars, activists, and the DOE itself tried to displace an ethos in which justification was needed to release information to one in which it required justification to keep information classified. The arguments for openness were several. Cost was one—as I mentioned, some $5.5 billion goes into maintaining the secret storehouse. But that isn't the only justification. As the national security establishment itself has long recognized, overclassification breeds disregard for classification procedures. Serious classifiers (as opposed to yahoo politicians desperately looking to classify everything in sight) want the arenas of real secrecy to be protected with higher walls and the vast penumbral gray range to be open.

Back in 1970, the Department of Defense Science Board Task Force on Secrecy, headed by Frederick Seitz, argued to the secretary of defense that there was vastly too much secrecy, and that even a unilateral set of disclosures were preferable to the current system. An all-out effort by the United States and the USSR to control thermonuclear weapons failed utterly as the United Kingdom and China followed soon on their heels. Conversely, when the nation decided to open certain areas of technical research, the results were powerful. The United States led in microwave electronics and computer technology, in nuclear reactors beginning in the mid-1950s, and in transistor technology.[16] Examples of secrecy run amok are legion, including some $2.7 billion that sank like a stone into an un-workable special access program aiming to produce the Navy A-12 attack aircraft. Secrecy contributed too in the protection of unworkable programs like the one outfitted to build the Tacit Rainbow antiradar missile and the ($3.9 billion) Tri-Service Standoff Attack Missile.[17]

Then there are the historians and journalists who clamor for access to documents about the history of the national security state. These groups join a chorus of others, from legislators and lawyers to former atomic workers, soldiers, and ordinary citizens, who have militated for a glimpse of records about radiological contamination, test sites, radiological experimentation on humans, and nuclear working conditions. Scientists themselves—especially those the national laboratories want to recruit from elite universities—want a degree of openness in which they can encounter other ideas and publish their own. But my own judgment is that none of these constituencies would have made even the limited progress they made during the Clinton years had it not been for the demands of industry insisting loud and clear that they no longer be excluded from the trove of secret (objective) information. Declassification makes it easier and cheaper for industry to produce, and, needless to say, opens the vast civilian and, within the constraints of export controls, the huge foreign military market.

TRADE SECRET LEGITIMACY

But within the secret world, managing the flood of data has presented ever greater problems. There is a nervousness in the classifying community, a sense that the rising mountain of classified materials is unstable. The absence of a principled basis for classification weighs heavily, and classification itself makes it hard to provide such a systematic understanding. "Need to know" compartmentalization leaves classifiers in different domains unable to communicate with one another, and each isolated branch forms its own routines of hiding. When the Department of Energy commissioned Oak Ridge classifier Arvin S. Quist to do a massive study of security classification, he commented throughout his several-volume report that there simply were no principles on which classification could be staked. And he wanted such a foundation.

Trade secrets appeared to be the open society's equivalent of national security secrecy, and Quist, speaking both to and for the DOE, saw in trade secrecy law the possibility of establishing, at last, a ground. Addressing the army of classifiers, Quist put it this way:

Our legal system's roots go back millennia, thereby giving that system a solid foundation. Trade secret law is a part of that legal system. Trade secret law has developed over hundreds of years and has been a distinct area of the legal system for over a century—principles of trade secret law are widely accepted. Because trade secret law evolved as part of the "common law," it has a firm basis in our culture. Our extensive body of trade secret law has been developed by a very open process; the workings of our legal system are essentially completely open to the public, and the judicial decisions on trade secrets have been extensively published and discussed. Thus, trade secret law rests on a solid foundation, is consistent with our culture, and is known, understood, and accepted by our citizens.[18]

Establishing the isomorphism between national security and trade secrets then became the order of the day. For this was the holy grail: the exact mechanism for the Teller-Ulam idea, the scheme that first made possible the detonation of a true hydrogen bomb, would remain a fiercely guarded secret, one for which the government was willing to wage an all-out battle in court against the *Progressive* (a rather small left-leaning magazine that printed an article describing the rudiments of the Teller-Ulam scheme). The DOE's declassification guide RDD-7 reports the guarded release in 1979 of the idea this way: "The fact that, in thermonuclear weapons, radiation from a fission explosive can be contained and used to transfer energy to compress and ignite a physically separate component containing thermonuclear fuel. Note: *Any elaboration of this statement will be classified.*" And so it has remained for over half a century.[19] Just such secrets, says

Quist, ought to be understood by comparison with the holiest of trade secrets, that best kept of all commercial formulae, "the recipe for Coca-Cola Classic . . . has been kept a secret for over one hundred years. It is said that only two Coca-Cola company executives know that recipe [which] is in a safe deposit box in Atlanta, which may be opened only by vote of the company's board of directors. . . . We probably would not know if a national security secret was as well-kept as the secret of Coca-Cola."[20]

Schematizing Quist's argument, the parallelism between the secrets of nukes and nachos might look something like Table 2.1.[21]

TABLE 2.1

Characteristic	National security secret (objective)	Trade secret
Interest definition	Includes national security weapons-related "facts of nature," technical design and performance of weapons; method, process, technique, or device to create a weapon	Includes profits formula, pattern, compilation, program, device, method, technique, process that is of economic value and derives its value from secrecy
Availability of knowledge inside organization	Must in fact be secret; must be distributed on a need-to-know basis	Must in fact be secret; must be distributed on a need-to-know basis
Secrecy measures taken	*U.S. v. Heine*: exonerated Heine on grounds that if the United States had not protected the (aviation) secrets inside the United States then it could not convict Heine for having sent information to foreign power	Must take "reasonable" measures that might include restricted access, "no trespassing" signs, guards, restrictive covenants, briefings, badges, compartmentalization
Value of information	Must have actual or potential military advantage	Must have actual or potential economic advantage
Effort to develop secret	Must constitute a sufficient effort such that this investment in development "is a factor in its classification"	Must protect "the substantial investment of employers in their propriety information [trade secrets]"
Effort needed for others to develop	Must be such that the secret not be readily ascertainable by easy reverse engineering, reference books, trade journals, etc.	Must be such that the secret not be readily ascertainable by easy reverse engineering, reference books, trade journals, etc.
Former employees	Use classified solutions to classified problems to solve unclassified problems "outside the fence"	"Former employees can make use of general skills, knowledge, memory if they do not include 'special confidential knowledge obtained from the employer which belongs to the employer.'"

There are two fascinating aspects to Quist's recourse to trade secret law. First, of course, is the formal structure: he is able to develop a largely parallel structure between security and trade secrecy. But perhaps even more interesting is a second feature. At the end of the Cold War (the two volumes appeared in 1989 and 1993, respectively), a senior classification officer could see security secrecy as in need of legitimation from something exterior to the needs of the state. While the nuclear establishment could draw on the 1946 Atomic Energy Act and its successor legislation, trade secrecy carried the weight of a long history. And while the Atomic Energy Act was largely isolated from other bodies of law, and so much of the AEC's own comportment was shrouded in secrecy, trade secrecy law (so Quist argued) emerged from open judicial structures. Because it was hammered out on the anvil of common law, it was part of the wider culture in ways that the scientist- and executive-branch-created AEC never would be. It is hard, perhaps impossible, to imagine such a search for justification to have seemed necessary at the height of the Cold War. Yet here is a case, made from *inside* the Department of Energy, for its secret practices to find a grounding in the legal ethos of the corporation.

CONCLUSION: PRODUCING IGNORANCE

When the Establishment of Secrecy tries to block the transmission of dangerous knowledge, it faces a fundamental dilemma. If it blanket-classifies whole domains of learning (nuclear physics, microwave physics), the accumulated mass of guarded data piles up at a smothering rate: it impedes industry, it interferes with work within the defense establishment, and it degrades the very concept of secrecy by applying it indiscriminately. Yet when the guardians of secrets try to pick and choose, to hunt for the critical number, essential technique, or irreplaceable specification; when they try to classify this fact, that property, or those circumstances, they find themselves in an impossible situation. They find themselves struggling to halt or at least stall the spread of vital, large-scale sectors of the technical-scientific sphere through the protocol-driven excision of bits of language and technique. It is as if they want to make an image unreadable by picking off just the *vital* pixels one by one. Indeed such a digital metaphor may be more than allusive. Faced with the proliferation of electronically registered data, the government is now embarking on a massive effort to recruit AI (artificial intelligence) to automate the classification (and declassification) of the fiber-optic pipes of e-secrets pouring out of the national laboratories and their affiliates.

Philosophically, this puts us, oddly flipped (and through a deadly pun), in the footsteps of early twentieth-century philosophy, when Bertrand Russell and the young Ludwig Wittgenstein were struggling to articulate a vision of language in which communication would be reduced to the assembly of isolated "atomic propositions." These elemental bits of meaning, "Red patch here now" or "Smell of ozone 12:00 noon in this room," were to be assembled into "molecular" and then into ever more complex concatenations. The effort failed back in the early 1900s because facts never did remain within their confines; as even its staunchest advocates eventually conceded, facts could *not* be defined without theory, and theory, ever spreading, refused to congeal into the isolable knowledge-islands of which seventeenth-century natural philosophers dreamed.

For both practical and theoretical reasons, the atomic statements of the 2003 Department of Energy are no more likely than Russell's atomic statements of 1903 to stay in their place. At some level, even the DOE and its sister agencies know this. DOE exempts prototype development of isotope separation technology from the maw of classification because the DOE desperately needs industrial and university-based work to produce each next generation of devices that will spew out the special materials for nuclear weapons. Think of tunable die lasers. But, then, just as the lasers actually start sorting the U-235 from the U-238, the secrecy lid slams down and the knowledge becomes adolescent classified. Too bad for us, though, because the techniques, skilled operators, businesses, journal articles, and graduate students are by then on the hoof. Is it a surprise that the West Germans with no nuclear weapons program were able in the mid-1970s to export the technology to apartheid South Africa, which immediately began assembling and eventually detonating a nuclear bomb? Or for that matter is it really astonishing that DOE's claim that they could contain "any elaboration" of why the Teller-Ulam idea eventually failed?

Back in 1966 when Thomas Pynchon finished his great *Crying of Lot 49*, he sketched a paranoid and disjointed society, a universe so obsessed with concealment and conspiracy, with government and corporate monopoly control of information, that the causal structure and even the raw sequence of events hovered perpetually out of reach. Now that the secret world has begun to exceed the open one, Pynchon's fantasy stands ever nearer to hand. In the midst of his protagonist Oedipa Maas's efforts to understand what was happening to her, she stumbles across a cryptogram scrawled onto a latrine wall, inscribed into postage stamps, present, if one looked carefully, just about anywhere. It was, as she soon discovers, the old post horn, symbol of the late medieval Thurn and Taxis state monopoly postal system. But there is a twist. Pynchon's post horn has a mute jammed into it; communication was blocked.[22]

Secret societies with private communication desperately tried to counter the monopoly on information; Pynchon's world crawls with disaffected engineers trying to patent Maxwell's demon, would-be suicides, and isolated lovers all seeking to break the out-of-control monopoly of knowledge transmission. Mad as it sounds, is it madder than it must feel to the radio astronomers who discover that important bits of what they know about their best instruments have long been clear to the National Reconnaissance Organization (NRO) and the NSA? That one of the main objects of astrophysical inquiry (gamma ray bursters) emerged not in the groves of academe but through secret efforts to monitor potential Russian violations of the Nuclear Test Ban Treaty using satellites built to find H-bomb detonations on the far side of the moon?

Contra the logical positivists and their allies, it is precisely *not* possible to reduce meaningful language to discrete enunciations. Communication—at least meaningful, verifiable communication—cannot be rendered into a sequence of protocol statements. But such a conception of knowledge is exactly what lies behind the classifiers' imaginary. To block the transmission of knowledge, to impede communication about the most deadly edge of modern science and technology, the security services of the United States (and for that matter NATO, the Warsaw Pact, China, and dozens of other countries) have chosen to list facts, circumstances, associations, and effects that would be banned from utterance.

At the root of this theory of punctiform knowledge excision stands a fundamental instability. To truly cover an arena of knowledge one is drawn ever outward, removing from the public sphere entire domains until one is in fact cutting out such a vast multiple of the original classification that the derivative censorship covers 330 million pages a year and growing. Even that number is one kept "low" by beating down the classified domain by its inverse, the classification of particular points. But then one is caught in the manifestly peculiar position of trying to stanch knowledge flow by punctiform excision.

On the one side is an unaffordable, intractable, holist antiepistemology, on the other a ludicrously naive punctiform one. If this were just a theoretical matter it would be fascinating but delimited. It is not. At stake for the national security establishment is the broad interference that compartmentalization is causing, manifest most recently in the world-changing failures of intelligence leading up to 9/11 and weapons of mass destruction that were or weren't in Iraq. Industry chafes under the restriction of classification, and vast resources are needed to defend excessive retention of information. For universities, the effects of the new order of secrecy are just beginning to be felt. The Patriot Act restricts laboratory access to people coming from certain countries, a direct clash with universities' own statutes that expressly forbid denying access to certain categories of laboratories on the basis of race, creed, or national origin. More broadly, for all the conceptual and practical problems with classification behind the fence at Los Alamos or Livermore, the problem of restricting research in the open university may be far greater. But it is not "just" the rights and culture of universities that are at stake. Billions of dollars have been spent on projects that scientifically or technically would not have, could not have, survived the gimbal-eyed scrutiny of international and open review. Whatever their strategic use or uselessness might have been, the atomic airplane and the x-ray laser were not just over budget, they were over a doomed set of assumptions about science and technology.

In the end, however, the broadest problem is not merely that of the weapons laboratory, industry, or the university. It is that, if pressed too hard and too deeply, secrecy, measured in the staggering units of Libraries of Congress, is a threat to democracy. And that is not a problem to be resolved by an automated original classifier or declassifier. It is political at every scale, from attempts to excise a single critical idea to the vain efforts to remove whole domains of knowledge.

NOTES

1. Assuming 3,000 pages per foot and 15 million pages per mile, the LOC contains approximately 500 miles of shelf and thus about 7.5 billion pages. This averages 60 pages per document, in contrast to the Joint Security Commission, which in 1994 estimated 3 pages per classified document. I take this to have been superseded by the Department of Energy, Analysis of Declassification Efforts, December 12, 1996, http://www.fas.org/sgp/othergov/doerep.html, which uses a mean of 10 pages per classified document.

2. According to the Annual Report for fiscal 2001: Harvard College Library, 11 libraries including Widener, net added 139,834 volumes for fiscal 2001. Librarians at Harvard estimate 30 volumes per three feet, so 10 volumes per foot or 300 pages per volume. In the fiscal year 2001, it contained 8.9 million volumes; the total university library systemnet added 218,507 volumes to a total of 14.7 million volumes.

3. See 2001 ISOO Report to President, http://www.fas.org/sgp/isoo/2001rpt.html [accessed February 16, 2004].

4. See 2002 ISOO Report to the President, http://www.fas.org/sgp/isoo/2002rpt.pdf [accessed February 16, 2004].

5. U.S. Department of Energy, Office of Declassification, "Restricted Data Declassification Decisions 1946 to the Present," RDD-7, 1 Jan. 20051, http://ww.fas.org/sgp/othergov/doe/rdd-7. html; hereafter abbreviated "RDD."

6. Arvin S. Quist, "Security Classification of Information," 2 vols., http://www/fas/org/sgp/library/quist2/index.html, vol. 2, chap. 3; hereafter abbreviated "SC."

7. See National Research Council, *A Review of the Department of Energy Classification: Policy and Practice* (Washington, DC: National Academies Press, 1995), 7–8.

8. Quist, vol. 2, ch. 2, 1–3.

9. Quist, vol. 2, ch. 2, 21–23.

10. Quist, vol. 2, ch. 2, 32.

11. Assistant Secretary of Defense for Command, Control, Communications, and Intelligence, "Department of Defense Handbook for Writing Security Classification Guidance," DoD 5200.1-H, November 1999, http://www.dtic.mil/whs/directives/corres/pdf/52001h_1199/p52001h.pdf, p. 8; hereafter abbreviated "DD."

12. "Handbook," DoD 5200.1-H, C3.3.

13. "Handbook," DoD 5200.1-H, C3.5.1.

14. "Handbook," DoD 5200.1-H, AP2.5, AP2.7.

15. Secretary of Energy Advisory Board website, http://www.seab.energy.gov/sub/openpanl .html.

16. See Steven Aftergood, "Government Secrecy and Knowledge Production: A Survey of Some General Issues," http://ciaonet.org/wps/rej02.html, p. 5 [accessed April 8, 2003].

17. See ibid., p. 3.

18. Quist, vol. 2, app. A, "Classification of Information Principles and Trade Secret Law," p. 1; following chart builds on this appendix.

19. "Restricted Data Declassification Decisions 1946 to the Present," RDD-7, 1 Jan. 2001, U.S. Department of Energy, pp. 61–62.

20. Quist, vol. 2, app. A, 3.

21. The following chart builds on "SC," vol. 2, appendix A.

22. See Thomas Pynchon, *The Crying of Lot 49* (1966; New York: HarperCollins, 1999).

CHAPTER 3

Challenging Knowledge:

How Climate Science Became
a Victim of the Cold War

NAOMI ORESKES AND ERIK M. CONWAY

ON JUNE 2, 2005, California governor Arnold Schwarzenegger announced an initiative to curb greenhouse gas emissions in California as a step toward addressing global warming. In his speech, the governor declared: "The debate is over. We know the science. We see the threat, and we know the time for action is now."[1]

Schwarzenegger had his science right: the scientific debate *is* over. In fact, it has been for quite some time. Since the early to mid-1990s there has been a consensus in the scientific community about the basic facts of global warming, which is why the Intergovernmental Panel on Climate Change (IPCC) is able to say with assurance that "most of the warming observed over the last 50 years is attributable to human activities."[2]

THE CONSENSUS ON CLIMATE CHANGE

What scientific knowledge lies behind this statement? First, that humans have changed the chemistry of the earth's atmosphere, most notably by changing the concentration of carbon dioxide from a pre–industrial revolution level of about 280 parts per million to its current level of 385 and rising. (For his systematic work on the measurement of atmospheric CO_2 since 1958, Charles David Keeling won the 2002 National Medal of Science.) Second, that this carbon dioxide is largely the result of the burning of fossil fuels—coal, oil, and natural gas—since the industrial revolution.[3] Third, that carbon dioxide is a greenhouse gas, meaning that it is highly transparent to visible light and less so to infrared; so if you change its concentration, it affects the radiative balance of the atmosphere. (This point was first made in the nineteenth century by John Tyndall and subsequently reaffirmed by various scientists, including Gustav Arrhenius, G. S. Callendar, Gilbert Plass, Hans Suess, and Roger Revelle.)[4] Physical theory predicts that given the steady increase in atmospheric CO_2 (and other greenhouse gases), we may reasonably expect to see the earth's climate change. And we have.

Instrumental measurements reveal an increased average global surface temperature of approximately 0.8° C since the 1860s, when sustained systematic record keeping began, and these data are independently corroborated by studies of tree rings, coral reefs, and ice cores.[5]

Physical theory and computer models predict that the effects of global warming will be seen first, and most strongly, in the Arctic, due to what is known as "ice-albedo feedback." Ice and snow strongly reflect solar radiation, helping to keep cold regions cold. But if you melt some of this snow or ice, exposing bare land or seawater, then more solar radiation is absorbed, leading to more rapid warming, more melting, more warming, and so on. So a given amount of warming has a bigger impact in the Arctic than in temperate regions. This is known as "polar amplification," and predicted effects included thinning and decreased extent of sea ice and the Greenland ice sheet, decreased extent of permafrost regions, earlier spring thaws, and ramifying effects of these changes on indigenous peoples who depend on native species for their survival. All of these effects have now been observed.[6]

Physical theory and climate models also suggest that global warming may lead to an increase in either the frequency or intensity of extreme weather events such as hurricanes, heat waves, and droughts. In the wake of the record-breaking Atlantic hurricane season of 2005, many people have wondered if this prediction has also come true. Hurricane seasons are notoriously variable, so no single storm or season can confirm or deny this prediction, but statistical studies suggest an increase in hurricane intensity in the Atlantic, Pacific, and Indian oceans, and in recent years numerous records have been broken around the globe.[7] While there is still some argument over whether this is a real change or an artifact of poor record keeping, many scientists believe that this prediction is coming true as well.

In short, both theory and evidence support the claim that anthropogenic global warming is underway.

Climate models based on our current scientific understanding predict that unabated increases in greenhouse gases will have serious and irreversible effects, including sea level rise, further melting of Arctic (and worse, Antarctic) ice, changes in ocean chemistry and circulation, habitat destruction, and more. Some of these changes may be mitigated by human actions, but mitigation is typically difficult and expensive, and in many cases will be unlikely to protect non-human species. The most recent scientific literature concludes that if all human carbon emissions were to stop tomorrow, the earth would still warm at least another 0.5° C.[8] But emissions will not stop tomorrow, so the "climate commitment" we have already made to future warming is much larger—most likely 2–3° C or more, and perhaps substantially more.[9]

These concerns and results have been documented in the four assessment reports of the Intergovernmental Panel on Climate Change, an organization created by the United Nations Environment Programme and the World Meteorological Organization, representing the world's most prominent atmospheric scientists, meteorologists, geophysicists, geographers, and other scientists. The most recent report, issued in February 2007, represents the combined work of over 800 scientists and 1,000 peer reviewers from 130 countries. Virtually everyone who is anyone in climate research has had the opportunity to participate in the IPCC process.[10]

The IPCC conclusions have been ratified by every major scientific society in the United States with pertinent expertise, including the American Geophysical Union, the American Meteorological Society, and the American Association for the Advancement of Science.[11] Outside the United States, they have been affirmed by the Royal Society in its "Guide to Facts and Fiction about Climate Change"[12] and by a joint statement of the National Academies of Science of eleven nations, including France, Russia, Germany, Japan, Italy, Canada, China, and Brazil. Robert May, president of the Royal Society, recently summarized the view of academicians around the world: "The scientific evidence forcefully points to a need for a truly international effort. Make no mistake, we have to act now. And the longer we procrastinate, the more difficult the task of tackling climate change becomes."[13] And in October 2007, the IPCC shared with former U.S. vice president Al Gore the Nobel Peace Prize for their "efforts to build up and disseminate greater knowledge about man-made climate change."[14]

Some critics have suggested that the IPCC, an international organization with links to the United Nations, might be politicized and not accurately reflect the consensus of expert scientific opinion. In 2001, the White House, under George W. Bush, commissioned a report on climate change from the National Academy of Sciences, addressing this question. The academy laid this argument to rest: "The IPCC's conclusion that most of the observed warming of the last 50 years is likely to have been due to the increase in greenhouse gas concentrations accurately reflects the current thinking of the scientific community on this issue."[15]

This conclusion should not have been surprising. The scientific community was in broad agreement that global warming would likely become a problem as early as 1979, when the National Academy of Sciences commissioned a study under the leadership of the distinguished MIT meteorologist Jule Charney. Charney's committee concluded that "If carbon dioxide continues to increase, [we] find no reason to doubt that climate changes will result, and no reason to believe that these changes will be negligible."[16]

Many people are surprised to learn that scientists recognized so early the dangers of global warming from greenhouse gases, and some might suppose that Charney's group was an outlier, sounding an early warning on warming much like British engineer Guy Callendar in the 1930s.[17] But the panel's work was a *review* of numerous studies undertaken throughout the 1970s, and so the accompanying press release declared: "A plethora of studies from diverse sources indicates a consensus that climate changes will result from man's combustion of fossil fuels and changes in land use."[18]

The academy's concern was expressed by way of a prediction—"climate changes will result"—changes that some scientists thought would be evident by the end of the century. In the proposal written to the White House Office of Science and Technology Policy, outlining the scope of the report, the academy wrote, "Plausible projections of future carbon dioxide concentrations suggest several-fold increases by the middle of the next century; experiments with models of the earth's climate system suggest major associated climate changes that might become evident in our own century."[19]

They were right. In 1995, the IPCC concluded that effects on climate from human activities were now "discernible." The evidence leading to this conclusion was the motivation for the United Nations "earth summit" in Rio de Janeiro in 1992, which led to the UN Framework Convention on Climate Change, signed by President George H. W. Bush.

For the overwhelming majority of research scientists, global warming is no longer a *prediction*, but an *observation*. In the summer of 2005, for example, the new president of the National Academy of Sciences, Ralph Cicerone, affirmed in testimony to the U.S. Congress: "Carbon dioxide in the atmosphere is now at its highest level in 400,000 years and it continues to rise. Nearly all climate scientists today believe that much of Earth's current warming has been caused by increases in the amount of greenhouse gases in the atmosphere, mostly from the burning of fuels."[20]

So why should anyone be confused about the facts of global climate change? The earth *is* warming—this is an observation, not a matter of political persuasion—and scientists agree that human activities are largely the cause. They have been in agreement over these matters for some time. Yet, as recently as 2006, polls showed show that a majority of the American people thought scientists were still arguing the point, and only about a third believed that global warming is "mainly caused by things people do."[21]

In fact, climate change is a profoundly polarized issue. Throughout the 1990s, on the Internet and AM radio, in the pages of *Forbes*, *Fortune*, and the *Wall Street Journal*, and even in the U.S. Congress, one could find adamant denials that global warming was real, or that if it was real, that it was caused by human activities. These denials emanated almost entirely from the right wing of the American political spectrum. In a letter to the editor of the *New York Times*, Robert Berkman of Rochester, New York, summarized the situation aptly:

What I fail to understand is why global warming has come to be viewed as a political or ideological issue. . . . If you are in a house where there's a strong burning smell and the air is getting smoky, the sane response is to acknowledge that there is a fire somewhere and do something about it—no matter what one's political ideology might be.[22]

Current confusion and political polarization has often been blamed on the administration of U.S President George W. Bush, which has often suggested that the scientific basis for understanding global warming is insufficient to warrant action, emphasizing the uncertainties rather than the accepted and established scientific relationships.[23] But the problem is quite a bit deeper, with historical roots in a little known organization called the George C. Marshall Institute. Examining the origins of the Marshall Institute suggests that the answer to Mr. Berkman's question is, at least in part, that climate science became a victim of the Cold War.

THE GEORGE C. MARSHALL INSTITUTE

Throughout the 1990s, a major source of statements in opposition to the scientific consensus on climate change was a Washington, DC, think tank known as the George C. Marshall Institute. Today, the institute continues to argue that there are major unresolved scientific uncertainties and significant scientific debate, suggesting that these uncertainties are sufficient justification for continuing to delay action to control greenhouse gas emissions and deforestation.[24]

The institute's stated mission is "to encourage the use of sound science in making public policy about important issues for which science and technology are major considerations." Examination of their positions, however, reveals that their view of "sound" science frequently clashes with the results of scientific research published in refereed journals, and with the stated positions of leading professional scientific societies.

Since the early 1990s, the Marshall Institute has insisted that the evidence of global climate change is uncertain, incomplete, insufficient, or otherwise inadequate. Its spokesmen and members have argued that there is no proof that global warming is real or, if it is real, that there is no proof that it is caused by human activities or, if it is real and anthropogenic, that there is no proof that it matters.[25] The institute suggests that regulatory action is premature at best, foolish and damaging at worst. Individuals with links to the institute have written extensively in mass media outlets and popular magazines such as the *Wall Street Journal, American Spectator, Forbes*, and *National Review*.[26] They have appeared on television and on radio, and on sponsored websites and listservs promoting views diametrically opposed to the mainstream of scientific opinion.

One recent report by the institute argues that natural variability is insufficiently understood to permit us to say that current global warming is not natural:

Climate varies naturally on time scales ranging from seasons to the tens of thousands of years between ice ages. Knowledge of the natural variability of the climate system is needed to assess the extent of human impact on the climate system. At present there are no robust estimates of natural climate variability on the decades to centuries time scale that is essential for evaluating the extent to which human activities have already affected the climate system, and to provide the baseline of knowledge needed to assess how they might affect it in the future.[27]

This position is of course at odds with the scientific consensus described above. Scientists have looked extensively at the issue of natural variability and concluded that it is insufficient to account for the observed changes.[28]

Why does the Marshall Institute insist on opposing professional expert opinion? Why do they deny anthropogenic global warming? A possible answer is suggested in the second sentence in their mission statement, as currently posted on their website's home page: "Our current program emphasizes issues in national security and the environment." The connection between national security and the environment is clarified by considering the history of the institute, and its founders.

THE GEORGE C. MARSHALL INSTITUTE:
ROBERT JASTROW AND SDI

The founder and long-time director of the Marshall Institute was Robert Jastrow. Born in 1925, Jastrow enjoyed a thirty-year career as a distinguished astrophysicist. He played a leading role in the U.S. space program, chairing NASA's lunar exploration committee. In 1961, he became the founding director of the Goddard Institute for Space Studies. On retiring in 1981, he became an adjunct professor of Earth Sciences at Dartmouth, a position he held until 1991.

While at Dartmouth, Jastrow had taken up another cause: the defense of Ronald Reagan's Strategic Defense Initiative (SDI). Proposed in March of 1983, the SDI concept was to develop a missile "shield" through the use of space-based lasers to defend the United States from incoming inter-continental ballistic missiles. Within weeks of its announcement, academic scientists began to express opposition, criticizing the program as unrealistic, undesirable, and potentially destabilizing, as it could undermine the principle of Mutual Assured Destruction on which the Cold War balance of power had long hung. By the end of the year, a few voices of opposition had swollen to a chorus, causing considerable consternation in the Reagan administration.

As historian Rebecca Slayton has discussed, academic physicists organized a historically unprecedented effort to resist the program. While most had long been accepting military research and development funds, they reacted differently to SDI, fomenting a coordinated effort to block the program that culminated in a boycott of program funds. By May of 1986, 6,500 academic scientists had signed a pledge not to solicit or accept funds from the missile defense research program, a pledge that received abundant media coverage.[29]

Jastrow was appalled by both his colleagues' actions and the media coverage of it, which he felt made it seem as if all scientists opposed SDI. A man with strong administrative and communicative skills, and plenty of contacts in Washington, he decided to act. Writing on Dartmouth College letterhead in December of 1984, he invited William (Bill) Nierenberg, director of the Scripps Institution of Oceanography, to join him and Frederick Seitz on the board of directors of a new institute, named after the military commander from World War II who, as Eisenhower's secretary of state, gave his name to the "Marshall Plan" to rebuild Europe.

Frederick Seitz was a solid-state physicist who had trained under Eugene Wigner at Princeton, with whom he developed the concept of the Wigner-Seitz unit cell, a now-standard way of understanding crystal lattices. From 1965 until 1968, Seitz was also president of the National Academy of Sciences, and in 1968 became president of Rockefeller University, a position he held until retiring in 1978.

Bill Nierenberg was also a physicist, having studied with I. I. Rabi at

Columbia and worked on uranium isotope separation for the Manhattan Project before joining the physics department at Berkeley. In 1953, he became the director of Columbia University's Hudson Laboratory, created to continue scientific projects begun on behalf of the U.S. Navy during World War II. He subsequently held a series of positions at the interface between science and politics, including NATO's assistant secretary general for scientific affairs, and in 1965, he became the director of the Scripps Institution of Oceanography.

Both Seitz and Nierenberg served on numerous government panels dealing with national security issues: Seitz had served on the U.S. President's Science Advisory Committee; Nierenberg had a longtime association with JASON, the committee of scientists with high-level security clearances who advise the Department of Defense on matters of science related to national security. Here were three prominent physicists with extensive links to the military-scientific complex, joining forces to counter the anti-SDI stance of most of their colleagues.[30]

Their principal focus was the mass media. The institute set up workshops and programs, and wrote reports and press releases, to counter the prevailing negative opinion of SDI. Jastrow had taken a first step with articles for *Commentary* and the *Wall Street Journal*. "It seems to have been effective," he told Nierenberg, "*Commentary* and the *Wall Street Journal* have been getting calls and letters from Sagan, Bethe, Carter, etc." A debate was now on.

Jastrow believed that if the American people understood SDI, they would support it, but for this to happen journalists had to present it correctly. The institute's first initiative, therefore, would be a "two-day training seminar for journalists on the fundamental technologies of Strategic Defense."[31] Over the next two years, the institute built up its program activities in the manner that Jastrow had hoped. By 1986, it had clarified its goal and was moving toward getting its message directly to where it counted, namely, Congress. Through press briefings, reports, and seminars directly aimed at Congress members and their staff, the institute promoted its message.

Jastrow's approach was underlined by a strongly anti-communist orientation. He believed that the opponents of SDI—particularly the Union of Concerned Scientists—were playing into Soviet hands.[32] As evidence, he cited a letter written by Soviet Secretary General Mikhail Gorbachev to MIT professor and Union of Concerned Scientists' founder Henry Kendall, congratulating him on the union's "noble activities in the cause of peace."[33] If Gorbachev approved of Kendall's work, then something was wrong. Jastrow suggested that Kendall and the union were stooges of the Soviets, noting "the intensification—one could say almost, the ferocity—of the efforts by the UCS and Soviet leaders to undermine domestic support for SDI."[34]

A major debating point was whether SDI violated the Anti-Ballistic Missile Treaty. The institute insisted that it did not, an argument used in England by Conservative MP Ian Lloyd in a House of Commons debate. Quoting directly from Marshall Institute materials, Lloyd insisted that SDI did not violate the ABM treaty because the treaty did not prohibit *research*. Lloyd closed with the familiar Cold War argument that the goal of the arms race was not simply to maintain a balance of terror, but rather to free the Soviet people. SDI was a means to achieve that goal:

[A] fundamental Western interest is the survival of the Russian people as a whole long enough for them to understand, evaluate, and eventually escape from the yoke of their self-imposed tyranny. That is in the interests of the civilised world. The perspective of this decision on SDI on both sides is one that extends well into the next century and clearly embraces that possibility. Our purpose is not merely the survival, but ultimately the legitimate enlargement, of the free world by the voluntary actions of convinced peoples.[35]

A consistent theme of Marshall Institute materials was the demand for "balance"—that the UCS position papers on SDI were one-sided, and journalists were obligated to present "both sides." Fair enough, there were two sides of SDI, conceptually—support and opposition—but those two sides had very different *numbers* of experts associated with them. One was a large majority position, the other a small minority position. If journalists were to give both sides equal weight or space, this would effectively misrepresent the situation in the scientific community. Yet the institute's insistence on gaining equal time for their (minority) views proved to be highly effective, and they later used the "balance" card in a host of other debates, including global climate change.

THE INSTITUTE TURNS TO GLOBAL WARMING

In 1986, global warming was not on the institute's radar screen. Besides SDI, other issues under consideration included nuclear winter, seismic verification, and the relative merits of manned and unmanned space flight. But 1989 saw the fall of the Berlin Wall, and by the early 1990s the Soviet empire was in collapse. On at least one reading, the Cold War was over.

Perhaps not coincidentally, the Marshall Institute began that very year to address global warming. By the early 1990s climate had become a major focus. As scientists began to consolidate around a consensus position and world leaders to converge on Rio, the institute scientists pursued the same strategy they had used with SDI: they claimed that the majority position was mistaken, that the science on which it was based was incomplete, inaccurate, or just plain wrong, and they demanded equal time for their views.

In the case of SDI, the demand for equal time had a certain logic: many scientists' objections to SDI were not exactly *scientific*, based as they were on moral and ethical qualms about destabilizing the balance of power. SDI *was* a political issue, and a great deal of opposition to it was political—so it was fair to insist on an open political debate. Moreover, SDI did not yet exist, so in a certain sense there were no facts about it.

Global warming was different. The question of whether or not warming was happening was an empirical matter—separable at least in principle from political decisions over how to respond. This was the position taken by most scientists in the U.S. Global Climate Research Program, who drew on the traditional fact/value distinction to defend their own objectivity and political neutrality. So when the Marshall Institute began to attack the scientific *evidence*, mainstream scientists were appalled. Consider one example.

In 1995, Robert S. Walker, chairman of the House Committee on Science, issued a press release quoting directly from a Marshall Institute report attacking the U.S. Global Climate Research Program. The press release was accompanied not by any statements from the leaders of that program, but from the Marshall Institute, whose leaders attacked NASA's Mission to Planet Earth—the very program designed to determine the facts about global warming—and called the U.S. Global Climate Research Program a "perversion of the scientific process."

John McElroy, dean of Engineering at the University of Texas, Arlington, and a member of the National Academy of Sciences Space Science Board, was enraged by the accusations and penned a three-page, single-spaced letter to Walker to register his indignation, and to defend the "many sober, careful scientists who are attempting to unravel one of the most challenging scientific puzzles that one can conceive." The Marshall Institute report

seriously understates the complexity of the problem and the time that will be required for its solution. [Its] political charge of "perversion of the scientific process" is reprehensible, . . . and is unsupported by evidence that would lend credence to such an allegation.[36]

The allegations, he concluded, were "scurrilous."[37]

That was in 1995. If you visit the Marshall Institute home page today, you will find "Environment" and "Climate Change" at the head of its agenda. How did climate change become the focus for an organization created to defend SDI? How did the Marshall Institute reach the position of offending mainstream scientists such as McElroy? And what does this tell us about the cultural production of ignorance? To answer these questions, we must consider some of the other activities of the institute's founders, Robert Jastrow and Frederick Seitz.

HOW SDI, TOBACCO, ACID RAIN, CFCS, AND GLOBAL WARMING CAME TOGETHER

Frederick Seitz was the first chairman of the board of the institute and continues to be listed as their chair, emeritus. He is well known in the scientific community as a past president of the National Academy of Sciences and president emeritus of the Rockefeller University. Less well known is the fact that he served as a principal advisor in the 1980s to the R. J. Reynolds Tobacco Company.[38]

In the mid-1970s, RJR Nabisco, the parent company of R. J. Reynolds Tobacco, established a "Medical Research Program" to support research that might help them avoid legal liability, either by establishing causes of cancer other than smoking, or by complicating the causal links between lifestyle and cancer. Much of the funded work can fairly be described as basic research—dealing with mechanisms of cell mutation, lung physiology, genetic predispositions, and the like—and a great deal was done at leading American research universities. But was this simple philanthropy, aimed at advancing basic science? Not exactly.

Documents released through tobacco litigation discovery show that the program goal was to find evidence or arguments that might cast doubt on the links between tobacco use and adverse health effects, by emphasizing other causal factors such as stress, hypertension, personality traits, and genetic background.[39] These documents also show that between 1975 and 1989, RJR Nabisco spent $45 million dollars on this program, and a principal advisor in establishing and running it was Frederick Seitz.[40]

In May 1979, Seitz explained how, when, and why he became associated with R. J. Reynolds Industries:

About a year ago, when my period as President of the Rockefeller University was nearing its end, [I was] asked if I would be willing to serve as advisor to the Board of Directors of R. J. Reynolds Industries, Inc., as it developed its program on the support of biomedical research related to degenerative diseases in man—a program which would enlarge upon the work supported through the consortium of tobacco industries. Since . . . R. J. Reynolds had provided very generous support for the biomedical work at the Rockefeller University, I was more than glad to accept.[41]

Among others involved in the program was Maclyn McCarty, the man who along with Ostwald Avery and Colin MacLeod had first demonstrated that DNA is the material that carries hereditary information in cells. McCarty, a Rockefeller colleague, worked with Seitz to establish the guidelines for the research program.[42] Seitz had been appointed to an advisory group to the board of directors, a group that also included former Reynolds chairman Colin Stokes.

In what appears to have been the introductory remarks to a speech by Seitz, Stokes elaborated on the research program. He asserted that the charges that tobacco was linked to lung cancer, hardening of the arteries, and carbon monoxide poisoning were "tenuous" (despite their repeated affirmation in Surgeon General's reports) and that "Reynolds and other cigarette makers have reacted to these scientifically unproven claims by intensifying our funding of objective research into these matters." Stokes claimed that "science really knows little about the causes or development mechanisms of chronic degenerative diseases imputed to cigarettes, including lung cancer, emphysema, and cardiovascular disorders" and that many of the studies linking smoking to these diseases were either "incomplete" or "relied on dubious methods or hypotheses and faulty interpretations."[43]

The intent of the program was to develop "a strong body of scientific data or opinion in defense of the product," which Stokes stressed had helped the industry avoid legal liability in the past. "Due to favorable scientific testimony, no plaintiff has ever collected a penny from any tobacco company in lawsuits claiming that smoking causes lung cancer or cardiovascular illness—even though one hundred and seventeen such cases have been brought since 1954 [sic]."[44] To evaluate and monitor these research projects, R. J. Reynolds had "secured the services of a permanent consultant—Dr. Frederick Seitz, former president of Rockefeller University."[45]

The impact of these research programs is hard to assess, but their purpose is not. The goal was to develop arguments to confound the causal links between tobacco and cancer by emphasizing epidemiological uncertainties and biochemical complexities—in effect, to construct ignorance.[46] The emphasis on uncertainty and complexity would characterize subsequent efforts to challenge the scientific evidence of anthropogenic global warming.

Seitz's work for R. J. Reynolds seems to have ended around 1989, just when the Marshall Institute began its campaign to deny the link between greenhouse gas emissions and global warming. Seitz by this time was 78 years old, and perhaps not as energetic as he had once been, and the project was taken up by another retired physicist: S. Fred Singer.

Like Jastrow, Seitz, and Nierenberg, Singer was a prominent physicist and career science administrator. Like Seitz, he received his PhD in physics at Princeton, from which he moved into a research career in the Upper Atmosphere Rocket Program at the Applied Physics Laboratory at Johns Hopkins University. Throughout the 1950s and early 1960s he worked on topics in atmospheric physics, astrophysics, and rocket and satellite technology, and in 1962 became the first director of the National Weather Satellite Center. From there he moved increasingly into the policy dimensions of environmental issues, serving as deputy assistant administrator at the U.S. EPA, where he chaired the Interagency Work Group on the Environmental Impacts of the Super-Sonic Transport and later served as chief scientist at the U.S. Department of Transportation in the second Reagan administration (1987–1989).[47]

In 1989, Singer founded the Science and Environment Policy Project (SEPP) in his home in Virginia. Echoing the mission statement of the Marshall Institute, SEPP was founded to "advance environment and health policies through sound science." Following the pattern established by Jastrow, Singer wrote numerous popular and semi-popular articles, op-ed pieces, and letters to editors challenging the emerging scientific consensus on global warming.[48]

Between 1989 and 2003, Singer published at least thirty-five articles, letters, and op-ed pieces, many of which disputed the reality or significance of anthropogenic warming. Meanwhile, many websites and listservs developed on the Internet citing arguments found in his work, and that of other individuals affiliated with the Marshall Institute.[49] This, of course, coincided with the period in which the mainstream scientific community reached consensus over global climate change. In short, the pattern was identical with that pursued for SDI: attempt to convince the public, through mass media campaigns, to accept an interpretation well outside the mainstream of professional science.

Singer's campaign culminated in 1997 with the publication of a book, *Hot Talk, Cold Science: Global Warming's Unfinished Debate*, published by the Independent Institute, a conservative think tank with links to the Hoover Institution, and whose board of academic advisors included the economist Julian Simon, famous for his "cornucopian" theory that, given truly free markets, technological innovation can and will solve any environmental or social problem. Government intervention is not only unnecessary but counterproductive.

Two years before, the IPCC had issued its Second Assessment Report in which it concluded that the balance of evidence suggested that climate change due to human activity, particularly fossil fuel burning and land use changes, was now "discernible."[50] While the IPCC report has since been ratified by virtually all relevant major scientific societies, Singer's book claimed that the evidence for warming was "neither settled, nor compelling, nor even convincing." Focusing on instabilities and uncertainties, he claimed that "scientists continue to discover new mechanisms for climate change and to put forth new theories to try to account for the fact that global temperature is not rising, even though greenhouse theory says it should."[51]

This was wrong on one count and at best misleading on another. The IPCC summaries made clear that the weight of the available evidence showed that global temperature *was* rising. Climate scientists were continuing to address the diverse mechanisms of climate change, but not because they doubted that greenhouse gases were implicated. It was to better understand the contributions of various possible forces, to understand how their effects ramify through Earth systems, and to determine whether severe climate change might happen abruptly.

The book's foreword claimed that global warming was simply a scare tactic, the result of pandering to irrational fears of environmental calamity by scientists seeking fame and fortune. A more sober analysis purportedly showed that "we do not at present have convincing evidence of any significant climate change other than from natural causes."[52] Who was the author of this sober foreword? Frederick Seitz.

Again Seitz was challenging the consensus of the expert scientific community to take a position that favored industry positions. And Singer was following a similar pattern, applying the strategy of challenging knowledge to several other issues as well: that acid rain was linked to power plant emissions, that stratospheric ozone depletion was linked to chlorinated fluorocarbons (CFCs), and that adverse health effects could be attributed to environmental tobacco smoke.[53]

In the early 1980s, Singer had served on the White House Office of Science and Technology (OSTP) Acid Rain Panel. In 1983, two major scientific reports affirmed that acid precipitation was largely the result of sulfate emissions from power plants, as well as nitrous emissions from automobile exhaust, and that policy steps should be taken to curb those emissions. One report came from the National Academy of Sciences, the other from OSTP itself. When the OSTP report was completed, the Reagan White House stalled the report's release, arguing that "more research" was needed. Administration spokesmen argued that the science was too uncertain to justify immediate action.[54]

This was the same argument that Singer would make a few years later in *Hot Talk, Cold Science*, and no wonder: Singer was apparently involved in the White House decision. According to one member of an acid rain panel on which Singer served, Singer was persistently skeptical of the scientific evidence and eventually went along with the majority only when it became clear that no one else on the committee would support his position.[55]

By the early 1990s, acid rain legislation had been adopted, and a parallel environmental issue had gained public attention: the depletion of stratospheric ozone by CFCs, chemicals used in refrigerators, air conditioners, and hair spray. Singer was involved in this issue, too.

Many chemicals break down rapidly in the natural environment, but CFCs are extraordinarily long-lived and stable. This had led atmospheric chemists Sherwood Rowland and Mario Molina to propose, in an article in *Nature* in 1974, that CFCs might reach the stratosphere where they would finally break down, releasing free chlorine that could combine with and destroy stratospheric ozone. Rowland and Molina's hypothesis stimulated vigorous scientific debate. More than a few scientists agreed that the potential for damage was significant, but the relevant empirical evidence was contradictory. So the U.S. government established a research program in 1977 to investigate the potential for CFC-induced ozone destruction. This program's Second Ozone Assessment, issued in 1985, became the scientific basis for the 1987 Montreal Protocol on Substances That Deplete the Ozone Layer, requiring 50 percent cuts in chlorofluorocarbon production by 2000. It also required the signatory parties to revisit the Montreal Protocol periodically in the light of new evidence, so that it could be tightened or loosened if the scientific case for CFC-induced depletion changed.[56]

In 1985, as the assessment was being finalized, British measurements in Antarctica revealed the now-famous ozone "hole," a continental-size region with depletion rates far higher than those expected by the scientific community. In 1986 and 1987, the American Chemical Association, the

National Oceanic and Atmospheric Administration, and NASA mounted joint expeditions to the Antarctic to investigate further. The expedition scientists concluded that the combination of high levels of anthropogenic chlorine and extremely low Antarctic stratospheric temperatures produced the large ozone losses.[57] The 1989 international ozone assessment document puts it this way: "The weight of scientific evidence strongly indicates that chlorinated (largely man-made) and brominated chemicals are primarily responsible for the recently discovered substantial decreases of stratospheric ozone over Antarctica in springtime."[58]

In 1989, President George H. W. Bush acted on this evidence, calling for a complete phaseout of chlorofluorocarbon production by 2000. In 1992, he acted again on new findings to accelerate the ban.[59] Instead of weakening the Montreal Protocol in the light of new scientific results, world leaders used its adaptive nature to tighten the protocol. Rowland, Molina, and Paul Crutzen shared the 1995 Nobel Prize in Chemistry for their work on demonstrating the relation between CFCs and the depletion of stratospheric ozone.

Singer, meanwhile, had been arguing that the scientific basis for regulatory action on CFCs was insufficient. In the late 1980s, as the ozone hole was discovered and monitored, and in the early 1990s, as the Bush administration signed the Montreal Protocol, Singer wrote popular articles and letters challenging the science, with titles such as "Ozone Scare Generates Much Heat, Little Light," published in the *Wall Street Journal*, and "The Hole Truth about CFCs," published in *Chemistry and Industry*.[60] These articles suggested that the observed depletions might just be natural variability and that the environmental arguments were nothing more than scare tactics.

In 1995, the House Energy and Environment Subcommittee on Science, chaired by Republican Robert Walker (the same Walker mentioned above), held hearings on "scientific integrity" focusing on three issues: ozone depletion, climate change, and dioxin. In the very year that Rowland and Molina would win their Nobel Prize—indeed, just weeks before the prize was announced—Singer testified to the U.S. Congress: "[T]here is no scientific consensus on ozone depletion or its consequences."[61]

DEFENDING SMOKE

There was yet another area in which Singer challenged science: environmental tobacco smoke (ETS). Today, the Department of Health and Human Services says that "there is no risk-free level of exposure to secondhand smoke: even small amounts . . . can be harmful to people's health," and this is not a new conclusion.[62] The 1986 Surgeon General's report, "Health Consequences of Involuntary Smoking," concluded that secondhand smoke is a cause of disease, including lung cancer, in healthy nonsmokers. Yet in 1994 Singer challenged this scientific evidence, too.

In a report, "EPA and the Science of Environmental Tobacco Smoke," written on behalf of the Alexis de Tocqueville Institute, an anti-regulatory think tank, and funded by a $20,000 grant from the Tobacco Institute, Singer asserted that "scientific standards were seriously violated" in concluding that ETS was a hazard. In finding such a risk, the U.S. Environmental Protection Agency had assumed a "linear dose-response curve"—that is to say, had assumed that the risk was directly proportional to exposure, even at very low levels. Singer rejected this idea, and argued that the EPA should assume a "threshold effect"—presuming that low doses would have no effect.[63]

Singer had a point: some substances that are clearly harmful at high doses do appear to be innocuous at very low levels. But he provided no *evidence* that this was the case for ETS; he merely asserted that it *might* be and used this to challenge the science on which the EPA (and, indirectly) the surgeon general had relied. But the EPA had followed normal scientific practice, as recommended in the well-known "Red Book" on risk assessment, published by the U.S. National Research Council.[64] One chemist who has worked closely with the EPA for many years put it this way: "Linear dose-response is the 'official' EPA default [position]. If there is sufficient evidence for a non-linear mode of action then that is used. Otherwise, it is linear. I think it is always linear. . . . This is [also] laid out in EPA's cancer guidelines."[65] But Singer's coauthor on the report turned that around, noting in a letter to his Tobacco Institute sponsors, "I can't prove that ETS is not a risk of lung cancer, but EPA can't prove that it is."[66]

Today, the home page of the Sierra Club of Canada compares the denial of global warming to the denial of the scientific evidence that smoking causes cancer. In both cases, there is strong scientific evidence supporting current scientific understandings, and the vast majority of scientific experts support the reality of the alleged links. But what the Sierra Club doesn't say, and perhaps doesn't know, is that the similarity in these positions is no coincidence. The same tactics, and in some cases even the same individuals, have been responsible for both.

WHAT IMPACT HAS THIS HAD?

In the early 1990s, underscoring uncertainty became the official strategy of the U.S. Republican Party. In a now-famous memo, leaked to the press in 2003, Republican pollster and media advisor Frank Luntz urged candidates in the 1992 mid-term elections to use scientific uncertainty as a political tactic. "*The scientific debate remains open,*" he wrote emphatically. "Voters believe that there is *no consensus* about global warming. Should the public come to believe that the scientific issues are settled, their views about global warming will change accordingly. Therefore, *you need to continue to make the lack of scientific certainty a primary issue in the debate.*"[67]

Evidence suggests that this tactic was successful. A 2007 Gallup–Yale University poll showed that while a large majority of Americans now believe that global warming is happening, 40 percent think that there is still "a lot of disagreement among scientists."[68]

In 1979, scientists had a consensus that warming would happen, and by the mid-1990s they had a consensus that it was beginning. The lion's share of this work was done in the United States. Yet, in 1997, the U.S. Senate voted 95–0 for the Byrd-Hagel Resolution (S. Res. 98), which rejected any protocol that did not impose binding targets on developing nations. The Kyoto Protocol does not impose emissions limits on India or the People's Republic of China, both major sources of carbon dioxide emissions, so the Resolution effectively scuttled the Kyoto Treaty before the Clinton administration had the opportunity to submit it for ratification. Today, the United States is the only major industrialized country to refuse to participate in the Kyoto agreement.

Polls also show that Americans have been consistently less concerned about global warming than citizens of other nations. Sociologists Aaron McCright and Riley Dunlap note that, at a minimum, the arguments of climate change deniers have aligned with the anti-regulatory ambitions of the U.S. Republican Party, in control of Congress from 1994 to 2006.[69]

Fred Singer continues to write articles for business journals such as the *Wall Street Journal*, *Forbes*, and *Business Investor's Weekly*, and to challenge the work of scientists (and others) who represent the consensus view.[70] He continues to be widely quoted in the popular media by reporters seeking "balance" for their stories.[71] And his arguments have been extended by others, some of whom have been influential.

In 2001, for example, Cambridge University Press released *The Skeptical Environmentalist*, written by a young Danish political scientist, Bjørn Lomborg. Covering everything from acid rain to overpopulation, the book's chapter on climate change echoed the Marshall Institute's stance that the science was uncertain and the likelihood of serious harm grossly exaggerated. Echoing Julian Simon, Lomborg argued that government regulation was the wrong way to address whatever real problems might exist, because it inhibits the economic growth and technological innovation that are the real solutions to human misery. Environmental challenges may lie ahead, but free markets will provide the appropriate solutions.

Prominent scientists criticized the book for misrepresenting the scientific evidence and for its flagrantly anthropocentric weltanschauung. *Scientific American* dedicated a large part of its January 2002 issue to a rebuttal, titled "Misleading Math about the Earth," in which four experts—Stephen Schneider, John Holdren, John Bongaarts, and Thomas Lovejoy—critiqued Lomborg's arguments on global warming, energy, overpopulation, and biodiversity.[72] While Lomborg claimed that his book was based on an extensive review of the relevant scientific literature—and Cambridge University Press championed the book for its nearly 3,000 endnotes—his critics noted that a very large proportion of his citations were to media articles and secondary sources rather than to refereed scientific literature.[73] Schneider characterized Lomborg's strategy as one of "selective inattention," ignoring reams of relevant scientific evidence that undermine his views.[74]

While it is impossible to say how much actual impact—as opposed to media flurry—Lomborg's book had, in 2004 he was named by *Time* as one of the most influential thinkers of the year.[75] At minimum, it took up many hours of the time of distinguished scientists like Schneider to refute Lomborg's erroneous claims. In Schneider's words, "What a monumental waste of busy people's time."[76]

Much of the debate over Lomborg's work concerned whether he had gotten the facts straight, but another book would soon suggest that, when it came to climate change, facts didn't matter. In 2005, science fiction writer Michael Crichton's novel, *State of Fear*, reached number three on the *New York Times* bestseller list, its premise being that global warming is a hoax perpetrated by radical environmentalists bent on bringing down Western capitalism. The book is a work of fiction, but it includes an appendix alleging that its central premise is correct, supported with a long list of claims highly redolent of Marshall Institute reports. Crichton has spoken at the American Enterprise Institute and many other venues promoting his claims, which have in turn been taken up by Oklahoma Senator James Inhofe. In 2005, Crichton was invited to the White House to meet President George W. Bush.[77]

James Inhofe, chair of the Senate Committee on Environment and Public Works until 2007, has suggested that global warming might be the "greatest hoax ever perpetrated on the American people." On September 28, 2005, he sponsored hearings on science in environmental decision making in the wake of Hurricane Katrina. Who was the star witness? Michael Crichton.[78] Vermont Senator James Jeffords summed up the cultural construction of ignorance perfectly when he asked: "Mr. Chairman, . . . why are we having a hearing that features a fiction writer as our key witness?"[79]

HOW CLIMATE SCIENCE BECAME A VICTIM OF THE COLD WAR

On first glance, it seems just plain weird that several of the same individuals—all retired physicists—were involved in denying that cancer causes smoking, that pollution causes acid rain, that CFCs destroy ozone, and that greenhouse gas emissions are causing global warming. But when you put these things together—tobacco regulation, banning of CFCs, delay of controls on CO_2 emissions—a pattern does emerge, insofar as all are expressions of a radical free market ideology opposing any kind of restriction on the pursuit of market capitalism, no matter the justification.

Throughout the literature of climate change denial, a recurrent theme is that environmentalists are motivated by a desire to bring down capitalism and to replace it with socialism or communism. There is also the implication—and sometimes the overt accusation—that the environmentalists' goal is some kind of world government.

In a 1991 piece on global warming, for example, Fred Singer suggested that the threat of global warming had been manufactured by environmentalists based on a "hidden political agenda" against "business, the free market, and the capitalistic system."[80] The true goal of those involved in the global warming issue was not so much to stop global warming—which he insisted did not exist—but rather to foster "international action, preferably with lots of treaties and protocols."[81]

A similar argument was made by political scientist Aaron Wildavsky in a 1992 preface to a book denying global warming.[82] Wildavsky suggested that the true goal of the environmentalist movement was the redistribution of wealth, and that characterizing environmentalists this way was "an accurate rendition of what environmentalist-cum-postenvironmentalist leaders are trying to accomplish."[83] This, he suggests, is why environmentalists are so enamored of international treaties and regulation: they view them as levers toward achieving a new world order.

As the basis for his view that global warming is a fiction, Wildavsky credited the Marshall Institute report, "Scientific Perspectives on the Greenhouse Problem," written by Seitz, Jastrow, and Nierenberg. But the real issue at stake, he continued, is not science, but "central planning versus free enterprise, regulation versus free enterprise, spontaneity versus control."[84] Evidently this is what Wildavsky believes is at stake.

In her PhD dissertation, anthropologist Myanna Lahsen studied the phenomenon of physicists who deny global warming and suggested that their actions were driven in large part by the downfall of physics as America's "prestige science." The reduction of funding and opportunity in physics, and its succession by biological and earth sciences as the dominant sciences of the era, led them to challenge climate science in a kind of turf war. Moreover, these physicists had little regard for the distinctively different methodologies and standards of evidence of these sciences, seeing them as less rigorous than the methods and standards of physics. Members of an "old guard" no longer connected to the highest levels of science, they could not accept that a new generation of scientific leaders, from "lesser" sciences, were replacing them in the role of speaking truth to power.[85]

To be sure, the men in this story were used to having their opinions sought and heeded on many important issues over the better part of three decades. To some extent, they may have been addicted to the limelight. By challenging climate science, they were able to remain in the center of attention long after their opinions were sought in government circles. However, we find little evidence in the historical documents that their actions were *motivated* by epistemic concerns about scientific methods. Robert Jastrow had built the climate modeling effort at Goddard, and hired the man who has since become America's premier voice on climate models: James E. Hansen. William Nierenberg similarly built the Climate Research Division at Scripps, hiring numerous climate modelers and other scientists directly engaged in developing the evidence of global warming. It simply does not seem plausible that they would attack the science they helped to build because it was the wrong kind of science, methodologically or even disciplinarily.

We believe that Lahsen is closer to the mark with another point. Following Richard Hofstader, she situates these men within the political tradition that Hofstader called "the paranoid style" in American politics: a style that sees grand conspiracies to undermine America's free market system and constant threats to American liberty. The political preferences of climate change "contrarians," including Singer, Nierenberg, and Seitz, can be characterized, Lahsen argues, as anti-communist, pro-capitalist, and anti–government interference[86] We agree. Indeed, philanthropist George Soros has given this perspective a succinct label: "market fundamentalism."[87] Market fundamentalists hold a dogmatic, quasi-religious belief in unfettered market capitalism, and therefore oppose *anything* that restrains the business community, be it restrictions on the use of tobacco or the emission of greenhouse gases.[88]

There is something very peculiar about this, because many people believe in the merits of free markets but still accept the reality of global climate change. One can argue the merits or demerits of carbon taxes, emissions control, carbon credits, and all kinds of other potential responses to climate change without denying the scientific facts—and indeed, all over the world, people are doing just that.

Political scientist Roger Pielke Jr. has emphasized that knowing scientific facts does not determine what policy actions should follow.[89] The widely held "linear model" of science-policy interaction—which assumes that facts do lead directly to policy—is simplistic and inaccurate. It is perfectly possible to accept the reality of global warming and believe that nothing should be done about it.[90] That was in fact Nierenberg's position in 1983, when he chaired a major National Academy of Sciences study of climate change—and before he became involved with the Marshall Institute.[91]

Pielke's critique of the linear model has been largely directed at scientists who, he suggests, have a naive faith in the power and virtue of science. And yet, in their own way, these climate change deniers presumed the linear model, too: that if global warming were proven true, then government interference in free markets would necessarily follow. Thus, they *had* to fight against the emerging consensus, either by challenging the scientific evidence directly or by creating the impression of ongoing scientific debate. As Republican pollster and media advisor Frank Luntz put it prior to the 2002 elections, "The science is closing against us but not yet closed. There is still a window of opportunity to challenge the science."[92] *This* was the linear model in action.

The Cold War, however, is over. We face now not a binary choice between communism and capitalism (if ever we did) but rather the realization that capitalism has had unintended consequences. When humans began to burn fossil fuels, no one intended to create global warming. But they (and we) did. Capitalism triumphed over communism, but now must deal with its own waste products.

In this sense, the anxieties of climate change deniers are not wholly unfounded. Capitalism *will* need to be adjusted, or adapted to address its own impacts, and this is the part that the deniers simply cannot accept. The United States won the Cold War—and Nierenberg, Jastrow, and Seitz played a role in that victory—but now we have to figure out a way to win the (ever-warmer) peace.

The connection to the Cold War and its legacies helps account for the origins of this story in the debate over SDI—a late–Cold War response to the perceived continued threat of communism. Most physicists opposed SDI on either technical or political grounds, but its defenders believed that the Soviet threat continued, and that the science that had contained it throughout the Cold War—namely, physics—could and should continue to do so. SDI was one more way in which physicists could defend America.

While the United States was different from the Soviet Union in various ways, to the physicists in this story the crucial difference was its defense of capitalism against communism, free markets against government control of the economy. Marshall Institute initiatives make sense when read as an expression of an uncompromising commitment to market capitalism—indeed, market fundamentalism—and a willingness to do whatever is necessary to prevent creeping government control. To accept that the free market may be creating profound problems that it cannot solve would be, as one of us has argued elsewhere, "ideologically shattering."[93] When scientific knowledge challenged their worldview, these men responded by challenging that knowledge.

Believing in free market capitalism does not *require* one to dispute the scientific evidence of global warming or to misrepresent the state of scientific debate. But in the hands of the Marshall Institute, and those it has influenced, climate science has been profoundly misrepresented and a great deal of confusion and ignorance produced.

The great economist John Maynard Keynes famously noted that there is no free lunch. The western world has experienced 150 years of unprecedented prosperity built by tapping the energy stored in fossil fuels. That was our lunch. Global warming is the bill.

NOTES

1. "Feeling the Heat," *New York Times*, June 14, 2005 (late edition), A22.

2. IPCC, *Climate Change 2001: Synthesis Report, A Contribution of Working Groups I, II, and III to the Third Assessment Report of the Intergovernmental Panel on Climate Change* (Cambridge, UK: Cambridge University Press, 2001), 5. For discussion of global warming as a discovery or realization, in the mid-1990s, see Spencer Weart, *The Discovery of Global Warming* (Cambridge, MA: Harvard University Press, 2003). For background on early recognition of the potential for greenhouse gas emissions to affect

climate, see James Roger Fleming, *Historical Perspectives on Climate Change* (New York: Oxford University Press, 1998; and idem, *Callendar Effect: The Life and Times of Guy Stewart Callendar, the Scientist Who Established the Carbon Dioxide Theory of Climate Change* (Boston: American Meteorological Society, 2006). On the role of the fossil fuel industry in challenging the scientific knowledge, see Ross Gelbspan, *The Heat Is On: The Climate Crisis, the Cover-Up, the Prescription* (New York: Perseus, 1995); and idem, *Boiling Point: How Politicians, Big Oil and Coal, Journalists and Activists Are Fueling the Climate Crisis—and What We Can Do to Avert Disaster* (New York: Basic Books, 2005); Jeremy Leggett, *The Carbon War: Global Warming and the End of the Oil Era* (London: Routledge, 2001); and George Monbiot, *Heat: How to Stop the Planet from Burning* (London: South End, 2007).

3. On the evidence that the observed CO_2 has been produced by burning fossil fuels (and not, for example, by volcanoes), see Prosenjit Ghosh and Willi A. Brand, "Stable Isotope Ratio Mass Spectrometry in Global Climate Change Research," *International Journal of Mass Spectrometry* 228 (August 2003): 1–33; and Taro Takahashi, "The Fate of Industrial Carbon Dioxide," *Science* 305 (July 2004): 352–353.

4. The best historical studies of climate change are Fleming's *Historical Perspectives on Climate Change* and Weart's *The Discovery of Global Warming*.

5. IPCC, *Climate Change 2001*, 30–34, 47–50.

6. *Impacts of a Warming Arctic: Arctic Climate Impact Assessment* (New York: Cambridge University Press, 2005). See also Andrew C. Revkin, "In a Melting Trend, Less Arctic Ice to Go Around," *New York Times*, September 25, 2005 (late edition), A1.

7. P. J. Webster, G. J. Holland, J. A. Curry, and H.-R. Chang, "Changes in Tropical Cyclone Number, Duration, and Intensity in a Warming Environment," *Science* 309 (2005): 1844–1846; Kerry Emanuel, "Increasing Destructiveness of Tropical Cyclones over the Past 30 Years," *Nature* 436 (2005): 686–688. For a discussion of the controversy over interpreting recent hurricane events and the resistance of some elements of the hurricane forecasting community to recognizing the role of global warming, see Chris Mooney, *Storm World: Hurricanes, Politics, and the Battle over Global Warming* (New York: Harcourt, 2007).

8. T. M. L. Wigley, "The Climate Change Commitment," *Science* 307 (2005): 1766–1769. Wigley states that the extant commitment "may exceed 1 C." In the same issue of *Science*, a multiauthored paper puts it at a half degree C for no further increase of carbon dioxide. See Gerald A. Meehl, Warren M. Washington, William D. Collins, Julie M. Arblaster, Aixue Hu, Lawrence E. Buja, Warren G. Strand, and Haiyan Teng, "How Much More Global Warming and Sea Level Rise?" *Science* 307 (2005): 1769–1772.

9. James E. Hansen, director of the Goddard Institute for Space Studies, places the earth's climate sensitivity to a doubling of the pre-industrial carbon dioxide levels as 3 C, based on paleoclimate data. The last time the earth was this warm, 3 million years ago, sea level was about 25 meters higher than it is today. See James E. Hansen, "Is There Still Time to Avoid 'Dangerous Anthropogenic Interference' with Global Climate?" (Keeling Lecture, American Geophysical Union annual meeting, San Francisco, December 6, 2005).

10. For the report itself and information about it, see http://www.ipcc.ch/.

11. Naomi Oreskes, "Beyond the Ivory Tower: The Scientific Consensus on Climate Change," *Science* 306 (2004): 1686.

12. The Royal Society, "A Guide to Facts and Fictions about Climate Change," http://www .royalsoc.ac.uk/page.asp?id=2986 [accessed February 16, 2006].

13. Stephen Pincock, "Scientists Demand Action on Climate," *Scientist* 19 (July 2005): 47.

14. http://www.guardian.co.uk/environment/2007/oct/12/gorecitation.

15. Committee on the Science of Climate Change, Division on Earth and Life Studies, National Research Council, *Climate Change Science: An Analysis of Some Key Questions* (Washington, DC: National Academies Press, 2001); see also Oreskes, "Beyond the Ivory Tower," 1686.

16. U.S. National Academy of Sciences, "Carbon Dioxide and Climate: A Scientific Assessment" (Charney report), 1979.

17. Fleming, *Callendar Effect*.

18. National Academy of Sciences Archives, An Evaluation of the Evidence for CO_2-Induced Climate Change, Assembly of Mathematical and Physical Sciences, Climate Research Board, Study Group on Carbon Dioxide, 1979, Film Label: CO_2 and Climate Change: Ad Hoc: General.

19. Proposal for Support of Carbon Dioxide and Climate Change: A Scientific Assessment, submitted by the National Academy of Sciences, to the White House Office of Science and Technology Policy, June 26, 1979, 1. Massachusetts Institute of Technology Archives, Papers of Jule M. Charney. box 11, folder 364: Climate Research Board.

20. Senate Committee on Energy and Natural Resources, *Climate Change*, 109th Cong., 1st sess., 2005, CIS S 31-20050721-01.

21. ABC News Poll, March 2006, Abcnews.go.com/technology/GlobalWarming/Story?id-1750492; see also Pew Research Center for The People and the Press, July 2006, http://people-press.org/reports/display.php3?ReportID=280. See Anthony Leiserowitz, "American Opinions on Global Warming," http://environment.yale.edu/news/5305-american-opinions-on-global-warming/.

22. Robert Berkman, "It's Time to Talk about Global Warming," *New York Times*, October 1, 2005 (late edition), A14.

23. Chris Mooney, *The Republican War on Science* (New York: Basic Books, 2005). It is also true that a lot of conflicting and contradictory claims have emanated from the current administration. On misrepresentation of the scientific work on climate change prior to the administration of George W. Bush, including the role of the Marshall Institute, see Gelbspan, *The Heat Is On;* and idem, *Boiling Point*. Gelbspan's focus is primarily on the role of the fossil fuel industry and its link to the administration of President George W. Bush, whose motivations are obvious. Our question is slightly different: why would distinguished *scientists* challenge scientific knowledge?

24. http://www.marshall.org/subcategory.php?id=9. For example, in October 2007, the site was highlighting the book *Shattered Consensus: The True State of Global Warming*, which insists on "disparities between what has been predicted about climate change and what has actually been observed," and "highlight[s] substantial anomalies and new information not generally discussed in mainstream reports about climate science." http://www.marshall.org/article.php?id=357. The editor of the book is Patrick J. Michaels, a well-known contrarian who, before he became involved in global warming, was also a contrarian who opposed the growing scientific consensus that a meteorite was largely responsible for the demise of the dinosaurs (Brooks Hansen, pers. comm., February 2006). Other authors include other well-known contrarians, including Sallie Baliunas, who testified along with Fred Singer in Congress in 1995 against the mainstream scientific

view on CFCs and ozone. Baliunas, an astrophysicist, testified that ozone depletion would not lead to increases in skin cancer, a position that directly contradicted the statement submitted by the American Academy of Dermatology that ozone depletion would lead to increases in both basal cell carcinomas and malignant melanomas (Scientific Integrity hearings, note 63, Baliunas testimony on 123–133. Cf. statement from American Academy of Dermatology on pp. 7–11).

25. We focus here on the Marshall Institute, one of the first think tanks to engage the contrarian position on global warming. Aaron M. McCright and Riley Dunlap note that between 1990 and 1997 this strategy was taken up broadly by "prominent conservative think tanks." These authors emphasize that while science studies scholars have emphasized the social construction of scientific knowledge, and sought to understand how scientists established the reality problem of global warming, conservatives constructed a parallel narrative of "non-problematicity," which few scholars have analyzed. We quite agree, except for departing from accepting the label of "conservative" to describe the individuals and ideology involved. We consider it radical market fundamentalism, discussed below. McCright and Dunlap, "Challenging Global Warming as a Social Problem: An Analysis of the Conservative Movement's Counter-Claims," *Social Problems* 47 (2000): 499–522.

26. These include particularly Patrick Michaels, Frederick Seitz, and S. Fred Singer. Michaels has been a visiting scientist at the Marshall Institute, Seitz was the founding director (as discussed below), and Singer is the author of a chapter in a book recently published by the Marshall Institute. Some characteristic articles include Patrick Michaels, "Benign Greenhouse," *Research & Exploration* 9 (1993): 222–233; idem, "Global Warming—Failed Forecasts and Politicized Science," *Waste Management* 14 (1994): 89–95; idem, "Global Warming Warnings: A Lot of Hot Air," *USA Today Magazine* 129 (2001): 18–20; Patrick Michaels and Robert C. Balling, *The Satanic Gases: Clearing the Air about Global Warming* (Washington, DC: Cato Institute, 2000); Frederick Seitz, S. Fred Singer, and H. W. Ellsaesser, "Coverup in the Greenhouse? (Letter to the Editor)" *Wall Street Journal*, July 11, 1996 (eastern edition), 15; S. Fred Singer, "The Science behind Environmental Scares," *Consumers Research Magazine* 74 (1991): 17–21; idem, "No Scientific Consensus on Greenhouse Warming (commentary)," *Wall Street Journal*, September 23, 1991 (eastern edition), 14; idem, "Global Warming Remains Unproved (Letter to the Editor)," *New York Times*, September 19, 1995 (late edition), A20.

27. George C. Marshall Institute, "Natural Climate Variability," http://www.marshall.org/article.php?id=340 [accessed on February 16, 2006].

28. See, for example, IPCC 4: "The observed widespread warming of the atmosphere and ocean, together with ice mass loss, support the conclusion that it is *extremely unlikely* that global climate change of the past fifty years can be explained without external forcing." *IPCC Climate Change 2007: The Physical Science Basis*, Summary for Policy-makers, on p. 10, released February 2007.

29. Rebecca Slayton, "Discursive Choices: Boycotting Star Wars between Science and Politics," *Social Studies of Science* 37:1 (2007), 27–66.

30. Robert Jastrow to Robert Walker, December 1, 1986, Box 21, George Marshall Institute 9/86–1/88, S.I.O. Office of the Director (Nierenberg) Records, 1904–1992, AC2, Scripps Institution of Oceanography, University of California, San Diego.

31. George C. Marshall Institute to William Nierenberg, Draft Proposal, December 12, 1984, 75:6, George Marshall Institute 9/86–1/88, S.I.O. Office of the Director (Nierenberg)

Records, 1904–1992, AC2, Scripps Institution of Oceanography, University of California, San Diego.

32. Robert Jastrow to Robert Walker, 1986.

33. Ibid. 1986.

34. Ibid. Kendall would win the 1990 Nobel Prize in Physics for his work on inelastic electron scattering.

35. James Frelk to William Nierenberg, Enclosure of an excerpt of Strategic Defense Initiative of February 19, 1986, Box 21, George Marshall Institute 9/86–1/88, S.I.O. Office of the Director (Nierenberg) Records, 1904–1992, AC2, Scripps Institution of Oceanography, University of California, San Diego.

36. John McElroy to Robert Walker, June 19, 1995, Box 21, Marshall Institute Correspondence, 1993–1995, S.I.O. Office of the Director (Nierenberg) Records, 1904–1992, AC2, Scripps Institution of Oceanography, University of California, San Diego. A copy was faxed to Nierenberg from the Marshall Institute, raising the interesting question of how the institute got a copy.

37. John McElroy to F. James Sensenbremmer, June 20, 1995, Box 21, Marshall Institute Correspondence, 1993–1995, S.I.O. Office of the Director (Nierenberg) Records, 1904–1992, AC2, Scripps Institution of Oceanography, University of California, San Diego.

38. Stanton A. Glantz, John Slade, Lisa A. Bero, Peter Hanauer, and Deborah E. Barnes, eds., *The Cigarette Papers* (Berkeley: University of California Press, 1996). This book is the best available entry into the copious online documents regarding tobacco industry activities made public during litigation.

39. For general background on the tobacco industry activities, see Glantz et al.; *The Cigarette Papers*. For a discussion of the role of the research program in exploring other causes of cancer, such as stress and "personality traits," see Executive Summary, and Summary of the RJR Nabisco, Inc., Biomedical Research Grants Program for 1987, http://tobaccodocuments.org/rjr/507720494-0525.html [accessed on February 16, 2006; rechecked on August 3, 2007].

40. Executive Summary and Summary of the RJR Nabisco, Inc., Biomedical Research Grants Program for 1987, http://tobaccodocuments.org/rjr/507720494-0525.html [accessed on February 16, 2006; rechecked on August 3, 2007]; see also Frederick Seitz to H. C. Roemer, Vice President and General Counsel, RJ Reynolds Industries, May 1, 1978, Summary of RJR Nabisco, Inc., Biomedical Research Grants Program for 1987, in http://tobaccodocuments.org/tplp/504480670-0672.html [accessed February 19, 2006; rechecked August 3, 2007].

41. Frederick Seitz, "Presentation to International Advisory Committee—R.J. Reynolds Industries by Frederick Seitz," May 9, 1979, pp. 1–2, at http://tobaccodocuments.org/tplp/504480541-0562.html [accessed on February 16, 2006; checked on August 2, 2007, and November 7, 2007].

42. Ibid., on p. 2 of the document, p. 3 of the website.

43. Colin Stokes, "Draft Presentation Prepared by RJR Managerial Employee for Review and Approval by RJR In-House Legal Counsel Concerning a Scientific Research Program and Containing Hand-written Marginalia of RJR In-House Legal Counsel Concerning Same," August 24, 1979, http://tobaccodocuments.org/bliley_rjr/504480518-0529.html [accessed on February 19, 2006].

44. Ibid.

45. Ibid.

46. Robert N. Proctor, *Cancer Wars: How Politics Shapes What We Know and Don't Know about Cancer* (New York: HarperCollins, 1996); Glantz et al., *The Cigarette Papers.*

47. On the history of the SST, see Erik Conway, *High-Speed Dreams: NASA and the Technopolitics of Supersonic Transportation, 1945–1999* (Baltimore: Johns Hopkins University Press, 2005).

48. S. Fred Singer, "No Scientific Consensus on Greenhouse Warming (Letter to the Editor)," *Wall Street Journal*, September 23, 1991, 14; idem, "Global Warming's Doomsday Nowhere in Sight (Letter to the Editor)," *New York Times*, September 28, 1993, 18.

49. See http://www.sepp.org/ [accessed on February 16, 2006]; http://heartland.org/ [accessed on February 19, 2006]; http://www.aei.org/ [accessed on February 19, 2006]; http://www .marshall.org/ [accessed on February 16, 2006].

50. Summary for Policy-makers: The Science of Climate Change, IPCC Working Group I, 1995, http://www.ipcc.ch/pub/sarsyn.htm [accessed on February 19, 2006].

51. S. Fred Singer, *Hot Talk, Cold Science: Global Warming's Unfinished Debate* (Oakland, CA: Independent Institute, 1997), ix.

52. Ibid.

53. S. Fred Singer, "Ozone Scare Generates Much Heat, Little Light," *Wall Street Journal*, April 16, 1987 (eastern edition), 30; idem, "Drastic Remedies Are Not Needed," *Consumer Research Magazine* 71 (1988): 32–33; idem, "My Adventures in the Ozone Layer," *National Review* (June 30, 1989), 34–38; idem, "Hot Words on Global Warming (Letter to the Editor)," *Wall Street Journal*, January 15, 1996 (eastern edition), 13; idem, "Climatic Change: Hasty Action Unwarranted," *Consumer Research Magazine* 80 (1997): 16–20; idem, "Global Warming: What We're Not Told (Letter to the Editor)." *Washington Post*, January 26, 1998, 22. See also the discussion in Mooney, *The Republican War*, 56–59; Gelbspan, *The Heat Is On*, 34–36, 46–49; William K. Stevens, *The Change in the Weather: People, Weather, and the Science of Climate* (New York: Delta, 1999), 245–249.

54. Mooney, *The Republican War*, 41–43.

55. F. Sherwood Rowland, personal interview, September 7, 2005.

56. Richard Elliot Benedick, *Ozone Diplomacy: New Directions in Safeguarding the Planet* (Cambridge, MA: Harvard University Press, 1991), 99. On the protocol as an "adaptive regime," see Edward A. Parson, *Protecting the Ozone Layer: Science and Strategy* (New York: Oxford University Press, 2003), 197–244.

57. The "missing science" from the 1985 assessment was that the scientific community had not considered the possibility that the chemical reactions taking place on ice and particle surfaces might be significantly different from those taking place solely in the gas phase. The presence of ice accelerated the release of active chlorine, producing higher ozone destruction rates. Cold temperatures in the Antarctic stratosphere allowed the formation of "polar stratospheric clouds," which were composed primarily of ice crystals. Several different research groups demonstrated this phenomenon in laboratory experiments during 1986. See Parson, *Protecting the Ozone Layer*, 149–153.

58. World Meteorological Organization Global Ozone Research and Monitoring Project, *Scientific Assessment of Stratospheric Ozone: 1989*, no. 20, vol. 1 (Washington, DC: National Aeronautics and Space Administration, 1989), vii.

59. Parson, *Protecting the Ozone Layer*, 163, 214–216; see also http://ozone.unep .org/ pdfs/Montreal-Protocol2000.pdf.

60. Singer, "Ozone Scare Generates Much Heat, Little Light," 1; idem, "The Hole Truth about CFCs," *Chemistry and Industry* 6 (1994): 240.

61. Mooney, *The Republican War*, 57.

62. http://www.hhs.gov/news/press/2006pres/20060627.html.

63. "Draft Only the EPA and the Science of Environmental Tobacco Smoke [*sic*], http :tobaccodocuments.org/nysa_ti_m2/ti40481951.html, NYSA Numbers 0221 B1793 04A, Box 9017 Walter Woodson files, Executive Committee Meeting Mailings and meetings, May 1994 [loaded January 27, 2005, accessed June 26, 2006].

64. *Risk Assessment in the Federal Government: Managing the Process* (Washington, DC: National Academies Press, 1983). This is the book that first firmly established definitions for hazard identification, dose-response assessment, exposure assessment, risk assessment, and risk management. At the time of this paper, a new NRC committee was "revising" the Red Book, "Improving Risk Analysis Approaches Used by the US EPA," chaired by Tom Burke.

65. http://cfpub.epa.gov/ncea/cfm/recordisplay.cfm?deid=116283; Judith Graham, email comm., August 6, 2007, 7:03:12 AM PDT.

66. August 11, 1994, letter from Samuel D. Chilcote to the Tobacco Institute, Members of the Executive Committee, http://legacy.library.ucsf.edu/tid/chf03foo/pdf [accessed July 10, 2006, and rechecked November 7, 2007]. See also Chilcote to the Tobacco Institute, July 26, 1994, http://legacy.library.ucsf.edu/action/document/page?tid=fif03foo.

67. "The Luntz Research Companies—Straight Talk," p. 137, http://www2.bc.edu/ ~plater/Newpublicsite06/suppmats/02.6.pdf. See also Mooney, *The Republican War*.

68. American Opinions on Global Warming, Anthony Leiserowitz, Principal Investigator, http://environment.yale.edu/news/5305-american-opinions-on-global-warming/. Polls also show that Americans have known about global warming for a long time, but in the late 1990s the issue became more politicized—with Republicans much more likely to disbelieve the scientific evidence, suggesting that the disinformation campaigns were effective, having reached their intended audience. See, for example, Jon A. Krosnick, Penny S. Visser, and Allyson L. Holbrook, "American Opinion on Global Warming: The Impact of the Fall 1997 Debate," *Resources* 5: 133 (Fall 1998), 5–9.

69. McCright and Dunlap note that surveys show that most Americans *do* believe that global warming is a serious problem, suggesting that the misinformation campaigns were not entirely successful in producing public ignorance. However, the Leiserowitz work demonstrates that they *were* effective in convincing the public that the scientific jury was still out, and for a sector of the population this was consistent with believing that action was still "premature." See, for example, Pew Research Center for the People and the Press, July 2006, "Little Consensus on Warming," July 12, 2006, http://people-press.org/reports/display .php3?ReportID=280 [re-accessed October 15, 2007]. In February 2007, on the release of the Fourth Assessment Report of the Intergovernmental Panel on Climate Change, Vice President Richard Cheney continued to insist on the uncertainty, saying in an interview with ABC news, "I think there's an emerging consensus that we do have global warming. . . . Where there does not appear to be a consensus . . . is the extent to which that's part of a normal cycle versus the extent to which it's caused by man, greenhouse gases, etc." Yet, the IPCC had explicitly addressed the causal issue, writing, "most of the observed warming over the last 50 years is very likely to have been due to the increase in greenhouse gas concentrations. . . . The observed widespread warming of the atmosphere and ocean, together with ice mass loss,

support the conclusion that it is *extremely unlikely* that global climate change of the past fifty years can be explained without external forcing" (IPCC, Summary for Policymakers, in *Climate Change 2007: The Physical Science Basis. Contribution of Working Group I to the Fourth Assessment Report of the Intergovernmental Panel on Climate Change*, p. 10, http://www.ipcc.ch/pdf/assessment-report/ar4/wg1/ar4-wg1-spm.pdf). As of this writing (October 2007), the White House was continuing to reject all but voluntary action, citing scientific uncertainties as justification (see, for example, Elizabeth Kolbert, *Field Notes from a Catastrophe: Man, Nature, and Climate Change* [New York: Bloomsbury, 2006]). Perhaps the real effect of the climate agnotological campaign has been to provide political cover for inaction, and to generate sufficient confusion among the American public to make such inaction politically acceptable.

70. Including us.

71. For evidence that those presenting anti-consensus views have received press and political attention greatly disproportionate to their numbers, see Aaron M. McCright and Riley E. Dunlap, "Defeating Kyoto: The Conservative Movement's Impact on U.S. Climate Change Policy," *Social Problems* 50 (2003): 348–373; Maxwell T. Boykoff and Jules M. Boykoff, "Balance as Bias: Global Warming and the U.S. Prestige Press," *Global Environmental Change* 14 (2004): 125–136. This point has been underscored recently by Eugene Linden, *The Winds of Change: Climate, Weather, and the Destruction of Civilizations* (New York: Simon and Schuster, 2006), based on his own experience as a science writer.

72. *Scientific American*, "Skepticism toward *The Skeptical Environmentalist*," http://www.sciam.com/article.cfm?articleID=00000B96-9517-1CDA-B4A8809EC588EEDF [accessed February 16, 2006]; see also Stuart Pimm and Jeff Harvey, "The Skeptical Environmentalist: Measuring the Real State of the World," *Nature* 414 (2001): 149–150; Stephen Schneider, "Hostile Climate: On Bjørn Lomborg and Climate Change," *Grist Magazine*, December 12, 2001, http://www.grist.org/advice/books/2001/12/12/hostile/ [accessed February 19, 2006].

73. Committee for the Scientific Investigation of Claims of the Paranormal, "The Skeptical Environmentalist: A Case Study in the Manufacture of News," http://www.csicop.org/scienceandmedia/environmentalist/ [accessed February 16, 2006].

74. Schneider, "Hostile Climate."

75. *Time*, "The 2004 *Time* 100 Scientists and Thinkers," http://www.time.com/time/2004/time100/scientists/ [accessed February 16, 2006].

76. Schneider, "Hostile Climate." (In terms of full disclosure: the authors of this chapter have also spent significant amounts of time over the past two years answering phone calls and emails offering "skeptical" questions and perspectives.)

77. Michael Janofsky, "Bush's Chat with Novelist Alarms Environmentalists," *New York Times*, February 19, 2006, http://www.nytimes.com/2006/02/19/national/19warming.html?ei=5088&en=a7ab8a51ec6cf4df&ex=1298005200&partner=rssnyt&emc=rss&pagewanted=print.

78. Michael Janofsky, "Michael Crichton, Novelist, Becomes Senate Witness," *New York Times*, September 29, 2005 (late edition), E1; American Institute of Physics, "Senate Hearing Demonstrates Wide Disagreement about Climate Change," http://www.aip.org/fyi/2005/142.html [accessed February 16, 2006].

79. U.S. Senate Committee on Environment and Public Works, "Statement by Sen. Jeffords at EPW Hearing on Science and Environment," http://epw.senate.gov/pressitem.cfm?id=246511&party=dem [accessed February 16, 2006].

80. S. Fred Singer, "Global Warming: Do We Know Enough to Act?" *Environmental Protection: Regulating for Results*, eds. Kenneth Chilton and Melinda Warren (Boulder, CO: Westview, 1991), 45–46.

81. Ibid.

82. The book was by geographer Robert C. Balling, Jr., *The Heated Debate: Greenhouse Predictions versus Climate Reality* (San Francisco: Pacific Research Institute for Public Policy, 1992).

83. Aaron Wildavsky, "Global Warming as a Means of Achieving an Egalitarian Society: An Introduction," preface to Balling, *The Heated Debate*, xvi.

84. Wildavsky, "Global Warming," xxxi.

85. Myanna H. Lahsen, "Climate Rhetoric: Constructions of Climate Science in the Age of Environmentalism" (PhD dissertation, Rice University, 1998), 358–369, 372–373, 379. See also "Technocracy, Democracy and U.S. Climate Science Politics: The Need for Demarcations," *Science, Technology, and Human Values* 30: 1 (2005): 137–169; idem, "The Detection and Attribution of Conspiracies: The Controversy over Chapter 8," *Paranoia within Reason: A Casebook on Conspiracy as Explanation*, ed. George E. Marcus (Chicago: University of Chicago Press, 1999); idem, "Seductive Simulations: Uncertainty Distribution around Climate Models," *Social Studies of Science* 35 (2005): 895–922; and idem, "Experiences of Modernity in the Greenhouse: A Cultural Analysis of a Physicist 'Trio' Supporting the Conservative Backlash against Global Warming," *Global Environmental Change*, forthcoming.

86. Lahsen, "Climate Rhetoric, 358–369, 372–373, 379.

87. George Soros, "The Capitalist Threat," *Atlantic Monthly* 279 (February 1997): 45–58.

88. In her dissertation on the history of fisheries management, M. Carmel Finley shows how a similar ideology informed American fisheries policy, which shifted the burden of proof onto those arguing for regulation and helped to prevent meaningful restrictions on fishing that might have served to prevent the collapse of world fisheries. See "The Tragedy of Enclosure: U.S. Fisheries Science, Development, and Management, 1945–1995" (PhD dissertation, University of California, San Diego, 2007).

89. Roger Pielke Jr., "When Scientists Politicize Science: Making Sense of Controversy over the Skeptical Environmentalist," *Environmental Science and Policy* 7 (2004): 405–417.

90. It is also possible to be a communist and have no opinions whatsoever about global warming.

91. National Academy of Science, *Changing Climate: Report of the Carbon Dioxide Assessment Committee* (Washington, DC: National Academies Press, 1983), xiii–xvi, 1–4; William Nierenberg, "Climate, CO_2 and Acid Rain," presented at the 80th Anniversary of the Scripps Institution of Oceanography, October 13, 1983, Box 169, Folder 17, MC13, Papers of William Aaron Nierenberg, Scripps Institution of Oceanography Archives, University of California, San Diego; and see physicist Alvin Weinberg's scathing denunciation of the 1983 study's "do nothing" attitude: Alvin M. Weinberg, "Comments on NRC Draft Report of the Carbon Dioxide Assessment Committee," July 6, 1983, Box 86, Folder 7, MC 13, Papers of William Aaron Nierenberg, Scripps Institution of Oceanography Archives, University of California, San Diego. See also Naomi Oreskes and Erik M. Conway, "From Chicken Little to Dr. Pangloss: William Nierenberg, Global Warming, and the Social Deconstruction of Scientific Knowledge," *Historical Studies in the Natural Sciences* 38:1 (2008), in press.

92. Mooney, *The Republican War*, 74.

93. Erik M. Conway, *A History of Atmospheric Science in NASA* (Baltimore: Johns Hopkins University Press, 2008); see also idem, "Satellites and Security: Space in Service to Humanity," in *The Societal Impact of Space Flight*, NASA SP-2007-4800, eds. Steven J. Dick and Roger D. Launius (Washington, DC: NASA, 2007), esp. 282–283.

CHAPTER 4

Manufactured Uncertainty

Contested Science and the Protection of the Public's Health and Environment

DAVID MICHAELS

SINCE 1986, every bottle of aspirin sold in the United States has included a label advising parents that aspirin consumption by children with viral illnesses greatly increases their risk of developing Reye's syndrome. Before that mandatory warning was required by the U.S. Food and Drug Administration (FDA), the toll from this disease, for which the cause is unknown, was substantial: 555 cases reported in one year, 1980, and with many others probably missed, because the syndrome is easily misdiagnosed. One in three diagnosed children died.[1]

Today, less than a handful of Reye's Syndrome cases are reported each year. While the disappearance of Reye's Syndrome is often considered a public health triumph, it is a bittersweet one, because an untold number of children were disabled or died while the aspirin manufacturers delayed the FDA's regulation by arguing that the four scientific studies establishing the aspirin link were incomplete, uncertain, unclear. The industry raised seventeen specific "flaws" in the four studies and insisted that more reliable ones were needed.[2] The medical community knew of the danger, thanks to an alert issued by the Centers for Disease Control (CDC), but parents were kept in the dark. Despite a federal advisory committee's concurrence with the CDC's conclusions about the link, the industry issued a public service announcement claiming, "We *do* know that *no* medication has been *proven* to cause Reyes" (emphasis in the original).[3]

The manufacturer's campaign and the dilatory procedures of the White House's Office of Management and Budget delayed a public education program for two years and mandatory labels for two more.[4] Only litigation by Public Citizen's Health Research Group forced the recalcitrant Reagan administration to act. Thousands of lives have been saved—after hundreds had been lost.

Absolute certainty in the realm of medicine and public health is rare. Our public health programs will not be effective if absolute proof is required before we act; the best available evidence must be sufficient. Yet we see a growing trend that demands proof over precaution in the realm of public health.[5]

Few scientific challenges are more complex than understanding the cause of disease in humans. Scientists cannot feed toxic chemicals to people to see what dose causes cancer. Instead, we must harness the "natural experiments" where exposures have already happened in the field. In the laboratory, we can use only animals. Both epidemiologic and laboratory studies therefore have many uncertainties, and scientists must extrapolate from study-specific evidence to make causal inferences and recommend protective measures. Absolute certainty is rarely an option. Our regulatory programs will not be effective if such proof is required before we act; the best available evidence must be sufficient.

THE TOBACCO ROAD

Years ago, a tobacco executive unwisely committed to paper the perfect slogan for his industry's disinformation campaign: "Doubt is our product."[6] With tobacco, doubt turned out to be less addictive for the public than the leaf itself, and the industry finally abandoned its strategy.

I call this strategy "manufacturing uncertainty,"[7] and no industry manufactured more uncertainty over a longer period than the tobacco companies. Following a strategic plan developed in the mid-1950s by the public relations firm Hill and Knowlton—a firm that manufactured uncertainty on behalf of various industries over several decades—Big Tobacco hired scientists to challenge the growing consensus linking cigarette smoking with lung cancer and other adverse health effects. This industry campaign had three basic messages: cause-and-effect relationships have not been established; statistical data do not provide the answers; and more research is needed. As recently as 1989, a spokesperson appearing on national television dismissed claims that tobacco smoking causes disease, declaring that "the causative relationship has not yet been established."[8]

The industry even started its own "scientific" publication, *Tobacco and Health Research*, for which the main criterion for articles was straightforward: "The most important type of story is that which casts doubt on the cause and effect theory of disease and smoking." Editorial guidelines stated that headlines "should strongly call out the point—Controversy! Contradiction! Other Factors! Unknowns!"[9]

Learning from tobacco's success, other industries have discovered that debating the science is much easier and more effective than debating the policy. Witness the debate over global warming. Many studies link human activity, and especially burning of carbon fuels, with global warming.[10] Waiting for absolute certainty that the accumulation of greenhouse gases will result in dramatic changes in the climate seems far riskier, and potentially far more expensive to address, than acting now to control the causes of global warming. Opponents of preventive action, led by the fossil fuels industry, attempted to delay the inevitable policy debate by challenging the science instead with a classic uncertainty campaign. I need only cite a memo from the political consultant Frank Luntz, delivered to his clients in early 2003. In "Winning the Global Warming Debate," Luntz wrote:

Voters believe that there is *no consensus* about global warming within the scientific community. Should the public come to believe that the scientific issues are settled, their views about global warming will change accordingly. Therefore, *you need to continue to make the lack of scientific certainty a primary issue in the debate. . . . The scientific debate is closing [against us] but not yet closed. There is still a window of opportunity to challenge the science* (emphasis in original).[11]

There has been substantial media coverage of the political machinations behind the global warming debate, and the behavior of the tobacco industry has been well documented.[12] Less well known are the campaigns mounted to question studies documenting the adverse health effects of exposure to beryllium, lead, mercury, vinyl chloride, chromium, benzene, benzidine, nickel, and a long list of other toxic chemicals and pharmaceuticals. In fact, it is unusual for the science behind any proposed public health or environmental regulation not to be challenged, no matter how powerful the evidence.

Manufacturing uncertainty on behalf of big business has become a big business in itself. "Product defense" firms have become experienced, adept, and successful consultants in epidemiology, biostatistics, and toxicology. The work of these product-defense firms bears the same relationship to science as the Arthur Andersen Company's work for Enron and Worldcom did to accounting—or did, before it went bankrupt following the Enron debacle.

BERYLLIUM: NATIONAL DEFENSE OR "PRODUCT DEFENSE"?

The metal beryllium is extremely useful—and almost unimaginably toxic. Breathing the tiniest amount of this lightweight metal can cause disease and death. As a neutron moderator that increases the yield of nuclear explosions, it is vital to the production of weapons systems, and throughout the Cold War, the U.S. nuclear weapons complex was the nation's largest consumer of the substance. As a result, however, hundreds of weapons workers have developed chronic beryllium disease (CBD)—and not just machinists who worked directly with the metal, but also others simply in the vicinity of the milling and grinding processes, and often for very short periods of time.

As Assistant Secretary of Energy for Environment, Safety and Health from 1998 to 2001, I was the chief safety officer for the nuclear weapons complex, responsible for protecting the health of workers, the communities, and the environment around the production and research facilities. In 1998, the Department of Energy's (DOE) exposure standard had remained unchanged for almost fifty years, and there were hundreds of cases of beryllium disease in the nuclear weapons complex and in factories that supplied beryllium products.

The history of this original DOE beryllium standard is legendary. It was developed in a 1948 discussion held in the backseat of a taxi by Merril Eisenbud, an Atomic Energy Commission (AEC) industrial hygienist, and Willard Machle, a physician who was a consultant to the firm building the

Brookhaven Laboratory on Long Island, New York. Eisenbud discusses this history in his autobiography, noting that they selected the exposure limit "in the absence of an epidemiological basis for establishing a standard."[13] The AEC "tentatively" adopted a standard of 2 μg/m³ in 1949, and then reviewed it annually for seven years before permanently accepting it.

When first implemented, the 2 μg/m³ standard resulted in a dramatic decrease in new beryllium disease cases. But by 1951, Eisenbud recognized that "the distribution of the chronic form of beryllium disease did not follow the usual exposure-response model seen for most toxic substances" and hypothesized an immunological susceptibility.[14] Eventually, cases of CBD appeared among workers hired after the 1949 standard went into effect, and whose exposure appeared to be below the 2 μg/m³ standard.[15] Moreover, CBD had been diagnosed in persons with no workplace exposure to the metal, including individuals who simply laundered the clothes of workers, drove a milk delivery truck with a route near a beryllium plant, or tended cemetery graves near a beryllium factory.[16]

When the Occupational Safety and Health Administration (OSHA) was established in 1971 to protect the health of workers in the private sector, it simply adopted the taxicab standard. By the 1980s, however, it was clear that workers exposed to beryllium levels well below the standard were developing the disease. As both the DOE and OSHA began the time-consuming legal process of changing their standards, the beryllium industry objected. At one public meeting, the director of environmental health and safety of Brush Wellman, the leading U.S. producer of beryllium products, asserted (according to DOE's minutes of the meeting): "Brush Wellman is unaware of any scientific evidence that the standard is not protective. However, we do recognize that there have been sporadic reports of disease at less than 2 μg/m³. Brush Wellman has studied each of these reports and found them to be scientifically unsound."[17]

In 1991, Brush managers were told that if they were "asked in some fashion whether or not the 2 μg/m³ standard is still considered by the company to be reliable," they should answer, "In most cases involving our employees, we can point to circumstances of exposure (usually accidental), higher than the standard allows. In some cases, we have been unable (for lack of clear history) to identify such circumstances. However, in these cases we also cannot say that there was *not* excessive exposure" (emphasis in original).[18]

This was the industry's primary argument, and it was based on a flawed logic. Practically speaking, it was not difficult to go back into the work history of anyone with CBD and estimate that at some point in time, the airborne beryllium level must have exceeded the standard. Brush did this, and then reasoned that the 2 $\mu g/m^3$ standard must be fully protective since most people who had CBD had at some point been exposed to a higher level.

Yet, the ever-increasing number of CBD cases identified at facilities across the nuclear weapons complex, as well as in the beryllium industry's own factories, rendered the claim that the old standard was safe less and less plausible. In September 1999, Brush Wellman sponsored a conference, in collaboration with the American Conference of Governmental Industrial Hygienists, to bring "leading scientists together to present and discuss the current information and new research on the hazards posed by beryllium."[19] The papers were subsequently published together in an industrial hygiene journal.[20] Clearly, one purpose of the conference was to influence government standard setting on beryllium; at the time of the conference, DOE was a few months away from issuing its final rule and OSHA had signaled its intention to revise its outdated standard.

Several papers were presented by scientists employed by Exponent, Inc., the beryllium industry's product defense consultant, including a paper entitled "Identifying an Appropriate Occupational Exposure Limit (OEL) for Beryllium: Data Gaps and Current Research Initiatives." This paper promoted the industry's new rationale for opposing a new, stronger beryllium standard: that more research is needed on the effects of particle size, of exposure to beryllium compounds, and of skin exposure to CBD risk. The paper concluded: "At this time, it is difficult to identify a single new TLV [threshold limit value] for all forms of beryllium that will protect nearly all workers. It is likely that within three to four years, a series of TLVs might need to be considered. . . . In short, the beryllium OEL could easily be among the most complex yet established."[21]

After reviewing the public comments and the literature on beryllium's health effects, the DOE health and safety office concluded that, while more research is always desirable, we had more than enough information to warrant immediate implementation of a stronger beryllium disease prevention standard. Over the industry's objections, we issued a new rule, reducing the acceptable workplace exposure level by a factor of ten.

Simultaneously, OSHA also recognized the inadequacy of its own standard[22] and announced its commitment to issuing a stronger one.[23] However, when the George W. Bush administration took office in 2001, the commitment to strengthening its beryllium rule was dropped from the agency's formal regulatory agenda.

In November 2002, OSHA implicitly accepted the industry's approach by issuing a call for additional data on the relationship of beryllium disease to, among other things, particle size, particle surface area, particle number, and skin contact.[24] In the few years since DOE issued its standard, however, researchers have published several epidemiologic studies that demonstrate that the 2 $\mu g/m^3$ standard does not prevent the occurrence of CBD.[25]

In addition to CBD, the scientific community widely recognizes that beryllium also increases the risk of lung cancer; several studies conducted by epidemiologists at the CDC support this conclusion.[26] In 2002, however, scientists at a product defense firm published a ten-year-old reanalysis of one of the CDC studies.[27] By changing some parameters, the statistically significant elevation of lung cancer rates was no longer statistically significant. (Such alchemy is rather easily accomplished, of course, while the opposite—turning insignificance into significance—is extremely difficult.) Not coincidentally, this particular firm had done extensive work for the tobacco industry.[28] The new analysis was published in a peer-reviewed journal—not one with much experience in epidemiology, but peer-reviewed nevertheless, and the industry now touts its study as evidence that everyone else is wrong.

And so it goes today, in industry after industry, with study after study, year after year. Data is disputed, data has to be reanalyzed. Animal data is deemed not relevant, human data not representative, exposure data not reliable. More research is always needed. Uncertainty is manufactured. Its purpose is always the same: shielding corporate interests from the inconvenience and economic consequences of public health protections.

PPA: THE TRICKS OF THE TRADE

In order to attract new clients, some product defense firms even brag about their successes. Until I wrote about it in *Scientific American*,[29] the Weinberg Group (another firm that had worked extensively for the tobacco industry) advertised on its website its contribution to the effort to oppose the FDA's belated clampdown on phenylpropanolamine (PPA), the over-the-counter drug that was widely used as a decongestant and appetite suppressant until the FDA forced it off the market.

Here is a short version of the PPA saga. Reports of hemorrhagic strokes in young women who had taken a PPA-containing drug began circulating in the early 1970s. Twenty years later, when the FDA finally raised official questions about the safety of PPA, the manufacturers rejected them. Eventually, a compromise was reached. The drug manufacturers would select an investigator—they selected the Yale University School of Medicine—and fund an epidemiologic study whose design would be approved by the FDA. In October 1999, the manufacturers and the FDA learned that the study confirmed the causal relationship between PPA and hemorrhagic stroke.[30] The study was published the following year in the *New England Journal of Medicine*.[31]

When they were initially alerted to the study's findings, did the manufacturers immediately withdraw this drug, which by then had annual sales of more than $500 million, but was responsible, according to an FDA analysis, for between 200 and 500 strokes per year among 18- to 49-year-olds?[32] No. Instead, they turned to the Weinberg Group to attack the Yale study, focusing on "bias and areas of concern."[33] The manufacturers recognized that the FDA would eventually force the drug off the market, but they stalled for almost a year, enough time to reformulate their products. And when the FDA finally requested manufacturers to stop marketing PPA in November 2000, the industry was prepared to ship reformulated products immediately.[34]

Amazingly, the Weinberg group boasted about this work on their website:

Adverse Event Linked to OTC Product

A pharmaceutical company retained THE WEINBERG GROUP to audit the results of a FDA-requested, industry-sponsored case-control study that linked their over-the-counter (OTC) product and several others with a serious, life-threatening adverse event. There was a substantial concern from the FDA based on reports of adverse events that use of these OTC products would present a public health problem. The study was commissioned to answer the question of risk with a controlled investigation. According to the study investigators, the results of the study showed a strong association between these products and a severe, life-threatening adverse event. Epidemiologists at THE WEINBERG GROUP led experts and consultants to some of the other affected OTC companies, in an effort that included a reanalysis of the raw data from the case-control study, and an assessment of the study's methodological flaws. The unique ability of the experts at THE WEINBERG GROUP to combine their expertise in epidemiology and biostatistics with strategic thinking enabled them to lead the pharmaceutical company's effort in their dispute with the FDA.[35]

THE FUNDING EFFECT

The biomedical literature extensively discusses the "funding effect," a term used to describe the close correlation between the results of a study desired by a study's funders and the reported results of that study.[36] Recent reviews in leading biomedical journals found that pharmaceutical industry sponsorship was strongly associated with pro-industry conclusions.[37]

As researchers have examined the workings of the funding effect, it has become clear this is not the result of poorly done studies conducted by researchers apparently aiming for a preordained conclusion (although examples of this are not rare). The quality of the studies paid for by pharmaceutical manufacturers is at least as good and often better than ones they didn't fund.[38] This is not surprising, since drug makers have plentiful financial resources and more extensive experience conducting clinical trials. However, the failure to identify methodologic flaws that might explain the funding effect puzzled journal editors, who generally have strong scientific backgrounds and who pride themselves on their ability to identify poor-quality research.

What then explains the funding effect? It appears that the pharmaceutical industry is devoting sizable resources to the conduct of studies whose results will increase sales, but will not necessarily provide the information physicians need to select the best drug for their patients. This has been summarized most clearly by Dr. Richard Smith, who recently retired as editor of *British Medical Journal* (*BMJ*). Describing how it took him "almost a quarter of a century editing for the *BMJ* to wake up to what was happening," he wrote:

Why are pharmaceutical companies getting the results they want? . . . The companies seem to get the results they want not by fiddling the results, which would be far too crude and possibly detectable by peer review, but rather by asking the "right" questions—and there are many ways to do this [see list below]. . . . There are many ways to hugely increase the chance of producing favourable results, and there are many hired guns who will think up new ways and stay one jump ahead of peer reviewers.[39]

Smith went on to provide a series of examples of methods used by pharmaceutical manufacturers to obtain the results they want from clinical trials (the following is a quote):

- Conduct a trial of your drug against a treatment known to be inferior.
- Trial your drugs against too low a dose of a competitor drug.
- Conduct a trial of your drug against too high a dose of a competitor drug (making your drug seem less toxic).
- Conduct trials that are too small to show differences from competitor drugs.
- Use multiple endpoints in the trial and select for publication those that give favourable results.
- Do multicentre trials and select for publication results from centres that are favourable.
- Conduct subgroup analyses and select for publication those that are favourable.
- Present results that are most likely to impress—for example, reduction in relative rather than absolute risk.[40]

The funding effect has also been seen in studies that look at the toxic effects of chemical exposures. The disparity between the results of studies examining the risk of lung cancer among beryllium-exposed workers discussed above is an example of the funding effect: three government-funded analyses find an elevated risk while the one industry-funded analysis (actually a reanalysis) does not.

An even more striking example in the toxicology literature is the debate over the effects of low-dose exposure to bisphenol A (BPA), an environmental estrogen used in the manufacture of polycarbonate plastic, a resin widely used in food cans and dental sealants. Exposure to BPA had been reported in some studies to alter endocrine function at very low doses. In response, the American Plastics Council hired the Harvard Center for Risk Analysis (HCRA) to conduct a weight-of-the-evidence review of the toxicology. The HCRA panel reviewed nineteen animal studies and reported that it found no consistent affirmative evidence of low-dose BPA effects.[41]

This conclusion was challenged by scientists who felt that the HCRA had chosen to examine only a minority of the 47 studies available at the time. These scientists reviewed the 115 studies that had been published through December 2004 and found results that differed markedly from the HCRA analysis.[42] As can be seen in Table 4.1, 90 percent (94 of 104) of the studies paid for with government funds reported an effect associated with BPA exposure; not a single one of the 11 corporate-funded studies found an effect.

TABLE 4.1 Biased outcome due to source of funding in low-dose, in vivo BPA research as of December 2004

Source of funding	Number of studies and effect reported	
	Harm	No harm
Government	94	10
Chemical corporations	0	11
Total	94	22

SOURCE: Adapted from F. S. Vom Saal and C. Hughes, "An Extensive New Literature Concerning Low-Dose Effects of Bisphenol A Shows the Need for a New Risk Assessment," *Environmental Health Perspectives* 113 (2005): 926–933.

VIOXX: CONFLICTED SCIENCE
AND ITS CONSEQUENCES

I am not presuming here that the scientists involved in manufacturing uncertainty knowingly promote deadly products. More likely, scientists, along with the corporate executives and attorneys who hire them, convince themselves that the products they are defending are safe, and that the evidence of harm is inaccurate, or misleading, or trivial.

This can be seen in the recent evidence on the cardiac effects of Vioxx (rofecoxib), Merck's blockbuster pain reliever that was taken off the market in November 2004, making headlines around the world. Even before the FDA approved Vioxx in May 1999, agency scientists reviewed data that suggested Vioxx could increase heart disease risk. Several independent scientists (that is, not on Merck's payroll) also raised red flags, but for the most part, the FDA ignored them. Then the results of a clinical trial appeared in early 2000, just a few months after the drug was put on the market, linking Vioxx with an increased risk of heart attack.

Merck had chosen naproxen (sold under the brand name Aleve) as the comparison treatment in the trial because aspirin, perhaps a more obvious choice, was known to lower cardiovascular disease risk, and the company didn't want its trial to find more heart attacks among the study participants who took Vioxx. But the results showed that participants who took Vioxx for more than eighteen months had five times the risk of heart attack as those taking naproxen.[43]

Merck's scientists faced a dilemma. They could interpret this finding to mean either that Vioxx increased heart attack risk by 400 percent or that naproxen was beneficial in reducing the risk of heart attack by 80 percent. When a double-blind trial using a placebo control found seven excess heart attacks per every thousand users per year, the correct interpretation was clear: Vioxx causes heart attacks. One FDA analysis estimates that Vioxx caused between 88,000 and 139,000 heart attacks—30 to 40 percent of which were fatal—in the five years the drug was on the market.[44]

Subsequent litigation has uncovered memos documenting that Merck executives were concerned about the increased risk of heart attacks associated with Vioxx, but downplayed these concerns in their communications with physicians and resisted the FDA's efforts to add warnings to Vioxx's label.[45] It is hard to imagine that the drug maker's scientists were consciously promoting a product they knew would result in disease and death. At the same time, it is hard to imagine they honestly thought naproxen reduced the risk of heart attack by 80 percent. It is possible that their allegiances were so tightly linked with the products they'd worked on, as well as the financial health of their employers, that their judgment became fatally impaired.

A NEW REGULATORY PARADIGM

There are clear lessons from these repeated regulatory failures in recent years: a new regulatory paradigm is needed. Federal agencies must ensure that data and scientific analyses provided by manufacturers are independently verified. Opinions submitted to regulatory agencies by corporate scientists and, especially, the product defense industry must be taken as advocacy, primarily, not as science. Below are a few steps that begin to develop this new paradigm.

It has become apparent that some industry-supported research is never published because the sponsor didn't like the results. Following a series of alarming instances in which the sponsors of research used their financial control to the detriment of the public's health, a group of leading biomedical journals have established policies that make their published articles more transparent to commercial bias and that require authors to accept full control of and responsibility for their work.

These journals will now only publish studies done under contracts in which the investigators had the right to publish the findings without the consent or control of the sponsor. In a joint statement, the editors of the journals asserted that contractual arrangements allowing sponsor control of publication "erode the fabric of intellectual inquiry that has fostered so much high-quality clinical research."[46]

But the federal regulatory agencies that are charged with protecting our health and environment have no similar requirements. When studies are submitted to the EPA or OSHA, for example, the agencies do not have the authority to inquire who paid for the studies, and whether these studies would have seen the light of day if the sponsor didn't approve the results. Federal agencies should adopt, at a minimum, requirements for "research integrity" comparable to those used by biomedical journals: parties that submit data from research they have sponsored must disclose whether the investigators had the right to publish their findings without the consent or influence of the sponsor.[47]

It is also important to recognize that the opinions of virtually any scientist can be clouded by conflict of interest, even if it isn't apparent to the scientist herself. Conflict of interest inevitably shapes judgment—and this must be factored into the consideration of the analyses and opinions of scientists in the employ of industry.

Public health is not well served by the unequal treatment of public and private science. While raw data from government-funded studies are generally available to private parties for inspection and reanalysis, enabling product defense experts to conduct post hoc analyses that challenge troubling findings, industry is under no obligation to release comparable raw data from their own studies. When private sponsors conduct research to influence public regulatory proceedings, these studies should be subject to the same access and reporting provisions as those applied to publicly funded science.[48]

Apologists for polluters and manufacturers of dangerous products commonly complain about government regulation, asserting that the agencies are not using "sound science." In fact, many of these manufacturers of uncertainty do not want "sound science"; they want something that sounds like science, but lets them do exactly what they want.

We all recognize that the scientific evidence is just one part of policy making. In shaping rules and programs to protect the public health and environment, decision makers also have to consider economic issues, moral values, and a host of other factors. In our current regulatory system, debate over science has become a substitute for debate over policy and the values on which policy should be based.

Opponents of regulation use the existence of uncertainty, no matter its magnitude or importance, as a tool to counter imposition of public health protections that may increase their financial burden. It is important that those charged with protecting the public's health recognize that the desire for absolute scientific certainty is both counterproductive and futile. This recognition underlies the wise words of Sir Austin Bradford Hill delivered in an address to the Royal Society of Medicine in 1965:

All scientific work is incomplete—whether it be observational or experimental. All scientific work is liable to be upset or modified by advancing knowledge. That does not confer upon us a freedom to ignore the knowledge we already have, or to postpone action that it appears to demand at a given time.

Who knows, asked Robert Browning, but the world may end tonight? True, but on available evidence most of us make ready to commute on the 8:30 next day.[49]

NOTES

1. E. D. Belay, J. S. Bresee, R. C. Holman et al., "Reye's Syndrome in the United States from 1981 through 1997," *New England Journal of Medicine* 340 (1999): 1377–1382.

2. Food and Drug Administration, "Labeling for Salicylate-containing Products: Advanced Notice of Proposed Rulemaking," *Federal Register* 47 (1982): 57886.

3. P. Lurie and S. Wolfe, "Aspirin and Reye's Syndrome," *Paradigms for Change: A Public Health Textbook for Medical, Dental, Pharmacy and Nursing Students* (Washington, DC: Public Citizen Health Research Group, unpublished).

4. P. J. Hilts, *Protecting America's Health: The FDA, Business, and One Hundred Years of Regulation* (New York: Alfred A. Knopf, 2003).

5. D. Michaels, "Doubt Is Their Product," *Scientific American* 292 (2005): 96–101.

6. "Smoking and Health Proposal," Brown & Williamson Document No. 332506. Available at http://legacy.library.ucsf.edu/tid/nvs40foo [accessed November 12, 2007].

7. D. Michaels and C. Monforton, "Manufacturing Uncertainty: Contested Science and the Protection of the Public's Health and Environment," *American Journal of Public Health* 95 (2005): S39–S48.

8. B. Dawson, Tobacco Institute, in a January 11, 1989, interview on ABC's *Good Morning America*. Available at http://legacy.library.ucsf.edu/tid/ile92foo [accessed November 12, 2007].

9. C. Thompson, Hill and Knowlton, Inc., Memorandum to W. Kloepfer, Jr., Tobacco Institute, Inc. (October 18, 1968). Tobacco Institute Document TIMN0071488–1491. Available at http://legacy.library.ucsf.edu/tid/upv92foo [accessed November 12, 2007].

10. National Academy of Sciences, *Planning Climate and Global Change Research: A Review of the Draft U.S. Climate Change Science Program Strategic Plan* (Washington, DC: National Academies Press, 2003).

11. F. Luntz, Memorandum: "Winning the Global Warming Debate: An Overview." Available at Environmental Working Group http://www.ewg.org/files/LuntzResearch_environment.pdf [accessed November 12, 2007].

12. Robert N. Proctor, "'Doubt Is Our Product': Trade Association Science," *Cancer Wars* (New York: Basic Books, 1995); R. Kluger, *Ashes to Ashes* (New York: Vintage, 1996); S. A. Glantz, J. Slade, L. A. Bero, P. Hanauer, and D. Barnes, eds., *The Cigarette Papers* (Berkeley: University of California Press, 1996).

13. M. Eisenbud, *An Environmental Odyssey: People, Pollution, and Politics in the Life of a Practical Scientist* (Seattle: University of Washington Press, 1990), 55.

14. J. H. Sterner and M. Eisenbud, "Epidemiology of Beryllium Intoxication," *Archives of Industrial Hygiene and Occupational Medicine* 4 (1951): 123–151.

15. National Institute for Occupational Safety and Health, "Criteria for a Recommended Standard to Beryllium Exposure," DHEW HSM 72-10268 (1972): IV-21.

16. Ibid.

17. Department of Energy, Transcript: Beryllium Public Forum: January 15, 1997 (Albuquerque, NM). Available from the author.

18. J. J. Pallum, Brush Wellman, Memorandum (December 10, 1991): "Meeting Notes—December 6, 1991—BLTT Program," Attachment: "Redraft of Exhibit B: 'Efficacy of the 2 microgram per meter Standard.'" Available from the author.

19. D. J. Paustenbach, A. K. Madl, and J. F. Greene, "Identifying an Appropriate Occupational Exposure Limit (OEL) for Beryllium: Data Gaps and Current Research Initiatives," *Applied Occupational and Environmental Hygiene* 16 (2001): 527–538.

20. Beryllium: Effect on Worker Health. *Applied Occupational and Environmental Hygiene.* 16 (2001): 514–638.

21. Paustenbach, Madl, and Greene, "Identifying an Appropriate," 536.

22. C. N. Jeffress, Assistant Secretary for Occupational Safety and Health, Department of Labor, letter to Peter Brush, Acting Assistant Secretary, Department of Energy (August 27, 1998).

23. Department of Labor, "Semiannual Agenda of Regulations," *Federal Register* 63 (1998): 22257.

24. Occupational Safety and Health Administration, "Occupational Exposure to Beryllium; Request for Information," *Federal Register* 67 (2002): 70707.

25. A. W. Stange, D. E. Hilmas, F. J. Furman, and T. R. Gatliffe, "Beryllium Sensitization and Chronic Beryllium Disease at a Former Nuclear Weapons Facility," *Applied Occupational and Environmental Hygiene* 16 (2001): 405–417. P. K. Henneberger, D. Cumro, D. D. Deubner et al., "Beryllium Sensitization and Disease among Long-term and Short-term Workers in a Beryllium Ceramics Plant," *International Archives of Occupational and Environmental Health* 74 (2001): 167–176. P. C. Kelleher, J. W. Martyny, M. M. Mroz et al., "Beryllium Particulate Exposure and Disease Relations in a Beryllium Machining Plant," *Journal of Occupational and Environmental Medicine* 43 (2001): 238–249. K. Rosenman, V. Hertzberg, C. Rice et al., "Chronic Beryllium Disease and Sensitization at a Beryllium Processing Facility," *Environmental Health Perspectives* 113 (2005): 1366–1372; A. K. Madl, K. Unice, J. L. Brown et al., "Exposure-Response Analysis for Beryllium Sensitization and Chronic Beryllium Disease among Workers in a Beryllium Metal Machining Plant," *Journal of Occupational and Environmental Hygiene* 4 (2007): 448–466.

26. International Agency for Research on Cancer, *Beryllium and Beryllium Compounds,* vol. 58 (1993): 41. Available at http://monographs.iarc.fr/ENG/Monographs/vol58/volume58 .pdf, National Toxicology Program, *11th Report on Carcinogens,* 2005. Available at http://ntp. niehs.nih.gov/ntp/roc/eleventh/profiles/so22bery.pdf; K. Steenland and E. Ward, "Lung Cancer Incidence among Patients with Beryllium Disease: A Cohort Mortality Study," *Journal of the National Cancer Institute* 83 (1991): 1380–1385; E. Ward, A. Okun, A. Ruder, M. Fingerhut, and K. Steenland, "A Mortality Study of Workers at Seven Beryllium Processing Plants," *American Journal of Industrial Medicine* 22 (1992): 885–904; W. T. Sanderson, E. M. Ward, K. Steenland, and M. R. Petersen, "Lung Cancer Case-Control Study of Beryllium Workers," *American Journal of Industrial Medicine* 39 (2001): 133–144.

27. P. S. Levy, H. D. Roth, P. M. Hwang, and T. E. Powers, "Beryllium and Lung Cancer: A Reanalysis of a NIOSH Cohort Mortality Study" *Inhalation Toxicology* 14 (2002): 1003–1015.

28. Michaels, "Doubt Is Their Product," 96–101.

29. Ibid., 99.

30. K. Sack and A. Mundy, "A Dose of Denial," *Los Angeles Times*, March 28, 2004. Available at http://www.latimes.com/news/nationworld/nation/la-na-ppa28mar 28-1,1,4339482,print.htmlstory?coll=la-home-headlines&ctrack=1&cset=true [accessed November 12, 2007].

31. W. N. Kernan, C. M. Viscoli, L. M. Brass et al., "Phenylpropanolamine and the Risk of Hemorrhagic Stroke," *New England Journal of Medicine* 343 (2000): 1826–1832.

32. L. LaGrenade, P. Nourjah, R. Sherman et al., "Estimating Public Health Impact of Adverse Drug Events in Pharmacoepidemiology: Phenylpropanolamine and Hemorrhagic Stroke." Poster presentation at the 2001 FDA Science Forum: "Science across the Boundaries" (Washington, DC: February 15–16, 2001).

33. W. Kirton, Email to Bayer representatives, SUBJECT: CHPA Yale Study Meeting, January 21, 1999. Available through the *Los Angeles Times*, "A Dose of Denial," at http://www.latimes.com/news/nationworld/nation/la-na-ppa28mar28-1,1,2552623.htmlstory?coll=la-home-headlines [accessed November 12, 2007].

34. Sack and Mundy, "A Dose of Denial."

35. Weinberg Group, "Adverse event linked to OTC product," was available at http://www.weinberggroup.com. A screen shot is available from the author.

36. S. Krimsky, *Science in the Private Interest: Has the Lure of Profits Corrupted the Virtue of Biomedical Research?* (Lanham, MD: Rowman & Littlefield, 2003); S. Krimsky, "The Funding Effect in Science and Its Implications for the Judiciary," *Journal of Law and Policy* 8 (2005): 43–68; R. Smith, "Medical Journals Are an Extension of the Marketing Arm of Pharmaceutical Companies," *PLoS Medicine* 2 (2005): 0138.

37. J. E. Bekelman, Y. Li, and C. P. Gross, "Scope and Impact of Financial Conflicts of Interest in Biomedical Research: A Systematic Review," *JAMA* 289 (2003): 454–465; J. Lexchin, L. A. Bero, B. Djulbegovic, and O. Clark, "Pharmaceutical Industry Sponsorship and Research Outcome and Quality," *BMJ* 326 (2003): 1167–1170.

38. Lexchin, Bero, Djulbegovic, and Clark, "Pharmaceutical Industry Sponsorship," 1167–1170.

39. Smith, "Medical Journals Are an Extension," 0364–0366.

40. Ibid., 0365.

41. G. M. Gray, J. T. Cohen, G. Cunha et al., "Weight of the Evidence Evaluation of Low-Dose Reproductive and Developmental Effects of Bisphenol A," *Human and Ecological Risk Assessment* 10 (2004): 875–921.

42. F. S. Vom Saal and C. Hughes, "An Extensive New Literature Concerning Low-Dose Effects of Bisphenol A Shows the Need for a New Risk Assessment," *Environmental Health Perspectives* 113 (2005): 926–933.

43. C. Bombardier, L. Laine, A. Reicin et al., "Comparison of Upper Gastrointestinal Toxicity and Rofecoxib and Naproxen in Patients with Rheumatoid Arthritis," *New England Journal of Medicine* 343 (2000): 1520–1528.

44. D. Graham, Testimony before the U.S. Senate Finance Committee (November 18, 2004). Available at http://finance.senate.gov/hearings/testimony/2004test/111804dgtest .pdf.

45. A. Berenson, "For Merck, Vioxx Paper Trail Won't Go Away," *New York Times*, August 21, 2005.

46. F. Davidoff, C. D. DeAngelis, J. F. Drazen et al., "Sponsorship, Authorship, and Accountability," *JAMA* 286 (2001): 1232.

47. D. Michaels and W. Wagner, "Disclosures in Regulatory Science," *Science* 302 (2003): 2073.

48. W. Wagner and D. Michaels, "Equal Treatment for Regulatory Science: Extending the Controls Governing Public Research to Private Research," *Journal of Law & Medicine* 30 (2004): 119–154.

49. A. B. Hill, "The Environment and Disease: Association or Causation?" *Proceedings of the Royal Society of Medicine* 58 (1965): 295–300.

CHAPTER 5

Coming to Understand

Orgasm and the Epistemology of Ignorance

NANCY TUANA

IT IS A COMMON TENET of theorists working in the sociology of scientific knowledge (SSK) that an account of the conditions that result in scientists accepting apparently true beliefs and theories is as crucial as an analysis of those that result in their holding to apparently false theories and beliefs. In outlining the Strong Programme in SSK studies, David Bloor (1976) argues against the asymmetry position common to philosophies of science.[1] On such a position, only false beliefs that have had a history of influence on science, such as views about ether, humors, or phlogiston, are in need of a sociological account. True beliefs or theories, however, are viewed as in need of no such explanation in that their acceptance can be accounted for simply by their truth. Bloor and other SSK theorists argue that such appeals to truth are inadequate, insisting that the acceptance of a belief as true, even in science, involves social factors. The appeal to reality thus does not suffice in explaining why a belief has come to be accepted by scientists.

In a similar fashion it is important that our epistemologies not limit attention simply to what is known or believed to be known. If we are to fully understand the complex practices of knowledge production and the variety of features that account for why something is known, we must also understand the practices that account for *not* knowing, that is, for our *lack* of knowledge about a phenomena or, in some cases, an account of the practices that resulted in a group *unlearning* what was once a realm of knowledge. In other words, those who would strive to understand how we know must also develop epistemologies of ignorance.[2]

Ignorance, far from being a simple lack of knowledge that good science aims to banish, is better understood as a practice with supporting social causes as complex as those involved in knowledge practices. As Robert Proctor argued in his study of the politics of cancer research and dissemination, *Cancer Wars* (1995), we must "study the social construction of ignorance. The persistence of controversy is often not a natural consequence of imperfect knowledge but a political consequence of conflicting interests and structural apathies. Controversy can be engineered: ignorance and uncertainty can be manufactured, maintained, and disseminated."[3]

An important aspect of an epistemology of ignorance is the realization that ignorance should not be theorized as a simple omission or passive gap but is, in many cases, an active production. In her essay, "On Being White," Marilyn Frye explains that "ignorance is not something simple: it is not a simple lack, absence or emptiness, and it is not a passive state. Ignorance of this sort—the determined ignorance most white Americans have of American Indian tribes and clans, the ostrich-like ignorance most white Americans have of the histories of Asian peoples in this country, the impoverishing ignorance most white Americans have of Black language—ignorance of these sorts is a complex result of many acts and many negligences."[4]

And because ignorance is frequently constructed and actively preserved, and is linked to issues of cognitive authority, doubt, trust, silencing, and uncertainty, it often, as Frye clearly demonstrates, intersects with systems of oppression. Charles Mills, in his book *The Racial Contract* (1997), argues that matters related to race in Europe and the United States involve an active production and preservation of ignorance: "On matters related to race, the Racial Contract prescribes for its signatories an inverted epistemology, an epistemology of ignorance, a particular pattern of localized and global cognitive dysfunctions (which are psychologically and socially functional), producing the ironic outcome that whites will in general be unable to understand the world they themselves have made."[5]

Although such productions are not always linked to systems of oppression, it is important to be aware of how often oppression works through and is shadowed by ignorance. As Eve Kosofsky Sedgwick argues in her *Epistemology of the Closet* (1990), "ignorance effects can be harnessed, licensed, and regulated on a mass scale for striking enforcements."[6] Indeed, tracing what is not known and the politics of such ignorance should be a key element of epistemological *and* social/political analyses, for it has the potential to reveal the role of power in the construction of what is known and provide a lens for the political values at work in our knowledge practices.

Epistemologies that view ignorance as an arena of not-yet-knowing will also overlook those instances where knowledge once had has been lost. What was once common knowledge or even common scientific knowledge can be transferred to the realm of ignorance not because it is refuted and seen as false, but because such knowledge is no longer seen as valuable, important, or functional. Obstetricians in the United States, for example, no longer know how to turn a breech, not because such knowledge, in this case a knowing-how, is seen as false, but because medical practices, which are in large part fueled by business and malpractice concerns, have shifted knowledge practices in cases of breech births to Cesareans. Midwives in most settings and physicians in many other countries still possess this knowledge and employ it regularly. Epistemologies of ignorance must focus not only on cases where bodies of knowledge have been completely erased, or where a realm has never been subject to knowledge production, but also on these in-between cases where what was once common knowledge has been actively "disappeared" among certain groups. We must also ask the question now common to feminist and postcolonialist science studies of who benefits and who is disadvantaged by such ignorance.[7]

While we must abandon the assumption that ignorance is a passive gap in what we know, awaiting scientific progress and discovery, it would be premature to seek out a theory of ignorance with the expectation of finding some universal calculus of the "justified true belief" model. Why we do not know something, whether it has remained or been made unknown, who knows and who is ignorant, and how each of these shift historically or from realm to realm are all open to question. Furthermore, while the movements and productions of ignorance often parallel and track particular knowledge practices, we cannot assume that their logic is similar to the knowledges that they shadow. The question of how ignorance is sustained, cultivated, or allowed is one that must be asked explicitly and without assuming that the epistemic tools cultivated for understanding knowledge will be sufficient for understanding ignorance. The general point, however, still holds that we cannot fully account for what we know without also offering an account of what we do not know and who is privileged and disadvantaged by such knowledge/ignorance.

Female sexuality is a particularly fertile area for tracking the intersections of power/knowledge-ignorance.[8] Scientific and commonsense knowledge of female orgasm has a history that provides a rich lens for understanding the importance of explicitly including epistemologies of ignorance alongside our theories of knowledge. And so it is women's bodies and pleasures that I embrace.

EPISTEMOLOGIES OF ORGASM

No doubt it sounds strange to ears schooled by a Foucaultian sensitivity to things sexual for me to frame an epistemology of ignorance around women's sexuality in general and their orgasms in particular. Indeed, it was Michel Foucault who warned that the disciplining practices of the nineteenth century had constructed sex as "a problem of truth": "[T]he truth of sex became something fundamental, useful, or dangerous, precious or formidable; in short, that sex was constituted as a problem of truth."[9] Can my investigations of the power dimensions of ignorance concerning women's orgasms not fall prey to a constructed desire for the "truth of sex"?

One might suggest that I follow Foucault's admonition to attend to bodies and pleasures rather than sexual desire to avoid this epistemic trap. And, indeed, I do desire to trace bodies and pleasures as a source of subversion. The bodies of my attention are those of women; the pleasures those of orgasm. But bodies and pleasures are not outside the history and deployment of sex-desire. Bodies and pleasures will not remove me, the epistemic subject, from the practice of desiring truth. Bodies and pleasures, as Foucault well knew, have histories. Indeed the bodies that I trace are material-semiotic interactions of organisms/environments/cultures.[10] Bodies and their pleasures are not natural givens, not even deep down. Nor do I believe in a true female sexuality hidden deep beneath the layers of oppressive socialization. But women's bodies and pleasures provide a fertile lens for understanding the workings of power/knowledge-ignorance in which we can trace who desires what knowledge; that is, we can glimpse the construction of desire (or lack thereof) for knowledge of women's sexuality. I also believe that women's bodies and pleasures can, at this historical moment, be a wellspring for resisting sexual normalization.[11] Although my focus in this chapter will be on the former concern, I hope to provide sufficient development of the latter to tantalize.

I have no desire in this chapter to trace the normalizing and patholo-gizing of sexual subjectivities. My goal is to understand what "we" do and do not know about women's orgasms, and why. My "*we*'s" include scientific communities, both feminist and nonfeminist, and the common knowledges of everyday folk, both feminist and nonfeminist. Of course I cannot divorce normalizing sexualities from such a study of women's orgasms, for, as we will see, what we do and do not know of women's bodies and pleasures interact with these practices. Although part of my goal is to trace an epistemology of orgasm, I do so because of a firm belief that as we come to understand our orgasms, we will find a site of pleasure that serves as a resource for resisting sexual normalization through the practices of becoming sexual.

In coming to understand, I suggest that we begin at the site of the clitoris.

UNVEILING THE CLITORIS

What we do and do not know about women's genitalia is a case study of the politics of ignorance. The "*we*'s" I speak of here are both the "*we*'s" of the general population in the United States[12] and the "*we*'s" of scien-tists. Let me begin with the former. I teach a popular, large lecture course on sexuality. I have discovered that the students in the class know far more about male genitals than they do about female genitals. Take, for example, the clitoris. The vast majority of my female students have no idea how big their clitoris is, or how big the average clitoris is, or what types of variations there are among women. Compare to this the fact that most of my male students can tell you the length *and* diameter of their penis both flaccid and erect, though their information about the average size of erect penises is sometimes shockingly inflated—a consequence, I suspect, of the size of male erections in porn movies. An analogous pattern of knowledge-ignorance also holds across the sexes. That is, both women and men alike typically know far more about the structures of the penis than they do about those of the clitoris.

This is not to say that women do not know anything about their genitalia. But what they, and the typical male student, know consists primarily in a more or less detailed knowledge of the menstrual cycle and the reproductive organs. Women and men can typically draw a relatively accurate rendition of the vagina, uterus, fallopian tubes, and ovaries, but when asked to provide me with a drawing (from memory) of an external and an internal view of female sexual organs, they often do not include a sketch of the clitoris; and when they do, it is seldom detailed.

This pattern of knowledge-ignorance mirrors a similar pattern in scientific representations of female and male genitalia. Although the role of the clitoris in female sexual satisfaction is scientifically acknowledged, and well known by most of us, the anatomy and physiology of the clitoris, particularly its beginnings and ends, is still a contested terrain. A brief history of representations of the clitoris provides an interesting initial entry into this epistemology of ignorance. Let me begin with the "facts."

As I and many other theorists have argued, until the nineteenth century, men's bodies were believed to be the true form of human biology and the standard against which female structures—bones, brains, and genitalia alike—were to be compared.[13] The clitoris fared no differently. Medical science held the male genitals to be the true form, of which women's genitals were a colder, interior version (see Figure 5.1). As Luce Irigaray would say, through this speculum women's genitals were simply those of a man turned inside out and upside down.[14] It thus comes as no surprise that the clitoris would be depicted as, at best, a diminutive homologue to the penis. A history of medical views of the clitoris is not a simple tale. It includes those of Ambroise Paré, the sixteenth-century biologist, who, while quite content to chronicle and describe the various parts and functions of women's reproductive organs, refused to discuss what he called this "obscene part," and admonished "those which desire to know more of it" to read the work of anatomists such as Renaldus Columbus and Gabriello Fallopius.[15] A history of the clitoris must also include the subject, well dissected by Thomas Laqueur, whether, despite the proliferation of terms such as *kleitoris*, *columnella*, *virga* (rod), and *nympha* in texts

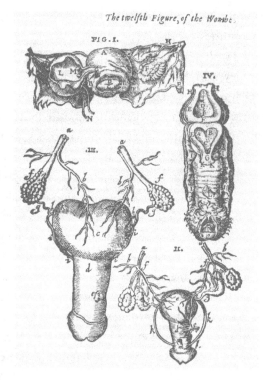

FIGURE 5.1 "The twelfth figure, Of the wombe."

SOURCE: *The workes of that famous chirurgion Ambrose Parey*, ed. Thomas Johnson (London: T. Cotes and R. Young, 1634), 127.

from Hippocrates to the sixteenth century, these meant anything quite like what "clitoris" meant after the sixteenth century when the link between it and pleasure were bridged.[16]

What was so "discovered" was, of course, complex. Renaldus Columbus (1559), self-heralded as he who discovered the clitoris, refers us to "protuberances, emerging from the uterus near that opening which is called the mouth of the womb." He described the function of these protuberances as "the seat of women's delight," which "while women are eager for sex and very excited as if in a frenzy and aroused to lust . . . you will find it a little harder and oblong to such a degree that it shows itself a sort of male member," and when rubbed or touched "semen swifter than air flows this way and that on account of the pleasure even with them unwilling."[17] Though a different clitoris than we are used to, I will later argue that Columbus provides an interesting rendition of this emerging flesh that is relevant to an epistemology of knowledge-ignorance.

While much pleasure can result from a thorough history of the clitoris, let me forebear and leap ahead to more contemporary renditions of this seat of pleasure. Even after the "two-sex" model became dominant in the nineteenth century, with its view of the female not as an underdeveloped male but as a second gender with distinctive gender differences, the clitoris got short shrift. It was often rendered a simple nub, which though carefully labeled, was seldom fleshed out or made a focus of attention. Even more striking is the emerging practice from the 1940s to the 1970s of simply omitting even the nub of this seat of pleasure when offering a cross-sectional image of female genitalia.[18] It is important to remember that this display, or lack thereof, is happening at a time when displays of the penis are becoming ever more complex.

Enter the women's health movement, and illustrations of women's genitals shift yet again, at least in some locations. Participants in the self-help women's movement, ever believers in taking matters into our own hands, not only took up the speculum as an instrument of knowledge and liberation but questioned standard representations of our anatomy. The nub that tended to disappear in standard anatomical texts took on complexity and structure in the hands of these feminists. In the 1984 edition of the Boston Women Health Collective's book, *Our Bodies, Ourselves*, the clitoris expanded in size and configuration to include three structures: the shaft, the glans, and the crura. This new model received its most loving rendition thanks to the leadership of the Federation of Feminist Women's Health Centers and the illustrative hands of Suzann Gage (1981) in *A New View of Woman's Body* (see Figure 5.2).

On such accounts, the lower two-thirds of the clitoris is hidden beneath the skin of the vulva. The clitoral glans surmounts the shaft, or body of the clitoris, which is partly visible, and then extends under the muscle tissue of the vulva (see Figure 5.3). To this is attached the crura, two stems of tissue, the corpora cavernosa, which arc out toward the thighs and obliquely toward the vagina. The glans of the clitoris, they explain, is a bundle of nerves containing 8,000 nerve fibers, twice the number in the penis, and

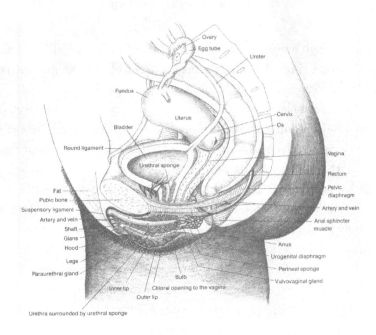

FIGURE 5.2 A cross section of the clitoris

SOURCE: Federation of Feminist Women's Health Centers, *A New View of a Woman's Body* (New York: Touchstone, 1981), illustrated by Suzann Gage, 41. Reprinted with permission of the Federation of Feminist Women's Health Centers.

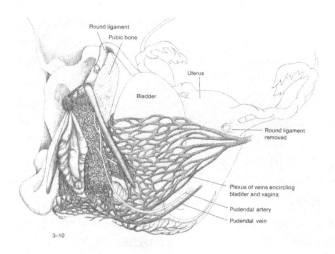

FIGURE 5.3 How the clitoris is situated in the pelvis

SOURCE: Federation of Feminist Women's Health Centers, *A New View of a Woman's Body* (New York: Touchstone, 1981), illustrated by Suzann Gage, 42. Reprinted with permission of the Federation of Feminist Women's Health Centers.

which, as you know, respond to pressure, temperature, and touch. The "new view" presented to us not only provides far more detail about the clitoral structures but also depicts the clitoris as large, and largely internal. Unlike typical nonfeminist depictions of the clitoris as largely an external genitalis, the new view rendered the divide between external and internal visible (see Figure 5.4).

Now to be fair, some very recent nonfeminist anatomical texts have included this trinity of shaft, glans, and crura.[19] But none of these texts focuses attention on coming to understand the sexual response patterns of these and other bits.[20] Feminist imagery diverges significantly from nonfeminist in providing us far more detailed views of the impact of sexual stimulation on the glans and crura of the clitoris, as well as the labia majora and the bulbs of the vestibule, the latter of which possess a very extensive blood vessel system that becomes very engorged during arousal, doubling, even tripling in size, we are told, during sexual arousal (see Figure 5.5). The always-found illustrations of male erections (see Figure 5.6) are now accompanied by an illustration of female erections (see Figure 5.7), something absent in nonfeminist texts. Feminist texts also lovingly

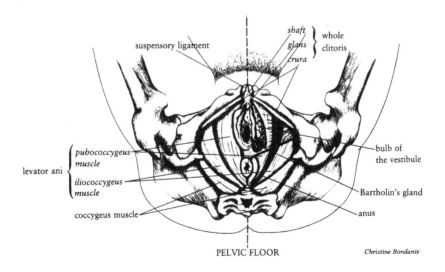

FIGURE 5.4 View of the pelvic floor and clitoris

SOURCE: Boston Women's Health Book Collective, *The New Our Bodies Ourselves* (New York, Simon & Schuster, 1984), illustrated by Christine Bondante, 206. Reprinted with permission of the Boston Women's Health Book Collective.

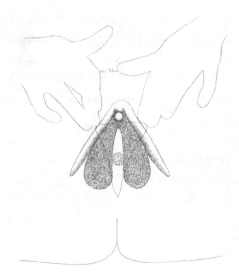

FIGURE 5.5   An inner view of the clitoris during the plateau phase

SOURCE: Federation of Feminist Women's Health Centers, *New View of a Woman's Body* (New York: Touchstone, 1981), illustrated by Suzann Gage, 51. Reprinted with permission of the Federation of Feminist Women's Health Centers.

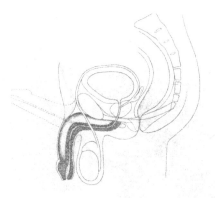

FIGURE 5.6 Side view of the penis

SOURCE: Federation of Feminist Women's Health Centers, *A New View of a Woman's Body* (New York: Touchstone, 1981), illustrated by Suzann Gage, 49. Reprinted with permission of the Federation of Feminist Women's Health Centers.

FIGURE 5.7 Side view of the clitoris

SOURCE: Federation of Feminist Women's Health Centers, *A New View of a Woman's Body* (New York: Touchstone, 1981), illustrated by Suzann Gage, 48. Reprinted with permission of the Federation of Feminist Women's Health Centers.

detail the other bits that are part of our seat of delight. Reminding us that the clitoris, impressive though it be, is not our only sensitive bit, feminists also provide us with images of the urethral sponge that lies between the front wall of the vagina and the urethra, which expands with blood during sexual arousal (see Figure 5.8). It was this structure that was allegedly "discovered" with Columbus-like gusto (Christopher, this time, not Renaldus) by Ernst Graffenburg and popularized as the "G-spot."[21] Although a few nonfeminist anatomical illustrators, post-Graffenburg, provide us glimpses of this pleasurable sponge, apparently neither they nor Graffenburg have gotten the hang of the feminist speculum, for they continue to overlook feminist presentations of the other sponge, the perineal sponge located between the vagina and the rectum, which also engorges when a woman is sexually aroused (see Figure 5.9). Pressure on any of these engorged structures can result in pleasure and orgasm.

We have a classic case of separate and unequal when it comes to contemporary nonfeminist depictions of female and male genitals. All the

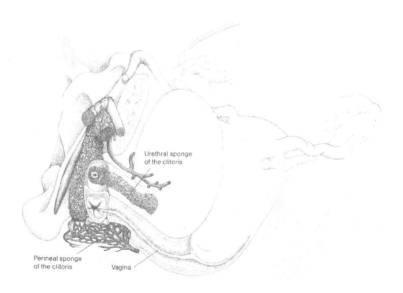

FIGURE 5.8 Urethral sponge

SOURCE: Federation of Feminist Women's Health Centers, *A New View of a Woman's Body* (New York: Touchstone, 1981), illustrated by Suzann Gage, 43. Reprinted with permission of the Federation of Feminist Women's Health Centers.

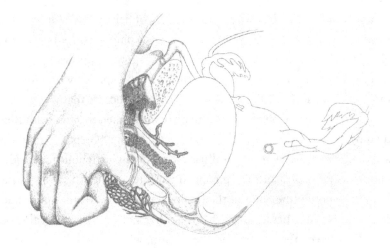

FIGURE 5.9 Self-examination of the perineal sponge

SOURCE: Federation of Feminist Women's Health Centers, *A New View of a Woman's Body* (New York: Touchstone, 1981), illustrated by Suzann Gage, 45. Reprinted with permission of the Federation of Feminist Women's Health Centers.

abovementioned contemporary anatomy textbooks include detailed renditions of the structures of the penis, with the *corpus cavernosum* and the *corpus spongiosum*, important sites of male engorgement, carefully drawn and labeled, while offering only the merest bit of a nub as a sufficient representation of the clitoris.

FINGERING TRUTH

So how do we put our finger on the truth of women's clitoral structures? Whose cartographies do we believe? For those of us who follow the speculum, the feminist-influenced model of the three-fold clitoral structures have become scripture, with each detail ever more lovingly drawn. But rather than follow desire and insist that the feminist depictions of the clitoris are the truth, let me rather trace the ebbs and flows of this knowledge-ignorance.

Despite fifteen years of clear illustrations of this new view of clitoral structures, our impact has been surprisingly minimal, at least so far. A review of anatomical illustrations in standard college human sexuality textbooks reveals a surprising lack of attention to the functions and structures of the clitoris.[22] No surprise, then, that my students have, at best, a passing knowledge of the depths and complexity of its structures. These are the very same students, I remind you, who have relatively detailed knowledge of the structures of female reproductive organs and of the structures of male genitalia, though the terminology they use to label those parts often turns to street talk rather than the high Latin of medical textbooks. The human sexuality textbook writers have clearly bought the line that "size doesn't matter," and continue to depict the clitoris as a modest, undifferentiated nub of flesh.

There is a politics of ignorance at work here, one that is linked to the politics of sex and reproduction. Whether female and male genitalia are seen as homologous or analogous (or somewhere in between), centuries of scientific theories and lay beliefs have treated their pleasures differently. There has been little dispute from the Greeks to the present of the importance of male pleasure and ejaculation for conception. In contrast, the question of female seed and the link between it and female pleasure was always a point of controversy. Many scientists, from the Greeks to well into the sixteenth century, disputed the very existence of female seed or semen, though those in the earlier centuries who did subscribe to the existence of female seed often argued for the importance of female pleasure as the vehicle for its release.[23] The infertility of prostitutes, for example, was often explained as due to a lack of pleasure in intercourse.[24] But by the thirteenth century and onward, the link between conception and female pleasure in sex was typically denied even by those who allowed for the existence of female seed. Women's sexual pleasure came to be seen as inessential to reproduction, although many scholars admitted that it might be useful in promoting the desire for intercourse.

Now to this view of the function (or lack thereof) of female erotic pleasure add the politics of sex, namely the view that the only or at least the main function of sex is reproduction. To this view add the politics of female sexuality, namely the tenet common in scientific and popular accounts well into the nineteenth century that women were more lustful than men and that their sexuality was a danger to men,[25] and a path is cleared to an understanding of why clitoral structures get lost in the process. The logic becomes quite clear: (a) There is no good reason to pay attention to the clitoris, given that it allegedly plays no role in reproduction and that sex is to be studied (only) in order to understand reproduction. (b) Worse, there is good reason to *not* pay attention to the clitoris lest we stir up a hornet's nest of stinging desire.[26] From Pandora on, and well into the nineteenth century, women's stinging desire and limb-gnawing passion had been branded the cause of the fall of mankind. What better reason to construct and maintain an epistemology of ignorance? What better way to disqualify and perhaps even control women's sexual satisfaction?[27]

But I simplify here to make my point. It is not true that there are no moments in the twentieth century when scientists focused their speculums on clitoral structures. Leaving Sigmund Freud aside for the moment, genitals came under scrutiny during the end of the nineteenth century as science constructed the category of the "invert," namely, those who mixed with members of their own sex. Evolutionary theory linked the newly "uncovered" sexual identity of the homosexual to degeneracy, and widespread societal fears of the degeneration of the race (that is, the white race) led to broadened support for eugenics movements. Scientists, now more intent than ever before on social control, began to examine bodies for signs of degeneration to provide support for proper "matings" and to discourage the dangerous mixing of people across racial or sexual boundaries. Belief in the degeneration of the race led many to believe that so-called inverts were proliferating. Anxiety led to a desire to be able to track such undesirables and an equally strong desire to believe that their perversity and devolution would be clearly marked on their bodies. Given the desire for such knowledge, it did not take long before genitals, or at least deviant genitals, would become a focus of the scientific gaze, hornet's nest or not. Although through images to be kept only for the eyes of professionals, whose objectivity and dispassionate nature would protect them from corruption, science began to turn its gaze on the structures of the clitoris to seek out and control deviancy.

The Sex Variant study, conducted in New York City from 1935 to 1941, was one example of scientific investigations launched to interrogate the marks of deviance that had been imprinted onto the structures of the body. The professed goal of the study was to identify inverts so that physicians could then try to stop them from reproducing and further contaminating the race. Gynecologist Robert Latou Dickinson, the principal investigator of the Sex Variant study, believed that deviance and degeneration would be mapped on women's genitals. Clitorises were examined, measured, and sketched, along with the various contours of vulva, breast, and nipple sizes. Dickinson concluded that, indeed, the genitals of inverts were a symbol of their deviance, arguing that their genitals were different from those of "normal" women—their vulvae, larger; their clitorises, notably erectile; their labia, longer and more protruding; their vaginas, distensible; their hymens, insensitive; and their uteruses, smaller (see Figure 5.10). This was also a period when the genitals of "inferior" races, particularly those of African descent, were examined and measured, with investigators once again believing that proof of inferiority would be marked on their genitals.[28]

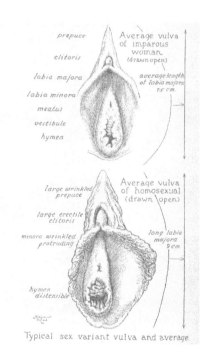

FIGURE 5.10 Typical sex variant vulva and average

SOURCE: Robert Latou Dickinson, "The Gynecology of Homosexuality," app. 6, in George W. Henry (ed.), *Sex Variants: A Study of Homosexual Patterns* (New York: P. B. Hoeber, 1941), 1102.

The point here is that this epistemology is not about truth. I am not arguing that the feminist model of the three-fold structures of the clitoris finally uncovered the long submerged truth of the clitoris. Nor am I arguing that feminists were, finally, practicing good science and being objective. These cartographies were and are fueled by our desire to transform normative heterosexuality's vagina-only attention to pleasure. Nor am I claiming that there were no discourses on the clitoris as a source of sexual pleasure in medical and popular literature until feminists and their speculums entered the scene. Indeed, one can find dozens, if not hundreds, of accounts of female orgasm resulting from this feminine seat of pleasure in texts as disparate as those written by midwives and those penned by pornographers. Nor am I arguing that the speculum was never focused on the female vulva. There is, however, a complex absence, a gap that I find important, one often repeated today. What is missing or only sketchily attended to in nonfeminist anatomies, at least when the focus is on the "normal" rather than the "deviant," is the desire to map the geographies and functions of the clitoris and our other pleasurable bits. What nonfeminist anatomists sketch seldom goes beyond the identification of this pleasurable (or dangerous) lump of flesh. What I am arguing is that the history of our knowledges-ignorances of the clitoris—indeed, our lived experiences of its beginnings and ends—is part of an embodied discourse and history of bodies and pleasures. It is a chapter in the tale of power/knowledge-ignorance.

THE ISSUE OF PLEASURE

Who would want a shotgun when you can have a semiautomatic?
Natalie Angier, *Woman: An Intimate Geography* (1999)

Let me remain a moment at this site of pleasure. Remember with me that until the nineteenth century not only women's desire for sex but the very pleasures they received from it were seen as far greater than those of men. In the words of Tiresias, he who had lived both as a woman and as a man, when it comes to the issue of pleasure:

> If the parts of love's pleasures be divided by ten,
> Thrice three go to women, one only to men.[29]

This image of women's sexuality shifts, at least for certain women, as we move into the nineteenth century, and with this move, we can locate a shift of knowledge-ignorance.

Many of our sociological surveys of sexuality, though not all, focus on heterosexual sexuality. Although this is far too narrow a story to tell if what we want is an account of bodies and pleasures, let me focus on the differences between Tiresias's abundant sexual pleasures when embodied as a woman and contemporary lived experiences of heterosexual female sexuality.

A 1994 survey of heterosexual women and men in the United States between the ages of 18 and 59 reveals that one out of every three women surveyed reported that she was uninterested in sex and one out of every five women reported that sex provided little pleasure, in both cases double the number of men reporting a lack of interest or of pleasure in sex.[30] Add to this the fact that almost 25 percent of the women surveyed reported being unable to reach orgasm, in comparison with 8 percent of men, and we begin to see an impact of knowledge-ignorance on bodies and pleasures. The pleasure gap surrounding heterosexual women's and men's first coital experiences is even more startling: 79 percent of men reported that they were certain they had an orgasm during their first sexual experience, while only 7 percent of the women could so report.[31]

These are astonishing figures in themselves, but they become all the more startling when set alongside women's multiorgasmic capacity. Women's capacity for multiple orgasm, though taken to be a revelation by contemporary scientists, was a commonplace in many scientific and popular circles in the past. What was once taken to be ordinary knowledge of women's more robust sexuality and her greater orgasmic capacity submerged into the mire of ignorance sometime during the turn of the nineteenth century, where it went dormant (or perhaps just pornographic) for about fifty years and then resurfaced in the new science of sexuality.

Woman's multiorgasmic capacity became a subject for contemporary scientific study when Kinsey's 1953 study, *Sexual Behavior in the Human Female*, revealed that almost half of the women studied reported the ability to experience multiple orgasms. Shere Hite's 1976 report on female sexuality confirmed Kinsey's results. In Hite's survey, 48 percent of the women reported that they often required more than one orgasm to be sexually satisfied.[32] William H. Masters and Virginia G. Johnson (1966) similarly documented women's ability to have more than one orgasm without a significant break. They noted that if proper stimulation continues after a woman's first climax, she will in most cases be capable of having additional orgasms—they report between five and six—within a matter of minutes. Masters and Johnson also report that with direct clitoral stimulation, such as an electric vibrator, many women have from twenty to fifty orgasms.

Despite having science and all those measuring tools on our side, efforts continue to suppress this bit of knowledge. As just one example, Donald Symons, in *The Evolution of Human Sexuality* (1979), strikes a typical pose when he assures his readers that the multiply orgasmic woman "is to be found primarily, if not exclusively, in the ideology of feminism, the hopes of boys, and the fears of men."[33]

Foucault warned us away from desire as a category implicated in the construction of human identities and cultures, but urged a greater attention to pleasure. His *History of Sexuality* (1990) documents the uses of pleasure in the practices of normalizing power and includes pleasure, not just desire, as fundamental to understanding the genealogy of sexuality. But Foucault's account also includes a creative, indeed resistant, aspect of pleasure, in which pleasure could be a site for resisting sexual normalization and a wellspring for enriching the art of living.[34]

At a time when popular culture and science alike are convinced of men's greater sexual drives, when a long-entrenched fear of the power of women's sexuality is still in the background, when a clear double standard of sexuality disciplines women and men alike, and when heterosexuality remains the normalized sexuality, it is perhaps no surprise that far more women than men are dissatisfied when it comes to the issue of pleasure. But I desire to flesh out pleasure in ways that have the potential to resist this type of normalization. As a first step, I stand Tiresias alongside the nineteenth century's passionless woman and the twentieth century's preorgasmic but sexually active woman, and by coming to understand the politics of knowledge-ignorance behind their presence, invoke the female orgasm.

THE EITHER/OR OF WOMEN'S ORGASMS

Let me return to my history of the clitoris. In this section I will complicate this study of the epistemology of ignorance-knowledge regarding female sexuality by bringing function to form, turning my attention to accounts of the role of the clitoris in female orgasm. To understand the almost complete circumcision of female orgasmic potentiality effected by labeling practically any clitoral "excitability" deviant during the first half of the twentieth century, we must turn to Freud. The longest-playing of the orgasm debates in the twentieth century began with Freud's declaration of not one but two types of orgasm: the vaginally adult kind and her immature kid sister, the clitoral orgasm.[35] From this one little act of counting to two erupted a huge, now almost century-long, debate.

Let me begin my account by returning to Reynaldus Columbus. While Columbus locates the clitoris inaccurately, the link he makes between it and sexual pleasure mark a movement I would like us to remember. His account bears repeating. He tells us that he discovered "protuberances, emerging from the uterus near that opening which is called the mouth of the womb" that were, in his words, "the seat of women's delight," which when rubbed or touched "semen swifter than air flows this way and that on account of the pleasure even with them unwilling."[36] Columbus functions according to an older economy in which women's pleasure in sex mattered because it was needed for conception.

While still marked by a male economy—both in representation ("it shows itself a sort of male member") and in function ("even with them unwilling")—Columbus's depiction of the clitoris evinces another economy, one that dissolves the boundary between inside and out, between the so-called external and internal genitalia. It also provides an interesting example of how knowledge once found can be lost. Columbus, a man of his time, viewed female genitalia as homologous to male genitalia but marked by a lack of heat that resulted in their remaining, for the most part, inside the body. In identifying a "protuberance" that emerges from the uterus, Columbus acknowledged that it, like the penis, grew in size when aroused, but he did not limit female pleasure to it. He acknowledged other sites of pleasure, such as "the circular folds of the cervix that cause a friction from which lovers experience wonderful pleasure" and the various bits of flesh closer to the vulva by which "pleasure or delight in intercourse is not a little increased."[37] Columbus's geography described various linked structures as contributing to women's pleasure, but he had no desire to determine where one part or orgasm stops and another begins. Nor was there a desire to locate pleasure in a clearly defined site. Protuberances, folds, and bits of flesh alike are, for Columbus, that from which pleasure flows.

What Columbus had put together, Freud would cast asunder. While Freud retained a remnant of the one-sex model, arguing that "portions of the male sexual apparatus also appear in women's bodies, though in an atrophied state," he argues for an important psychical difference between the pleasures of men and those of women.[38] In boys, there is a relatively unproblematic "accession of libido" during puberty. In girls, however, he tells us that there is "a fresh wave of repression in which it is precisely clitoroidal sexuality that is effected."[39] That is, to become a woman the girl must abandon the pleasures of the clitoris and discover those of the vagina. "When erotogenic susceptibility to stimulation has been successfully transferred by a woman from the clitoris to the vaginal orifice, it implies that she has adopted a new leading zone for the purposes of her later sexual activity."[40] This is an economy that requires a level of differentiation not found in Columbus. Freud's is a map of the female genitals that requires that we can, and do, distinguish between the clitoris and all its bits, on the one hand, and the vagina and its bits of flesh on the other. And it is here, despite the trace of the one-sex model, that Freud imposes a two-sex economy that divides the clitoris from the other bits. But he does so to perpetuate an even older economy that perceives the purpose of female pleasure, when properly channeled, to be heterosexual reproduction. Indeed, "the intensification of the brake upon sexuality brought about by pubertal repression in women serves as a stimulus to the libido of men and causes an increase in its activity."[41] In other words, repressed female sexuality increases male desire—quite a modern trope.

The story, of course, shifts in the 1960s with the tools of Masters and Johnson and the politics of feminism. Masters and Johnson (1966) rejected the purported distinction between clitoral and vaginal orgasm, arguing that physiologically speaking there was only one kind of orgasm. Peering through their speculums, they concluded that allegedly vaginal orgasms, which they revealingly identified as those experienced during intercourse (notice the functionality of the definition), were no different than allegedly clitoral orgasms, for both resulted from the same phenomenon, namely clitoral stimulation. We are told that penile coital thrusting draws the clitoral hood back and forth against the clitoris and vaginal pressure heightens blood flow in the clitoris, further setting the stage for orgasm.

These findings were, and still are, met with skepticism in the scientific community, but not in the feminist community. Following closely on the heels of Masters and Johnson's pronouncements and the second wave of feminism that hit in the late 1960s, feminist theorists such as Ann Koedt and Alex Shulman insisted that we women should all "think clitoris" and reject the myth of the vaginal orgasm.[42] Their concern was to discredit the vaginal orgasm and the years of pressure placed on women who did not have the "right kind." But to make the case, a frustrating reversal occurred where *only* the clitoris was *the* source of sensation—and remember we do not yet have the enlarged *Our Bodies, Ourselves* (1984) conception of the clitoris to turn to. Shulman tells us that the vagina has so little sensation that "women commonly wear a diaphragm or tampon in it, and even undergo surgery on it, without feeling any sensation at all."[43] And although Shulman does not deny that some women might sometimes experience orgasm through intercourse, for after all some women, she tells us, sometimes experience orgasm through breast stimulation or mental stimulation or even through dreams, she does disparage the level of pleasure intercourse can provide: "Masters and Johnson observe that the clitoris is automatically 'stimulated' in intercourse since the hood covering the clitoris is pulled over the clitoris with each thrust of the penis in the vagina—much, I suppose, as a penis is automatically 'stimulated' by a man's underwear whenever he takes a step. I wonder, however, if either is erotically stimulating by itself."[44]

Despite Masters and Johnson and feminist slogans, the days of vaginal orgasm are not (yet) numbered. Josephine Singer and Irving Singer (1972), for example, argue that there are still two types of orgasms, the vulval and the uterine.[45] They contend that what Masters and Johnson observed were vulval orgasms, which remain the same despite the source of stimulation, clitoral or vaginal. But they argue that the uterine orgasm occurs only in response to deep thrusting against the cervix, which slightly displaces the uterus and stimulates the tissues that cover the abdominal organs. This view of two types of orgasm has received additional support from scientists who argue that orgasms that result from deep cervical or uterine stimulation are controlled by a different neural pathway and produce different subjective experiences than do those generated through clitoral stimulation.[46]

One response to the orgasm debates is to ask what keeps them so entrenched? As breasts and other nongenital bits attest to, the origins of orgasms are a complex matter. Why the persistence in counting even when we are reassured (repeatedly) that they are all equally "good"?[47] Though I have no doubt that the answer to this question is complex, let me explore two of its components: the geography of the genitals and the persistence of the belief that the function of sex is reproduction.

Those who sketch anatomical renditions of male and female genitals insist on making a distinction between internal and external genitalia. There is a factor of arbitrariness clearly marked on this distinction. For males, the penis is wholly an external genital, but testicles get divided in two, with the scrotum being listed as an external sex organ and the testes as internal. Since a lot of bits of the penis are internal, one wonders why we even bother to make this distinction. But when it comes to the analogous division of female genitals, there is more than arbitrariness at play. The politics of reproduction gets written explicitly into this division, for in the female another descriptive phrase for the internal female sex organs is "the female reproductive system."[48] This division reinforces the orgasm debates and provides a way to "make sense" of the claim that there are different kinds of orgasms, those that originate from outside and those from inside.

What we have here is an instance of the politics of knowledge-ignorance. This division of female genitals evinces the persistence of a politics of viewing reproduction as central to sexuality, so that it becomes a defining element in the demarcation of female genitalia. If you set sail by Columbus's map, you would not arrive at the planned destination. Still, like his earlier navigator namesake, where you do arrive is interesting too. Seeing orgasm and reproduction as a piece of a whole cloth, Columbus had no desire to demarcate the clitoris as "external" and hence not part of the female reproductive system. But once the clitoris and its orgasmic pleasures were seen as inessential to reproduction, few anatomists saw any value in charting its contours and it was relegated into that little undifferentiated nub that could easily be deemed "external" and "nonreproductive," with the "true" genitals, those that matter, being the internal genitalia.[49]

This politics of knowledge-ignorance is in turn marked by a persistent refusal to admit that the new, feminist-inspired view of female genitals dissolves the basis for the internal/external divide, for, on its view, the clitoris is always already both. And once one has this richer understanding of all the bits involved in female orgasm, and little political commitment to retaining a teleology of reproduction in accounts of pleasure, then nothing turns on demarcating types of orgasm based on physiological location. In *Women's Experience of Sex* (1985), Sheila Kitzinger sums up this view thusly: "Asking whether orgasm is in the clitoris or in the vagina is really the wrong question."[50] But here, despite feminists' insistence that their accounts were about truth—"I think that we were revealing the truth. And how can you argue with anatomy?"[51]—we find ourselves in that complex intersection between knowledge-ignorance and power-politics. The desire to "cut nature at its joints" often requires value-laden, strategic decisions. Feminists cut nature at different joints than do others who represent the clitoris because their values concerning the politics of sex differ from the values of nonfeminist anatomists. Perhaps the body speaks, but understanding what it says requires interpretation.

What we learn from feminist explorations of our genital geography is twofold. First, if you view the clitoris as an important knowledge project, whether because you are convinced that orgasm is primarily clitoral and your geographies aim to understand pleasure or because, like Columbus, you think orgasm is central to reproduction and you aim to understand reproduction, then you will focus far more attention on the structures of the clitoris than if you see it as an uninteresting though pleasant nub. What we attend to and what we ignore are often complexly interwoven with values and politics. Second, if you discover new knowledge about something others do not take seriously, do not expect your knowledge projects to have much effect. The veil of ignorance is not so easily lifted.

SISTERHOOD IS POWERFUL

I've talked so far about scientific views of human female orgasm, but another way to enrich our understanding of this epistemology of ignorance-knowledge and attend to bodies and pleasures is to include in this account our simian sisters and how their stories and ours are woven together in theories of evolution. In making this move, I would like to return to the issue of pleasure and keep in the foreground why women's multiple orgasmic pleasures are so seldom acknowledged. Lest one think that only feminist accounts of orgasm are political, one need only look at the orgasm debates in evolutionary theory to see that nonfeminist accounts also wear their societal values on their sleeves.[52] First of all, and not at all surprising given what I've already pointed out, the typical evolutionary accounts of female sexuality explain all basic aspects of sexuality in terms of reproduction. It is rare to find an account in which sexuality is treated as an autonomous set of functions and activities only partially explained in terms of reproductive functions.

The reduction of sexuality to reproduction is well illustrated in primate studies. In reconstructing how early man and woman behaved, researchers have generally turned to chimpanzees, with whom we shared a common ancestor a mere 5 million years ago. Despite our kinship and some important similarities between humans and chimpanzees, such as the long period of infant dependency, social bonds that persist over generations, and the need to learn what to eat and how to obtain it, there is also a striking difference, namely, the fact that female chimps have sex only during estrus, which begins and ends during their fertile period. Add to this that such occurrences are comparatively rare in a chimpanzee community because females spend most of their adult lives either pregnant or lactating,[53] and the use of chimp sexual behavior as a blueprint for human sexual behavior becomes questionable. However, one effect of this comparison is to link all sexual behavior, chimpanzee and human alike, to reproductive success. The vast majority of chimpanzee sexual behavior occurs during the female fertile period, and thus it is easy to argue that it is linked to reproductive success.

But there is another contender for a snapshot of early hominid sexual behavior, the bonobos, who also shared that same 5-million-year-old ancestor. Bonobos, unlike chimpanzees and far more like humans, frequently separate sex from reproduction, and female bonobos' sexuality, like the sexuality of female humans, is not tied to their ovulation cycles. Though female bonobos have pink genital swellings as do chimps, theirs begin and end weeks before and after their fertile periods and last for approximately 70 percent of their cycle. Bonobo sexuality is not only *not* linked to fertile periods, but its functions and enactments go far beyond simple reproductive success. Bonobos use sex to decrease tensions caused by potential competition, typically competition for food. When bonobos find a food source such as a tree filled with ripe fruit, their initial response is a sexual freeplay that calms down the group before they turn to feeding. Sexual encounters also often follow displays of aggression, especially among males. After two males fight, one will often place his rump against the other's genitals or reach out and stroke the other's penis, again as a way to release social tension. Females also use sexual behavior to enhance bonding, both with males and with females. Females, who join new communities when they reach sexual maturity, will have sex with each member of the group as a way to gain acceptance. Females also maintain sexual relations with other females as a way to form alliances that will help ensure access to food and collaborative efforts to control male behavior.[54]

Lest this foraging in the jungles of primate sexuality has made it difficult to follow the logic of my analysis, my point here is that knowledge and ignorance production emerge from values and prior assumptions concerning proper ends. If we have for centuries insisted that the proper function of sexuality is reproduction, then it is crucial to "civilize" it, that is, to put it in service of family values. Given the persistence of the belief that the primary purpose of human sex is reproduction and, I would add, an equally imbedded fear of female sexuality, it comes as no surprise that our mostly male evolutionary theorists would pick the chimp over the bonobo to model the evolution of human sexuality. A female chimpanzee may have sex with more than one male, but at least she modestly reserves her passions for procreation.

Seeing how sex fares, it would be foolhardy to predict that female orgasms would fare any better. And indeed, if we turn our attention to evolutionary accounts of female orgasms, their existence and function, we find another story of family values. But to understand the plotline of this story, we have to return to our primate sisters. Although evolutionary theorists have accepted the existence of human female orgasms, until recently they wanted to make them *uniquely* human. In other words, although it was accepted that male primates exhibit orgasmic responses during ejaculation, most theorists denied that female nonhuman primates experienced orgasm, another piece in an epistemology of ignorance.

In asking why theorists denied our primate sisters their orgasms, let's begin with some of the facts. Donald Symons, in his influential book *The Evolution of Human Sexuality* (1979), chronicled the empirical data marshaled by those who wondered about such orgasms. He noted that numerous primatologists reported a "clutching reaction" in which female rhesus monkeys grasped the male, but only during the ejaculatory mount, the last of two to eight mounts. Though some argued that the timing of this clutch supported a possible ejaculation-triggering vaginal spasm, others denied any such association. Others studying rhesus monkeys noted rhythmic contractions of thigh muscles and around the base of the tail in females after a number of mounts and thrusts. Others studying stumptail monkeys noted that females who mount other females sometimes exhibit the same behavior patterns that a male stumptail exhibits as he ejaculates, namely "a pause followed by muscular body spasms accompanied by the characteristic frowning round-mouthed stare expression and the rhythmic expiration vocalization."[55] Others studying rhesus monkeys found that after sessions of clitoral and vaginal stimulation some of the monkeys had vaginal contractions.

Despite the mounting evidence for nonhuman primate orgasm, Symons concludes: "While the possibility that nonhuman female mammals experience orgasm during heterosexual copulation remains open, there is no compelling evidence that they do."[56] He argues that what evidence there is for nonhuman primate orgasm occurs only in "unnatural" settings such as laboratories or zoos in which primates experience "more intense and varied sexual behavior than occurs in natural circumstances."[57] Notice that the only orgasms that count for Symons are those that occur during heterosexual copulation in so-called natural settings.

The evidence is now turning against the view that orgasm is uniquely human, though the debates still rage. Alan Dixson (1998), for example, reports evidence of uterine contractions in female stumptail macaques during copulations with males as well as while engaging in so-called mounting behavior between females.[58] Studies also document elevated heart rates similar to those experienced in human females during orgasm, as well as vaginal contractions, clitoral tumescence, limb spasm, and body tension during normal bouts of pelvic thrusting. Jane Goodall, I would add, also notes that adolescent female chimpanzees laugh softly as they masturbate.[59] Dixson concludes that "orgasm should therefore be viewed as a phylogenetically ancient phenomenon among anthropoid primates; the capacity to exhibit orgasm in the human female being an inheritance from ape-like ancestors."[60]

So, again, why the decades of denial of orgasm to our primate sisters in the face of their embodied pleasures? What is the logic of this epistemology of knowledge-ignorance? The desire to make the human female orgasm unique was linked to the desire to argue for the so-called pair-bond, that is, monogamous heterosexual coupling—the family values script. Western sexual values and the sexual antics of bonobos are about as far afield from each other as they can get, but even the more sexually sedate chimpanzee female mates with multiple partners during her estrus. Evolutionary theorists opted instead for a picture right out of a Norman Rockwell painting, the idea being that orgasm evolved by sexual selection in the human female to facilitate bonding and long-term relationships between the sexes. According to David Barash, "sex may be such a device [to sustain the pair-bond], selected to be pleasurable for its own sake, in addition to its procreative function. This would help explain why the female orgasm seems to be unique to humans."[61] Female orgasm here serves as a female's reward and motivation to engage in frequent intercourse, but only with one partner, which helps cement the pair-bond, ensures reproduction, and increases male cooperation and assistance with rearing offspring. Here we see how an epistemology of ignorance surrounding female orgasms, in this case those of our simian sisters, can be put in the service of family values.

There are, as you might suspect, a number of problems with this story. Females of other primate species, such as gibbons, who do not exhibit obvious signs of female orgasm are primarily monogamous. But the theory also associates orgasm with intercourse in assuming that orgasm is a reward for engaging in frequent intercourse. In both humans and many nonhuman primates, heterosexual intercourse is a far less reliable path to orgasm than other types of genital stimulation. Orgasm through intercourse alone and apart from any additional clitoral stimulation is relatively rare for human females: somewhere between 20 to 35 percent of women in the United States report always or almost always experiencing orgasm from intercourse alone.[62] Evolutionary theorists want to wed the bonobo-like social bonding function of sexuality to gibbon-like monogamy, but without attending to when we human women are laughing softly.

Now introduce human female multiorgasmic capacity into the evolutionary picture, and the pair-bond story becomes even less credible, a patriarchal pipe dream, if you will. The human female stands before us, lacking any visible sign of estrus and a capacity for far more orgasmic pleasure than the human male. Now compare this to the oft-told evolutionary tale about the differences in the so-called cost of sex:

The unconscious evolutionary logic of males and females differs. Physiologically, if a man mated with a different woman every night he could sire thousands of children, whereas an equally promiscuous woman could bear at most some twenty children during her adult life. The dramatic variance in reproductive potential between males and females suggests that human males, unlike females, may have benefited significantly by copulating with as many lovers as possible. Thus, in males at least, the desire for "sex for sex's sake," the taste for sex without emotional attachment, very likely has been genetically reinforced.[63]

Where this tale goes awry yet again reflects the politics of ignorance. Let's begin by checking out these numbers. First of all, men do not have unlimited sperm supplies. The daily human sperm production is about 185 million sperm per day and most men ejaculate somewhere between 150 and 360 million sperm. A man's sperm count drops by 72 percent if he ejaculates more than once a day, and ejaculating more than 3.5 times a week significantly decreases total sperm supplies, compromising fertility.[64] Now remember he is consorting with females who show no visible signs of fertility and, if we accept the "sex for sex's sake" hypothesis, is competing with many other males. Assuming a generous window of 5 days in a 28-day cycle where fertilization is possible, then, even assuming that the male restricts all his ejaculations to intercourse and assuming he does not go over the 3.5 ejaculations per week to keep his sperm count up to peak performance, but allowing that he mates randomly with different females, it is unlikely that any of his 14 ejaculations per month will result in conception. Now add to this the supposition that other males, given their projected promiscuity, may also be having sex with the same females. This requires that we add sperm competition to the picture, yet again reducing male reproductive potential.[65] The facts, it seems, make the dramatic variance in reproductive potential postulated between males and females highly questionable.

Now stand this male whose ejaculations cannot go over 3.5 per week without reducing reproductive efficacy alongside the female who is capable of twenty to fifty orgasms in each of her sexual encounters. One way to retell this story is to account for the evolutionary advantage of female orgasmic capacity as an inducement to copulate with a variety of males rather than one partner and thus promote sperm competition. But another way to retell this story is to break sex off from its exclusively reproductive role and acknowledge that sex has other functions. Following the antics of the bonobos, we might see female sexual potency as a means of assuring societal harmony and diffusing tensions or as a way to ensure the assistance of others, and not just male others, in procuring food and assisting in the care of offspring. But these are stories that are very seldom told.

My point in all this is not to argue for the superiority of my "what if" story of human sexual evolution, but to point out as clearly as I can the dramatic suppression of female orgasmic capacity in current evolutionary accounts. Human women's orgasms are not denied, but they are carefully cultivated to avoid rupturing certain societal scripts. Returning to the issue of pleasure once again, I would ask what we might discover about bodies and pleasures if we cultivated our female sexuality through scripts from different disciplinary practices.

BODIES AND PLEASURES

I return to the figure of Tiresias, now standing beside a female bonobo, and add a third to this gathering, Annie Sprinkle, porn-star-turned-performance-artist/sex-educator. If bodies and pleasures are to be seen as a resource, it is important not to think that our goal is to find those pleasures that are free from sexual normalization, free from disciplinary practices. Here I follow LaDelle McWhorter, who claims that "instead of refusing normalization outright, we need to learn ways to use the power of its disciplines to propel us in new directions." Though we cannot simply remove ourselves from disciplinary practices, she argues that it is possible to affirm "development without affirming docility, [through] affirming the free, open playfulness of human possibility within regimes of sexuality without getting stuck in or succumbing to any one sexual discourse or formation."[66] McWhorter, following Foucault, suggests that one path to this playfulness is to deliberately separate practice from goal and simply engage in disciplinary practices for their own sake, for the pleasures they bring, rather than for some purpose beyond them. "What if we used our capacities for temporal development not for preparation for some task beyond that development but for the purpose of development itself, including the development of our capacities for pleasure? What if we used pleasure rather than pain as our primary disciplinary tool?"[67] Following Foucault, what we must work on "is not so much to liberate our desires but to make ourselves infinitely more susceptible to pleasure."[68]

Annie Sprinkle, in her one-woman show, "Herstory of Porn: Reel to Real," describes the new direction her work took in the mid-1980s when she devoted her talents to displaying the beauty of sex and the undiscovered power of orgasms. "Some people discover Jesus and want to spread the word. I discovered orgasms and want to spread the word." Sprinkle's new productions attempt to refocus attention from power to pleasure. "There's a lot of people who talk about violence, rape, and abuse. But, there's not a lot of people that talk about pleasure, bliss, orgasm, and ecstasy."[69] Sprinkle's work has transformed over time. At one point her performances focused attention on female orgasmic ejaculations, providing audiences with sights seldom before seen on stage and ones that were, as the title of her performance explains, real, not reel. She has also advocated and really performed the nongenital breath or energy orgasm in which one "can simply lie down, take a few breaths, and go into an orgasmic state."

Sprinkle is not advocating a new homologous model of female orgasm—women ejaculate too—or an ultimate radical feminist rejection of penetrative sex. Rather than setting up new disciplinary practices with clearly defined markers between "good" feminist sex and "bad" nonfeminist sex, Sprinkle explores pleasure and refers to herself as a "metamorphosexual." I am not here claiming that Sprinkle's pleasures are outside sexual normalization, but I do think she stands before us as one who explores pleasure for its own sake. I offer her pleasures as an example of how we might, in McWhorter's words, "live our bodies as who we are, to intensify our experiences of bodiliness and to think from our bodies, if we are going to push back against the narrow confines of the normalizing powers that constrict our freedom."[70]

Sprinkle's pleasures are themselves part of disciplinary practices. It is important if we go the way of pleasure that we not desire pleasures that escape power. For Sprinkle's body and pleasures are situated in economies partially shaped by the feminist speculum. A more complete story would situate Sprinkle in the decades of practices of the feminist health movement and feminist efforts to take back our bodies and our sexualities. This pleasurable account I must leave for another time. Here I will simply tantalize by repeating Sprinkle's gospel that we return to our bodies and to our orgasms, and spread the word.

CONCLUSION

It comes as no surprise that there is often a correlation between knowledge and pleasure. The feminist quest to enhance knowledge about women's bodies and their sexual experiences had as its goal the enhancement of women's pleasures. As should now be clear, ignorance and pleasure are complexly interrelated. Indeed the old adage that "ignorance is bliss" takes on new meanings when read through the lens of an epistemology attentive to both knowledge and ignorance. Whose pleasures were enhanced by ignorance and whose were suppressed by knowledge are complex questions that must be asked repeatedly in any study of the science of sexuality.

My goal in this chapter was twofold. First, I wanted to share a genuine fascination with the study of the science of sexuality, particularly in relation to female sexuality. While much effort has gone into studying the formation of sexual *identities*, far less has been devoted to the science of sexuality. While I do not want to suggest that this aspect of sexual science or our sexual experiences are divorced from the constructions of sexual identities, I do believe that a fascination with the latter has deferred full attention from the former. While sexual identity issues will always be an aspect of any study of the science of sexuality, it is my conviction that an inclusion of sexuality will highlight other axes of power.

My second goal was to begin to outline the importance and power of attending to what we do not know and the power-politics of such ignorances. Although my account is preliminary and suggestive, I have presented the following claims:

- Any complete epistemology must include a study of ignorance, not just knowledge.
- Ignorance—far from being a simple, innocent lack of knowledge—is a complex phenomenon, which, like knowledge, is interrelated with power. For example, ignorance is frequently constructed, and it is linked to issues of cognitive authority, trust, doubt, silencing, and so forth.
- While many feminist science studies theorists have embraced the interrelationship of knowledge and values, we must also see the ways in which ignorance, too, is so interrelated.
- The study of ignorance can provide a lens for the values at work in our knowledge practices.
- We should not assume that the epistemic tools we have developed for the study of knowledge or the theories we have developed concerning knowledge practices will transfer to the study of ignorance.

EPILOGUE

Inanna placed the shugurra, the crown of the steppe, on her head.
She went to the sheepfold, to the shepherd.
She leaned back against the apple tree.
When she leaned against the apple tree, her vulva was wondrous to behold.
Rejoicing at her wondrous vulva, the young woman Inanna applauded
herself.[71]

I hope by now you are laughing softly with me. Lean back against the apple tree. Feel the delicate fire running under your skin. Our vulvae are wondrous to behold.

NOTES

This essay benefited from helpful suggestions from Lynn Hankinson Nelson and Alison Wylie.

1. David Bloor, *Knowledge and Social Imagery* (London: Routledge and Kegan Paul, 1976).

2. I choose to employ the phrase "epistemologies of ignorance" despite its potential awkwardness (theories of knowledge of ignorance) for a number of reasons. One alternative term, *agnoiology*, has histories I have no desire to invoke. First employed by James Frederick Ferrier (1854) to refute William Hamilton's (1858–1860) thesis of the unknowableness of the Absolute Reality, Ferrier posits ignorance as properly attributable only to an *absence or lack* of knowledge of that which it is possible for us to know and precludes the term *ignorance* from being applied to anything that is unintelligible or self-contradictory. Ferrier used the term *agnoiology* to distinguish what was truly knowable—and thus the proper subject matter of epistemology—from that which was unknowable. James F. Ferrier, *Institutes of Metaphysic* (Edinburgh: Blackwood, 1854), 536; William Hamilton, "Lectures on Metaphysics and Logic," in *Works of William Hamilton*, ed. Savina Tropea (Bristol: Thoemmes, 1858–1860/2001).

The term *agnoiology* has been resuscitated by Keith Lehrer (1990) as part of an argument demonstrating that skepticism has not been philosophically refuted; he argues that the possible truth of the skeptical hypothesis entails that we can never achieve completely justified true belief. Hence, Lehrer concludes that we do not know anything, even that we do not know anything. His point is that rational belief and action do not require refuting the skeptical hypothesis, nor do they need the validating stamp of "knowledge." Keith Lehrer, *Theory of Knowledge* (Boulder, CO: Westview, 1990).

While *agnotology* does not carry this history, I wish to retain the rhetorical strength of "epistemology" when investigating ignorance. Too often, as evidenced by both Ferrier and Lehrer, ignorance is only a vehicle to reveal the proper workings of knowledge or, in the case of Lehrer, rational belief and action. Ignorance itself is not interrogated but is set up as the background against which one unfurls enriched knowledge. It is my desire to retain a focus on ignorance, to foreground ignorance as a location for understanding the workings of power. Just as we have epistemology/ies of science, of religion, and so on, I wish to argue for an epistemology of the complex phenomenon of ignorance as well as to suggest that no theory of knowledge is complete that ignores ignorance.

3. Robert N. Proctor, *Cancer Wars: How Politics Shapes What We Know and Don't Know about Cancer* (New York: Basic Books, 1995), 8.

4. Marilyn Frye, "On Being White: Thinking toward a Feminist Understanding of Race and Race Supremacy," in *The Politics of Reality: Essays in Feminist Theory* (Berkeley, CA: Crossing Press, 1983), 118.

5. Charles S. Mills, *The Racial Contract* (Ithaca, NY: Cornell University Press, 1997), 18.

6. Eve Kosofsky Sedgwick, *Epistemology of the Closet* (Berkeley: University of California Press, 1990), 5.

7. Sandra Harding, *Is Science Multi-Cultural? Postcolonialisms, Feminisms, and Epistemologies* (Bloomington: Indiana University Press, 1998); Nancy Tuana, "Re-Valuing Science," in *Feminism, Science, and the Philosophy of Science*, eds. Lynn Hankinson Nelson and Jack Nelson (Dordrecht, Netherlands: Kluwer, 1996).

8. I will use this particular rhetorical form both to visually remind readers of Foucault's notion of power/knowledge (1980) and to add to it my emphasis on ignorance. I am not here claiming that Foucault did not understand how the workings of power/knowledge served to suppress knowledge practices, but with our contemporary philosophical emphasis on what we do know, I think the constant reminder to attend to what we do not know is crucial. Without the reminder, the politics of ignorance are too often erased. Michel Foucault, *Power/Knowledge: Selected Interviews and Other Writings, 1972–1977*, ed. and trans. Colin Gordon (New York: Pantheon, 1980).

9. Michel Foucault, *The History of Sexuality, Volume 1: An Introduction*, trans. Robert Hurley (New York: Random House, 1990), 56.

10. This conception of bodily being was developed extensively in Nancy Tuana, "Fleshing Gender, Sexing the Body: Refiguring the Sex/Gender Distinction," *Spindel Conference Proceedings. Southern Journal of Philosophy*, vol. 35 (1996); Tuana, "Material Locations: An Interactionist Alternative to Realism/Social Constructivism," in *Engendering Rationalities*, eds. Nancy Tuana and Sandra Morgen (Bloomington: Indiana University Press, 2001).

11. McWhorter convincingly (and pleasurably) argues that a neglected aspect of Foucault's philosophy is his account of pleasure as creative and as a resource for political resistance. My use of Foucault in this chapter owes much to her reading. LaDelle McWhorter, *Bodies & Pleasures: Foucault and the Politics of Sexual Normalization* (Bloomington: Indiana University Press, 1999).

12. It is important to emphasize that what we do and do not know is often "local" to a particular group or a particular culture. I locate my "we" in this section as the common knowledge of laypeople in the United States both because the studies and surveys that I will employ were limited to this group and in recognition of the fact that knowledge-ignorance about women's sexuality varies tremendously from one culture/country to another.

13. Thomas Laqueur, *Making Sex: Body and Gender from the Greeks to Freud* (Cambridge, MA: Harvard University Press, 1990); Catherine Gallagher and Thomas Laqueur, eds., *The Making of the Modern Body: Sexuality and Society in the Nineteenth Century* (Berkeley: University of California Press, 1987); Londa Schiebinger, *The Mind Has No Sex? Women in the Origins of Modern Science* (Cambridge, MA: Harvard University Press, 1989); Nancy Tuana, *The Less Noble Sex: Scientific, Religious, and Philosophical Conceptions of Women's Nature* (Bloomington: Indiana University Press, 1993).

14. Luce Irigaray, *Speculum of the Other Woman*, trans. Gillian C. Gill (Ithaca, NY: Cornell University Press, 1985).

15. Ambroise Paré, *The Collected Works of Ambroise Paré*, trans. Thomas Johnson (New York: Milford House, 1968), 130.

16. Thomas Laqueur, "Orgasm, Generation, and the Politics of Reproductive Biology," *Representations* 14 (1986): 1–41; Laqueur, "Amor Veneris, vel Dulcedo Appeletur," in *Fragments for a History of the Human Body*, ed. Michel Feher (New York: Zone, 1989).

17. Renaldus Columbus, *De re anatomica* (Venice, 1559), 11.16.447–448; Laqueur, "Amor Veneris," 103.

18. For a careful study of this phenomenon see Lisa Jean Moore and Adele E. Clarke, "Clitoral Conventions and Transgressions: Graphic Representations in Anatomy Texts, c1900–1991," *Feminist Studies* 21.2 (1995): 255–301.

19. McAnulty and Burnette describe the clitoris as composed of shaft and glans, but make no effort to provide an illustration. Richard D. McAnulty and M. Michele Burnette, *Exploring Human Sexuality: Making Healthy Decisions* (Boston: Allyn and Bacon, 2001),

67. Rathus et al. (2002) is the first textbook designed for college human sexuality classrooms that includes an illustration of what they label the "whole clitoris," namely, the shaft, glans, and crura. Spencer A. Rathus, Jeffrey S. Nevid, and Lois Fichner-Rathus, *Human Sexuality in a World of Diversity*, 5th ed. (Boston: Allyn and Bacon, 2002).

20. McAnulty and Burnette, for example, while admitting a more complex structure for the clitoris, simply indicate that "the glans of the clitoris has a high concentration of touch and temperature receptors and should be the primary center of sexual stimulation and sensation in the female" (*Exploring Human Sexuality*, 67). Later, when discussing the female sexual response cycle, they simply note that the diameter of the clitoral shaft increases (*Exploring Human Sexuality*, 114).

21. Ernst Graffenburg, "The Role of the Urethra in Female Orgasm," *International Journal of Sexology* 3 (1950): 145–148.

22. I have examined the various editions of Albert Richard Allgeier and Elizabeth Rice Allgeier, *Sexual Interactions* (Lexington, MA: D. C. Heath, 1984/1988/1998); Curtis O. Byer and Louis W. Shainberg, *Dimensions of Human Sexuality* (Boston: McGraw Hill, 1985/1988/1991/1998/2001); Gary F. Kelly, *Sexuality Today: The Human Perspective* (Boston: McGraw Hill, 1988/1994/1998/2001); McAnulty and Burnette, *Exploring Human Sexuality*; and Rathus, Nevid, and Fichner-Rathus, *Human Sexuality*. Only Rathus, Nevid, and Fichner-Rathus include this expanded model of the clitoris. But while they provide the most detailed discussion of women's multiorgasmic capacity, their images and discussion of the female response phases are surprisingly traditional, with the clitoris once again relegated to a mere nub.

23. Nancy Tuana, "The Weaker Seed: The Sexist Bias of Reproductive Theory," *Hypatia: A Journal of Feminist Philosophy*, 3.1 (1988): 35–39; Tuana, *The Less Noble Sex*.

24. Joan Cadden, *Meanings of Sex Difference in the Middle Ages: Medicine, Science, and Culture* (Cambridge, UK: Cambridge University Press, 1993), 142–143.

25. I support these claims in my book, *The Less Noble Sex*.

26. The reference here is to Hesiod's depiction of the creation of the first woman, Pandora, in *Works and Days*. After she was molded in the shape of a goddess by Hephaistos, Zeus ordered Aphrodite to bequeath to her "stinging desire and limb-gnawing passion." Hesiod, *Theogony, Works and Days, and The Shield*, trans. Apostolos Athanassakis (Baltimore: Johns Hopkins University Press, 1983), p. 66, lines 66–67.

27. As just one of literally thousands of examples of the view that women's greater susceptibility to sexual temptation requires control, I refer the reader to David Hume's (1978) discussion of chastity and modesty. Hume argues that women have such a strong temptation to infidelity that the only way to reassure men that the children their wives bear are their own biological offspring is for society to "attach a peculiar degree of shame to their infidelity, above what arises merely from its injustice"; also, because women are particularly apt to overlook remote motives in favor of present temptations, he argues "'tis necessary, therefore, that, beside the infamy attending such licenses, there should be some preceding backwardness or dread, which may prevent their first approaches, and may give the female sex a repugnance to all expressions, and postures, and liberties, that have an immediate relation to that enjoyment." David Hume, *A Treatise of Human Nature*, ed. Lewis Amherst Selby-Bigge (New York: Oxford University Press, 1978), bk. 3, pt. 2, sec. 12, para. 6/9, 571–572.

28. Scientists believed that enlarged clitorises were both a result of and a reason for hypersexuality, and both sex deviants and racially "inferior" women were viewed as sexually deviant because of heightened sexual "excitability." For further discussion of these themes see

Anne Fausto-Sterling, "Gender, Race, and Nation: The Comparative Anatomy of 'Hottentot' Women in Europe, 1815–1817," in *Deviant Bodies: Critical Perspectives on Difference in Science and Popular Culture*, eds. Jennifer Terry and Jacqueline Urla (Bloomington: Indiana University Press, 1995); and Jennifer Terry, "Anxious Slippages between 'Us' and 'Them': A Brief History of the Scientific Search for Homosexual Bodies," in *Deviant Bodies*, 1995.

29. Apollodorus, *The Gods and Heroes of the Greeks: The Library of Apollodorus*, trans. Michael Simpson (Amherst: University of Massachusetts Press, 1976), 3.6.7.

30. Edward O. Laumann, John H. Gagnon, Robert T. Michael, and Stewart Michaels, *The Social Organization of Sexuality: Sexual Practices in the United States* (Chicago: University of Chicago Press, 1994).

31. Susan Sprecher, Anita Barbee, and Pepper Schwartz, "'Was It Good for You, Too?': Gender Differences in First Sexual Intercourse Experience," in *Social Psychology and Human Sexuality*, ed. Roy F. Baumeister (Philadelphia: Taylor and Francis, 2001).

32. Shere Hite, *The Hite Report: A Nationwide Study of Female Sexuality* (New York: Dell, 1976), 602–603.

33. Donald Symons, *The Evolution of Human Sexuality* (New York: Oxford University Press, 1979), 92.

34. See McWhorter, *Bodies & Pleasures*, for an insightful analysis of the difference between desire and pleasure. "The art of living" is, of course, Beauvoir's phrase.

35. Sigmund Freud, *Three Essays on the Theory of Sexuality*, trans. and ed. James Strachey (New York: Avon, 1962), 124.

36. Columbus, *De re anatomica*, 11.16.447–448; Laqueur, *Amor Veneris*, 103.

37. Columbus, *De re anatomica*, 11.16.445; Laqueur, *Amor Veneris*, 105.

38. Sigmund Freud, "Femininity," in *Standard Edition of the Complete Psychological Works*, vol. 22, trans. and ed. James Strachey (London: Hogarth, 1964), 114.

39. Freud, *Three Essays*, 123.

40. Freud, *Three Essays*, 124.

41. Freud, *Three Essays*, 123.

42. Ann Koedt, "The Myth of the Vaginal Orgasm," in *Notes from the Second Year: Women's Liberation*, eds. Shulamith Firestone and Ann Koedt (New York: Radical Feminism, 1970); Alex Shulman, "Organs and Orgasms," in *Women in Sexist Society*, eds. Vivian Gornick and Barbara K. Moran (New York: New American Library, 1971).

43. Schulman "Organs and Orgasms," 294.

44. Schulman, "Organs and Orgasms," 296.

45. Josephine Singer and Irving Singer, "Types of Female Orgasm," *Journal of Sex Research* 8.4 (1972): 2550–2567.

46. Heli Alzate, "Vaginal Eroticism: A Replication Study," *Archives of Sexual Behavior* 14.6 (1985): 529–537; John Delbert Perry and Beverly Whipple, "Pelvic Muscle Strength of Female Ejaculators: Evidence in Support of a New Theory of Orgasm," *Journal of Sex Research* 17.1 (1981): 22–39; Whipple, "Research Concerning Sexual Response in Women," *The Health Psychologist* 17.1 (1995): 16–18.

47. McAnulty and Burnette, *Exploring Human Sexuality*, 119.

48. Rathus, Nevid, and Fichner-Rathus, *Human Sexuality*, 106.

49. This view of female genitals is surprisingly resilient. A recent story in my local State College, Pennsylvania, newspaper, the *Center Daily Times*, reported that two women who were running nude were acquitted of charges of streaking. The story explains that the streaking law requires that the genitalia be exposed, something that the judge in this case

decided is nearly impossible for women, since, in the judge's view, female genitalia are all internal! My thanks to David O'Hara for calling this story to my attention.

50. Sheila Kitzinger, *Women's Experience of Sex: The Facts and Feelings of Female Sexuality at Every Stage of Life* (New York: Penguin, 1985), 76.

51. Suzann Gage, the illustrator of *A New View of a Women's Body* (1981), as reported in Moore and Clark, "Clitoral Conventions."

52. Elisabeth A. Lloyd, "Pre-Theoretical Assumptions in Evolutionary Explanations of Female Sexuality," *Philosophical Studies* 69 (1993): 139–153.

53. Alan Dixson, *Primate Sexuality: Comparative Studies of the Prosimians, Monkeys, Apes, and Human Beings* (Oxford: Oxford University Press, 1998), 43.

54. For a discussion of bonobo behavior as an evolutionary model for human sexuality, see Meredith F. Small, *What's Love Got to Do with It? The Evolution of Human Mating* (New York: Anchor, 1995).

55. Donald Symons, *The Evolution of Human Sexuality* (New York: Oxford University Press, 1979), 28.

56. Symons, *The Evolution*, 82.

57. Symons, *The Evolution*, 82–83.

58. Dixson, *Primate Sexuality*.

59. Jane Goodall, *In the Shadow of Man* (Boston: Houghton Mifflin, 1988).

60. Dixson, *Primate Sexuality*, 133.

61. David Barash, *Sociobiology and Behavior* (New York: Elsevier North-Holland, 1977), 296–297.

62. Hite, *The Hite Report*; William H. Masters and Virginia E. Johnson, *Human Sexual Response* (Boston: Little, Brown, 1966).

63. Lynn Margulis and Dorion Sagan, *Mystery Dance: On the Evolution of Human Sexuality* (New York: Summit, 1991), 43.

64. Small, *What's Love Got to Do With It?* 111.

65. For a discussion of current theories of sperm competition, see R. Robin Baker and Mark A. Bellis, *Human Sperm Competition: Copulation, Masturbation, and Infidelity* (London: Chapman and Hall, 1995).

66. McWhorter, *Bodies & Pleasures*, 181.

67. McWhorter, *Bodies & Pleasures*, 182.

68. Michel Foucault, "Friendship as a Way of Life," in *Foucault Live*, trans. John Johnston and ed. Sylvere Lotringer (New York: Semiotext(e), 1989), 310.

69. Sprinkle, "Herstory of Porn: Reel to Real" (1999).

70. McWhorter, *Bodies & Pleasures*, 185.

71. *Inanna: Queen of Heaven & Earth, Her Stories and Hymns from Sumer*, trans. Diane Wolkstein and Samuel Noah Kramer (New York: Harper and Row, 1983), 12.

PART II

Lost Knowledge, Lost Worlds

CHAPTER 6

West Indian Abortifacients and the Making of Ignorance

LONDA SCHIEBINGER

SINCE COLUMBUS'S VOYAGES, Europeans have scoured the Caribbean looking for useful and profitable drugs.[1] The greatest success story both in terms of efficacy and profit was *cinchona*, the anti-malarial, known variously as the Peruvian bark, Jesuits' bark, or, by its Quechua name, *quinquina*. Importing exotics from Europe's East and West Indian colonies was big business. President of the Royal Society of London Hans Sloane, for example, while in Jamaica as a young man invested the greatest part of his fortune in "the bark," a Jamaican knockoff of the Peruvian quinine, which he later promoted by prescription in his fashionable London practice. He did the same with chocolate, which he recommended for stomach upset and consumption.[2] A number of medicinal plants from the Americas—jalapa, quassia, ipecacuanha, and cacao, for example—became standard medicines in Europe.

Given this climate where Europeans enthusiastically culled New World flora for useful exotics for European markets, it is remarkable that a particular class of drugs—abortifacients (used to induce abortion)—did *not* transfer from the Caribbean into Europe. In this chapter I explore the movement, mixing, and extinction of botanic knowledge in early modern encounters between Europeans and the peoples of the Caribbean. I am particularly interested to see how gender relations in Europe and its West Indian colonies guided European naturalists as they selected particular plants and technologies for transport back to Europe. The plant whose history provides the leitmotif for this work is the "peacock flower," *Poinciana pulcherrima* or *Caesalpinia pulcherrima*. In the Caribbean, it is also known as the Pride of Barbados, Flower Fence, Red Bird-of-Paradise, and, on the Malabar coast, the *Tsjétti-Mandáru*—though it has dozens of other names specific to the particular cultures in which it has been culti-vated, suggesting the time-depth of its uses.

The peacock flower is not a heroic plant of the stature of cacao, the potato, quinine, coffee, tea, or even rhubarb, used extensively in the eigh-teenth century as a laxative.[3] I lavish attention on the peacock flower not because it is exquisitely beautiful, growing in stunningly inviting places, but because it was a highly political plant, deployed in the struggle against slavery throughout the eighteenth century by slave women in the West In-dies, who used it to abort offspring who otherwise would have been born into bondage. We know this from a number of sources, the most remarkable of which is a passage from Maria Sibylla Merian's 1705 *Metamorphosis of the Insects of Surinam*, recording how slave and Indian populations in Surinam used the seeds of this plant as an abortifacient:

The Indians and Africans, who are not treated well by their Dutch masters, use the seeds [of this plant] to abort their children, so that their children will not become slaves like they are. . . . They told me this themselves.[4]

I would love to recount in full the torrid tale of the peacock flower, but that is not my topic. Here I will discuss the agnotology surrounding West Indian abortifacients. Historians have rightly focused on the explosion of knowledge associated with the scientific revolution and global expansion, and the frantic transfer of trade goods and plants between Europe and its colonies.[5] Abortifacients, however, represent a body of knowledge and set of techniques that did not transfer from the New World into Europe. Knowledge ignored in the eighteenth century was by the nineteenth cen-tury largely forgotten.

The first thing to recall, though—and indeed this may seem surpris-ing—is that the use of herbs to induce abortion was well established in the West Indies in the eighteenth century. Europeans observed these practices immediately upon contact. They wrote about abortifacients often and in different contexts, and I have identified eight plants widely used for abortion in the Caribbean in this period. Many other "herbs" were used as well, but these remained unidentified. These abortifacients, however, were not among the medical plants collected and developed in Europe as mainstream medicines. In order to look at this in some detail, I focus on Maria Sibylla Merian's peacock flower.

One reason I chose the peacock flower for close study is that naturalists from three separate European countries each independently discovered its use as an abortive in the West Indies: Merian reported its use for this purpose in Surinam; Sloane described it in Jamaica; and some time later Michel Descourtilz, a French naturalist, observed this same use in Saint Domingue, now Haiti.[6] When analyzing whether the peacock flower moved into Europe, we need to distinguish clearly between movement of *knowledge* and movement of the plant itself. We find that the peacock flower *itself* did in fact move freely into Europe. From about 1666 onward, the plant was cultivated all across Europe, including in the Jardin du Roi in Paris and the famous Hortus Academicus in Leiden. Philip Miller at the Chelsea Physic Garden outside London noted that "the seeds of this plant are annually brought over in plenty from the West-Indies." With proper management, he wrote with remarkable hubris, this plant will grow much taller in England than in Barbados.[7]

While the peacock flower itself moved easily into Europe, the knowledge of its use as an abortifacient did not. Merian's report of its abortive qualities was published in 1705. Caspar Commelin, director of the Hortus Medicus and professor of botany in Amsterdam, prepared elaborate bibliographical notes for her book and was clearly familiar with its contents. If he and others had valued knowledge of how to manage women's fertility, knowledge of the peacock flower and its uses would have quickly spread throughout Europe. But it did not. Hermann Boerhaave, professor of botany at Leiden and the leading authority on Europe's materia medica, reported in 1727 "no known virtues" of this plant.[8]

Whereas the Peruvian bark and the quinine it yields represents a technology of conquest moving from America to Europe, we have here a technology of resistance moving from perhaps Amerindians to African slaves—and only then to Europeans, with the added twist that this latter technology that could have been of enormous value to women was ignored, left to languish increasingly in rumor and innuendo. Knowledge of abortifacients poured into the Caribbean in the eighteenth century— some from South America and others from Africa. European women even brought a few abortifacients with them from Europe (penny royal, for example). What I want to emphasize, though, is that knowledge that flowed into the Caribbean from Africa and South America did not transship out of the Caribbean and into Europe. Trade winds of prevailing opinion prevented shiploads of New World abortifacients and knowledge of their use from reaching European shores.

AGNOTOLOGIC FISSURES

Agnotology traces the cultural politics of ignorance. It takes the measure of our ignorance, and analyzes why some knowledges are suppressed, lost, ignored, or abandoned, while others are embraced and come to shape our lives. Ignorance is often not merely the absence of knowledge but an outcome of cultural struggles. In this section, I investigate two questions. First, whose knowledge was it that did not transfer into Europe? Amerindian? African? A hybrid knowledge created by colonial slaves through the crossing of African and Amerindian techniques? Second, what produced Europeans' neglect of abortifacients from abroad and the gradual vilification of induced abortion in their own medical traditions?

There are many forms of ignorance (see Proctor, this volume). I am here not interested in the sequestering of knowledge in the early modern period through secrecy, such as guild or trading company secrets, or the secrets of the Spanish who did not publish the intelligence gathered from their many royal expeditions into the New World so as to retain an advantage over their enemies, nor even the secrets of the many colonial slaves who hid their medicines from Europeans.[9] Nor am I interested in ignorance produced by overtly suppressing knowledge considered worthless or dangerous, as was the fate of Jamaican obeah and Saint Dominguan vodou. What I am interested in is how, in the eighteenth century, both European science and societies were structured to cultivate certain types of knowledge over others. Funding priorities, global strategies, national policies, structures of scientific institutions, trade patterns, configuration of technologies all pushed investigation toward certain parts of nature and away from others. Before turning to the agnotology of herbal abortifacients, let me discuss two other distinctive ignorances in eighteenth-century botany.

The distinguished English botanist William Stearn has drawn attention to a fundamental distortion in eighteenth-century botanical knowledge. A burning question for early modern European taxonomists, such as John Ray, was: how great is the uniformity of plants across continents? Ray queried Sloane in Jamaica, for instance, whether he found many species of plants that were common to both Europe and the Americas. Sloane himself realized that much of the floral uniformity he observed across the Caribbean was human-made, a result of cultigens carried from the South American mainland and elsewhere into the islands first by the Tainos, then by the Spanish, Dutch, and English. The impression of floral uniformity in the tropics was further heightened by the fact that Europeans who collected in these areas before 1753 did so mostly in ports and along coasts, regions highly disturbed by two hundred years of European voyaging and trade. Sacks of produce standing in harbors before being shipped often picked up soil and seeds of weedy species. By this means, European settlements around the globe eventually came to host much the same flora as a result of both intentional transport of useful plants and inadvertent conveyance of weeds. A collector, unaware of these mixings, might find the same plant in both the East and West Indies, and assume it to be indigenous to wherever it was found. This human-made uniformity led taxonomists erroneously to assume that tropical flora were highly uniform instead of regionally diverse.[10]

Stearn's observation raises an interesting example of agnotology in that the ignorance of the rich diversity in tropical flora was produced by distinctive cultural patterns, in this case plants following European trade routes. What distinguishes the type of ignorance Stearn discussed from that surrounding abortifacients is that in the former case, once the error was discovered, it was energetically corrected. Incorrect scientific conclusions were quickly revised when Alexander von Humboldt, Aimé Bonpland, James Cook, and Joseph Bank's voyages revealed great variety in tropical flora. European taxonomists were not invested in the notion of uniformity.

Other culturally induced ignorances were created by eighteenth-century technologies of conveyances. Until the early nineteenth century, for example, plants were better known in Europe than stones and minerals for the simple reason that plants were lighter and more easily transported.

Among plants, voyagers gave preference to succulents and bulbs because these were more likely to survive successfully the long and expensive passage back to Europe.[11] To the extent that Europeans consciously made these choices, they changed as ships became larger and speedier.

The ignorance surrounding abortifacients was different in kind. First, I should note that knowledge in this realm was rarely suppressed by decree. Instructions to travelers did not warn against collecting this knowledge. Physicians often cautioned against the dangers of the use of this class of drugs in Europe, but at the same time they knew and used different abortive techniques. Indeed, the lives of many women depended on this knowledge. When new exotic abortifacients were discovered, as indeed they were repeatedly by naturalists for over a century, knowledge of them was not cultivated. Unlike the two examples above, cultural forces closed Europe's borders to the importation of abortive techniques from abroad. When knowledge became available, it was not embraced.

Turning to my first question, whose knowledge was rebuffed? What characterized the chain of knowledge, and where was it broken? Who originally developed the peacock flower as an abortifacient whose use the Europeans observed? Merian reported that both Amerindians and African slaves used the peacock flower as an abortifacient—but by 1699, when she arrived in Surinam, these cultures had been mixing for over a century.

There are several different ways to explain the presence of this plant and its widespread use as an abortive in the Caribbean. One possibility is that the plant later known as the peacock flower moved without human agency from South America into the Caribbean. Seeds of the plant may have been swept from the Guiana coast and Orinoco valley into the Caribbean by the flood waters that divert the South Equatorial current northward, carrying plants and sometimes even animals into the Windward Islands.[12] The peacock flower's sturdy seed pod may have helped it make this watery voyage.

A second scenario suggests that the presence of the peacock flower in the Caribbean and the knowledge of its use as an abortifacient may have had African origins. Richard Ligon, a seventeenth-century plantation owner, reported having brought seeds of the plant from Saint Jago, in the Cape Verde archipelago off the west coast of Africa, to Barbados.[13]

The flaming yellows and reds of this elegant flower made it a favorite ornamental. It should be kept in mind, however, that Cape Verde was a shipping crossroads and entrepôt in this period. If Ligon carried the plant from St. Jago, it could have come earlier from anywhere in the world that the Europeans had ports.

Alternatively, the plant might have been carried to the Caribbean by African slaves themselves. Africans had long practiced herbal abortion, and may have brought the seeds with them when they were carried into slavery. A plant closely resembling Merian's peacock flower does in fact grow on the west coast of Africa and its seeds are well known in Senegal as an abortifacient.[14]

Finally (and I think this scenario the most likely), one might postulate a South American origin and an Amerindian discovery of its abortive virtues. The historical record of the peacock flower used as an abortive from Surinam up through the French Antilles to Jamaica suggests that the plant was known to the forebears of the Tainos, the Saladoid peoples, and followed their migration out of South America into the islands. Sometime around 4000 BC, the Saladoids moved from the northeast coast of South America into the Caribbean islands. This quick movement of peoples (in less than a century) may account for the similarities in the uses of plants found in the region.[15] While it is possible that displaced Africans taught the Tainos the use of the peacock flower, I find it more likely that the Tainos and Arawaks taught its uses to the newly arrived Africans.[16]

While much Amerindian and African knowledge entered Europe via the Caribbean in this period, their knowledge of abortifacients did not. To turn to my second question: Why was this so? Agnotology calls for an investigation into how societies are structured so that certain knowledges are embraced while others are reviled or slip by unnoticed. What, then, were the agnotological fissures that impeded transport of the knowledge of abortifacients into Europe? What induced this form of cultural ignorance?

The suppression of abortifacients was rarely overt (until the nineteenth century). The archives of the Académie des Sciences in Paris yield only one report of an abortifacient—a plant known to us only as the "potato with two roots"—in 1763. The report, sent by a M. De la Ruë from the Island of Bourbon, indicated that people there (*les gens du pays*) used a poultice made from a plant known as *la patate à deux rangs* (the potato with two roots) to abort dead fetuses. De la Ruë reported that he had experimented with the plant in a European woman (*une Dame*), a "Negresse," and also with a nanny goat, and found use of the poultice superior to the painful and dangerous surgical removal of the fetus. The report was read to the full Academy and passed to the Comité de Librairie, where it was marked "*supprimé attend le danger de la publication.*"[17] This example of explicit and direct suppression seems, however, to have been the exception—more common was a kind of cultured apathy or cultivated disinterest.

Many aspects of eighteenth-century European societies contributed to the induced ignorance of abortifacients. I should note first that abortion did not become illegal in Europe until the nineteenth century.[18] Throughout the early modern period, the general consensus was that for legal purposes a woman was *not* pregnant—not truly with child—until "quickening" or "ensoulment" took place, usually considered to occur near the midpoint of gestation, late in the fourth or early in the fifth month of pregnancy (or, according to Aristotle, forty days after conception for a male child and ninety days for a female child).[19] As Barbara Duden has emphasized, a fetus that had not quickened was not considered a person, but simply a part of the mother's own body (*ein Theil mütterlicher Eingeweide*).[20] Even though abortion was legal in this period, it was never undertaken lightly: moral trepidation and physical danger argued against it.

Cultivating knowledge of West Indian abortifacients in Europe was discouraged by the fact that European colonial enterprises were largely male. The majority of Caribbean planters and slaves were men, as were colonial administrators, naturalists, and physicians. Colonial governors, such as Hendrick van Reede and Philippe de Lonvilliers, chevalier de Poincy (for whom the *Poinciana pulcherrima* was named), were most interested in medicines to protect traders, planters, and trading company troops, among whom few women were found.

Developing abortifacients or any drugs used predominantly to control fertility also worked directly against the interests of mercantilist states. Mercantilist governments sought to augment the wealth of nations by producing growing and healthy populations. Within Europe, abundant population was to increase the production of crops and goods, fill the ranks of standing armies, and provide productive workers who would pay substantial taxes and rents. In the colonies, the practice of "growing negroes," as it was called, was seen as a key factor in securing the "wealth of nations." Slave women, whom planters had earlier used chiefly as "work units," became increasingly valued as "breeders," as abolitionists in Europe threatened to shut down the slave trade in the 1780s and 1790s.[21]

Finally, the culturally induced ignorance of abortifacients resulted also from newly cantankerous disciplinary hierarchies and professional divides. Abortion, like much female medicine, traditionally belonged to the domain of midwifery. Much knowledge of abortion was lost in the shift in the management of birthing in this period away from midwives to professionalized obstetricians. Physicians, of course, employed abortifacients in their practices but only when a woman's life was seriously in danger. As obstetricians sought professional standing, they pushed aside potentially tainted practices and knowledges.[22]

Alexander von Humboldt, writing at the turn of the nineteenth century, revealed in a single passage a great deal about how and why European scientific men did not collect abortifacients from the New World. Humboldt expressed his surprise at how safe the abortifacients were that the Amerindians living along the Orinoco river (he did not name the peoples) employed, and he discussed the need for such drugs in Europe, sympathizing with young mothers there who are "afraid of having children, because they know not how to feed, clothe, and provide for them." Yet he refused to transmit information about these efficacious herbs to Europe. While he was well aware that European women had a working knowledge of abortifacients (he listed savin, aloes, and the essential oils of cinnamon and clove), he feared that the introduction of New World abortives into Europe would increase "the depravity of manners in towns, where one quarter of the children see the light only to be abandoned by their parents."[23]

More importantly, Humboldt made clear that his reluctance to collect such knowledge had to do with neo-mercantilist concerns about population growth. Listing the causes of depopulation among these peoples, Humboldt dismissed smallpox, which had so ravished other Amerindians (according to Humboldt the smallpox had not yet penetrated inland to this remote area). Humboldt highlighted instead the Amerindian's "repugnance" of the Christian mission (as one reason for their decreasing numbers), the unhealthy hot and damp climate, the poor food they received, the severity of children's diseases, and, last but not least, women's control of their own fertility. These "guilty mothers," he wrote, prevent pregnancy and abort their children by the use of "deleterious herbs." Like many European medical men who by the end of the eighteenth century simply refused to discuss abortives, Humboldt concluded his remarks by adding, "I thought it necessary to enter into these pathological details [concerning abortion], far from agreeable as they are, because they make known a part of the causes, which in the rudest state of our species as well as in a high degree of civilization, render the progress of population almost imperceptible."[24]

CONCLUSION

The curious history of Merian's peacock flower shows, then, how voyagers selectively culled nature for knowledge responding to state policies, patterns of patronage and trade, and moral and professional imperatives. Gender politics both in Europe and its colonies gave recognizable contours to distinctive bodies of knowledge and of ignorance. The same forces feeding the *explosion* of knowledge we commonly associate with the scientific revolution and global expansion led to an *implosion* of knowledge of herbal abortifacients. There was no systematic attempt to introduce into Europe abortifacients gathered from cultures around the globe. European awareness of antifertility agents declined over the course of the eighteenth and nineteenth centuries largely because the development and testing of such agents did not become part of academic medicine or pharmacology in the eighteenth century. Many drugs no doubt *were* dangerous because they were not submitted to rigorous and systematic testing. The notorious hazards of abortion in the twentieth century must be traced partly to this process of forgetting and failure to test.

Traditions that did not travel to Europe remained alive in the Caribbean. In my travels to Belize, Jamaica, Costa Rica, Martinique, Guadeloupe, Dominica, Dominican Republic, and so forth, I queried numerous people concerning the use of abortifacients today. In Costa Rica I was told by a male guide of Spanish heritage that "everyone" knows these remedies and that they are still employed today. While hiking through the rain forest, he told me that "a little virgin" had recently aborted a child conceived out of wedlock. In Dominica, I had an animated, two-hour conversation about Carib history and culture with one of the approximately three thousand ethnic Caribs who have survived in the Caribbean basin. Feeling comfortable with this very open and interesting woman, I eventually turned to the topic of birth control. She launched into her answer, then shot me a glance and said quietly, "but it's secret." I did not press the issue. After a moment's reflection, she called her husband and together they picked a plant growing at their backdoor step. She told me that to prevent conception, after intercourse a woman ingests a tea made from the plant and also washes herself with it.

The closest I came to a firsthand account of Merian's peacock flower was from a woman of European origin about sixty years of age, whose family had been in the islands for over 300 years. She told me that when she was young, one of the serving girls in her household had become pregnant. In the kitchen, speaking to the other servants, the young woman said she planned "to do away with it." What did she plan to use? The peacock flower. I pressed my interlocutor for a recipe (which I had not found in the historical records). Unfortunately, she was only a child at the time and did not have details. Enthobotanists today tell us that the plant is still used as an abortifacient in the Caribbean. Pharmacologists tell us that it induces uterine contractions that could well bring on abortion.[25]

One sees in these casual meetings specters of the eighteenth-century encounters between European bioprospectors and the peoples of the Caribbean. There is the language problem: the Carib woman and I conversed in English (the Carib language has died out in Dominica and she works with Awaraks in Surinam in a project to revive it); nonetheless, we did not share the same names for plants. I could not ask her if she knew the peacock flower because I had not yet been in the country long enough to discover their local term for Merian's flowering bush. Then there was the problem of secrecy and fear because abortion in this largely Catholic country is illegal. One wonders what easy, safe, and effective methods of birth control and abortion have been lost to women because innocent plants have become entangled in the web of history and wide-ranging cultural politics.

NOTES

1. Portions of this chapter are drawn from my *Plants and Empires: Colonial Bioprospecting in the Atlantic World* (Cambridge, MA: Harvard University Press, 2004).

2. [Thomas Birch], "Memoirs relating to the Life of Sir Hans Sloane, formerly President of the Royal Society," British Library, Additional MS 4241, 25. See also Arthur MacGregor, "The Life, Character and Career of Sir Hans Sloane," in *Sir Hans Sloane: Collector, Scientist, Antiquary, Founding Father of the British Museum*, ed. Arthur MacGregor (London: British Museum, 1994), 11–44, esp. 15.

3. Henry Hobhouse, *Seeds of Change: Five Plants That Transformed Mankind* (New York: Harper & Row, 1985); Clifford Foust, *Rhubarb: The Wondrous Drug* (Princeton, NJ: Princeton University Press, 1992); Saul Jarcho, *Quinine's Predecessor: Francesco Torti and the Early History of Cinchona* (Baltimore: Johns Hopkins University Press, 1993); Larry Zuckerman, *The Potato: How the Humble Spud Rescued the Western World* (New York: North Point, 1999); Susan Terrio, *Crafting the Culture and History of French Chocolate* (Berkeley: University of California Press, 2000).

4. Maria Sibylla Merian, *Metamorphosis insectorum Surinamensium* (Amsterdam, 1705), commentary to plate no. 45.

5. Marie-Cécile Bénassy-Berling, ed., *Nouveau monde et renouveau de l'histoire naturelle*, 3 vols. (Paris: Université de la Sorbonne nouvelle, 1986–1994); John MacKenzie, ed., *Imperialism and the Natural World* (Manchester, UK: University of Manchester, 1990); James McClellan III, *Colonialism and Science: Saint Domingue in the Old Regime* (Baltimore: Johns Hopkins University Press, 1992); Mary Louise Pratt, *Imperial Eyes: Travel Writing and Transculturation* (London: Routledge, 1992); N. Jardine, J. A. Secord, E. C. Spary, eds., *Cultures of Natural History: From Curiosity to Crisis* (Cambridge, UK: Cambridge University Press, 1995); Yves Laisses, ed., *Les Naturalistes français en Amerique de sud* (Paris: Edition du CTHS, 1995); Richard Grove, *Green Imperialism: Colonial Expansion, Tropical Island Edens and the Origins of Environmentalism, 1600–1860* (Cambridge, UK: Cambridge University Press, 1995); David Miller and Peter Reill, eds., *Visions of Empire: Voyages, Botany, and Representations of Nature* (Cambridge, UK: Cambridge University Press, 1996); Tony Rice, *Voyages: Three Centuries of Natural History Exploration* (London: Museum of Natural History, 1999); Londa Schiebinger and Claudia Swan, *Colonial Botany: Science, Commerce, and Politics* (Philadelphia: University of Pennsylvania Press, 2005); Londa Schiebinger, ed., "Colonial Science," *Isis, Journal of the History of Science Society* 96 (2005): 52–87; Jorge Cañizares-Esguerra, *Nature, Empire, and Nation: Explorations of the History of Science in the Iberian World* (Stanford: Stanford University Press, 2006); Antonio Barrera-Osorio, *Experiencing Nature: The Spanish American Empire and the Early Scientific Revolution* (Austin: University of Texas Press, 2006).

6. Merian, *Metamorphosis*, commentary to plate no. 45. Hans Sloane, *A Voyage to the Islands Madera, Barbados, Nieves, St. Christophers, and Jamaica; with Natural History, etc.*, 2 vols. (London, 1707–1725), vol. 2, 49–50, 384. Michel-Étienne Descourtilz, *Flore pittoresque et médicale des Antilles*, 8 vols. (Paris, 1833), vol. 1, 27–30.

7. Philip Miller, *The Gardeners Dictionary* (London, 1768), s.v. "Poinciana (Pulcherrima)."

8. Hermann Boerhaave, *Historia plantarum* (Rome, 1727), 488–489. Clearly much information concerning the use of contraceptives and abortifacients passed from woman to woman, neighbor to neighbor, midwife to client, and may have passed from the Caribbean to Europe in this fashion. If it did, however, it was not recorded, or at least I have not found

letters, notices, or other traces of these otherwise vibrant largely oral cultures.

9. Iris Engstrand, *Spanish Scientists in the New World: The Eighteenth-Century Expeditions* (Seattle: University of Washington Press, 1981), 3.

10. William Stearn, "Carl Linnaeus's Acquaintance with Tropical Plants," *Taxon* 37 (1988): 776–781.

11. Mary Gunn and L. E. Codd, *Botanical Exploration of Southern Africa* (Cape Town: A. A. Balkema, 1981), 25.

12. Irving Rouse, *The Taino: Rise and Decline of the People Who Greeted Columbus* (New Haven, CT: Yale University Press, 1992), 3–4.

13. Richard Ligon, *A True and Exact History of the Island of Barbados* (London, 1657), 15.

14. Hans Neuwinger, *African Ethnobotany* (London: Chapman & Hall, 1996), 321–324. Barbara Bush discusses some continuities between abortive practices in Africa and Caribbean slave societies in her *Slave Women in Caribbean Society, 1650–1832* (Bloomington: Indiana University Press, 1990).

15. William Keegan, "The Caribbean, Including Northern South America and Lowland Central America: Early History," in *The Cambridge World History of Food*, ed. Kenneth Kiple and Kriemhild Coneè Ornelas, 2 vols. (Cambridge, UK: Cambridge University Press, 2000), vol. 2, 1260–1278.

16. It may also have been that people periodically rediscovered this abortive virtue in the environment around them. It should also be pointed out that slave women combined African and New World techniques. It was reported at the time that female slaves who intend to abort lubricated themselves with a diet of okra, a plant of African origins. They then induced abortion using the gully-root or the "sensitive plant" (*Mimosa pudica*), a native of tropical America and most notably Brazil. Edward Bancroft, *An Essay on the Natural History of Guiana in South America* (London, 1769), 52–53, 371–372.

17. *Registres du Comité de Librairie* (March 1763), vol. 1, 122. I thank James E. McClellan III for this information.

18. Günter Jerouschek, "Zur Geschichte des Abtreibungsverbots," in *Unter anderen Umständen: Zur Geschichte der Abtreibung*, ed. Gisela Staupe and Lisa Vieth (Dresden: Deutsches Hygiene-Museum, 1993), 11–26.

19. Aristotle, *History of Animals*, ed. D. M. Balme (Cambridge, MA: Harvard University Press, 1991), bk. 9, pt. 3, 583b. European medical traditions were influenced also by Arabic scientific traditions. Muslim jurists held that the fetus becomes a human being only after the fourth month of pregnancy (120 days); abortion was allowed up until that time. Basim Masallam, "The Human Embryo in Arabic Scientific and Religious Thought," in *The Human Embryo*, ed. G. R. Dunstan (Exeter: University of Exeter Press, 1990), 32–46, esp. 39. Michael Ryan objected in the 1830s that quickening did not occur until half the period of uterogestation had elapsed, even though the fetus was alive from the very moment of conception (*A Manual of Medical Jurisprudence* [London, 1831], 151). It was not until 1876 that Oskar Hertwig observed a sperm fertilize an egg. John Riddle, *Eve's Herb: A History of Contraception and Abortion in the West* (Cambridge, MA: Harvard University Press, 1997), 222.

20. Barbara Duden, *Disembodying Women: Perspectives on Pregnancy and the Unborn*, trans. Lee Hoinacki (Cambridge, MA: Harvard University Press, 1993), 79–82; Johann Peter Frank, *System einer vollständigen medicinischen Polizey*, 4 vols. (Mannheim, 1784), vol. 2, 61.

21. Bush, *Slave Women*.

22. For general information on midwives and anti-fertility agents, see Angus McLaren, *A History of Contraception: From Antiquity to the Present Day* (Oxford: B. Blackwell, 1990); Hilary Marland, ed., *The Art of Midwifery: Early Modern Midwives in Europe* (London: Routledge, 1993); and Riddle, *Eve's Herbs*.

23. Alexander von Humboldt (and Aimé Bonpland), *Personal Narrative of Travels to the Equinoctial Regions of the New Continent, during the Years 1799–1804*, trans. Helen Williams, 7 vols. (London, 1814–1829), vol. 5, 28–32. Frank also reported that women killed their infants because they feared poverty (*System einer vollständigen medicinischen Polizey*, vol. 2, 61).

24. Humboldt (and Bonpland), *Personal Narrative*, vol. 5, 28–32.

25. Julia Morton, *Atlas of Medicinal Plants of Middle America* (Springfield, IL: Charles Thomas, 1981), 284–285. *Caesalpinia pulcherrima* (another name for the *Poinciana pulcherrima*) is listed in Norman Farnsworth's large study as an abortifacient and emmenagogue ("Potential Value of Plants as Sources of New Antifertility Agents I," *Journal of Pharmaceutical Sciences* 64 (1975): 535–598, esp. 565; and in R. Casey, "Alleged Anti-Fertility Plants of India," *Indian Journal of Medical Science* 14 (1960): 590–600, esp. 593.

CHAPTER 7

Suppression of Indigenous Fossil Knowledge

From Claverack, New York, 1705
to Agate Springs, Nebraska, 2005

ADRIENNE MAYOR

LONG BEFORE EUROPEANS ARRIVED in the New World, indigenous people had encountered the remains of large extinct animals, from dinosaurs to mammoths. Native Americans kept oral records of their discoveries and created narratives to account for the remarkable fossilized creatures. Much was lost or forgotten during migrations and in post-contact epidemics, wars, and forced removals, but a surprisingly rich body of oral traditions about fossils was preserved in writing, by the Spanish beginning in 1519, and in the seventeenth to nineteenth centuries by French, English, and American colonists, explorers, and naturalists. Beginning in 1825, David Cusick (Iroquois), Richard Calmet Adams (Delaware), and others began to publish their nations' fossil folklore themselves.

Indigenous observations and interpretations were not scientific in the modern sense, but they offered an alternative explanation of large vertebrate fossils at a time when Euro-Americans were questioning their own mythic biblical explanations and beginning to develop theories of geological time and paleontology. Moreover, like the neglected literary evidence for fossil discoveries in classical antiquity that I have described elsewhere, some Native American fossil traditions contained concepts of deep time, extinction, fossils' relationships to living species, and successive ages marked by different landforms, climate, and life-forms—insights that anticipate or parallel modern scientific theories. Some classical and indigenous myths were revised to accommodate new information, and excavations and verification of fossil finds were carried out.[1]

From the Conquest through the Enlightenment, Native Americans brought major bone beds to the attention of Euro-Americans, who actively inquired about indigenous fossil discoveries and ideas in the struggle to understand "the fossil enigma."[2] North and South American Indian discoveries of large vertebrate fossils played a role in the thinking of Georges Cuvier, who established the modern science of paleontology. Later, Indian scouts guided the pioneer paleontologists to significant fossil beds in the American West. It is therefore striking that the contributions of Native Americans in the first scientific investigations of fossils are missing in modern histories of paleontology.

Why is the official history of paleontology silent on the earliest recorded fossil discoveries? In my analysis of classical Greek and Roman fossil interpretations, I found that passive neglect, misunderstanding of literary evidence, and ignorance of paleontology were the main reasons that ancient Mediterranean fossil knowledge was absent from the history of science. Modern classicists tended to ignore non-elite Greek and Latin sources; they read fossil folklore as fiction and were unaware of the rich Miocene-Pleistocene bones in the locales where ancients reported "giant" or "monster" remains.[3]

But the silencing of Native American fossil knowledge has been more active and deliberate. This chapter explores some motives and strategies of agnogenesis by considering five case studies to show why and how indigenous American discoveries and interpretations of large vertebrate fossils have been purposely omitted from the historical record.

Case 1 is Cotton Mather, one of the first authorities in North America to willfully censor Indian fossil knowledge. Case 2 presents a normative model, Georges Cuvier, the "father of paleontology," who compiled, analyzed, and published every available ancient Greco-Roman and Native American account of oversized animal bones; he considered these finds significant evidence to help support his theories. Yet Cuvier's interest in classical and Native American fossil knowledge is generally unknown today. Cuvier's works are translated and interpreted by the leading modern historian of geology, Martin J. S. Rudwick, whose significant omissions provide the third case study.

Case 4 is George Gaylord Simpson (1902–1984), the most eminent American paleontologist of the twentieth century. Simpson's two monographs of 1942–1943, chronicling North American fossil discoveries up to 1842, are considered *the* authoritative history of vertebrate paleontology in America. Simpson systematically denied Native Americans any role, going to great lengths to reject even their documented participation in historic events in paleontology.

But Euro-Americans are not the only ones to actively suppress indigenous fossil knowledge. A complex veil of ignorance surrounds some sacred or taboo fossil traditions, intentionally kept secret by Native American and non-Native authorities in an effort to control dangerous knowledge (see Chapters 1 and 9 in this volume). The concluding vignette centers on traditional Lakota Sioux knowledge of Miocene animal fossils at Agate Springs Fossil Beds in Nebraska to illustrate the well-meaning suppression of fossil knowledge by diverse groups over centuries.

COTTON MATHER AND THE
CLAVERACK GIANT, 1705–1712

In northeastern America, abundant remains of Pleistocene mastodons and mammoths, and giant species of sloths, bears, beavers, and bison that lived 10,000 to 2 million years ago attracted the attention of pre-contact Native observers. As detailed in my book, *Fossil Legends of the First Americans* (2005), these conspicuous fossils were featured in Iroquois, Delaware, Shawnee, Wyandot, and many other native oral traditions as evidence that enormous creatures lived and vanished before the era of present-day humans. European colonists first heard some of these stories in 1705, when mastodon remains appeared along the Hudson River.

At that time, no scientific theory existed in Europe to account for such bones. Europeans and Americans strove to explain the skeletons of startling magnitude coming to light around the New World. According to biblical traditions, the bones were wicked giants drowned in Noah's flood. But so many extraordinary skeletons in far-flung lands never mentioned in the Bible began to strain that claim. The idea of extinction was unacceptable. So, while many Euro-Americans believed the huge bones were drowned giants, others thought they were stranded whales or huge carnivores that must have migrated to the still-unexplored northwest. They also solicited the opinions of Native Americans, who had observed the bones for thousands of years.[4]

In 1705, when some enormous bones and teeth eroded from the banks of the Hudson River at Claverack, New York, curious crowds came from miles around. Two groups in particular—the Indians of the Hudson Valley region and the Dutch and English farmers—debated the identity of the Claverack giant. Word of the New World "giants" electrified intellectual circles in the Colonies and Europe. The Puritan poet Edward Taylor was fascinated by Indian tales of giants. In 1705, he examined the great bones and "fangs" (said to hold a pint of beer) at Claverack. He recounted the debate between the colonists and Indians "flocking to see the monstrous Bones." The Indians "upbraided" the Dutch farmers for not believing what the Indians had already told them, that giants had once inhabited the land. Indeed, thirty-five years earlier, in 1668, Taylor had heard Indians describe a "Gyant of incredible Magnitude" but "disbelieved it till he saw the Teeth" at Claverack. According to some of the unidentified Indians (probably Mohawks, Algonquian Mohicans, Abenakis, and Pequots, among others), the bones belonged to a giant being called *Maushops*, which had died out many centuries ago.[5]

In 1712, Taylor's fellow Puritan, the erudite minister Cotton Mather (see Figure 7.1), described the giant bones of Claverack in a letter to the Royal Society of London, founded in 1660 for the scientific study of natu-

FIGURE 7.1 Cotton Mather. Engraving by Peter Pelham (1727). Peter Pelham, Boston: 1728, restrike 1860. Prints & Photographs Division, Library of Congress.

ral history. Mather was a complex man: he demonized the "savages" as devil worshippers, but his writings show a keen interest in their knowledge of natural history, and Mather took the trouble to learn Algonquian. In his letter to the Royal Society, Mather argued that the bones belonged to a giant victim of the flood. This and similar finds in North and South America were "scientific proof" that giants had once inhabited the Americas and died when the flood inundated the whole world.

To support these claims, Mather referred to local Indian lore. "Upon the Discovery of this horrible *Giant*," Mather wrote, "the *Indians* within an Hundred Miles" maintained that giants were described in their ancient traditions, passed down over "hundreds of years." For example, among the "Albany Indians," continued Mather, the giant's "name was *Maughkompos*." But Mather suddenly breaks off to ridicule Native American languages, with their "disagreeable" sounds and ludicrously long names. He digresses to spell out a long Algonquian word of fifty-four letters, with a jocular aside to the poor printer who has to set the line of type. Mather dismisses the topic abruptly: "There is very Little in any Tradition of the Salvages [*sic*] to be relied upon."[6]

Notably, Mather was well versed in ancient and Native American fossil legends; he had previously cited Inca and Aztec discoveries, along with mythic interpretations, as reported by the Spanish in the 1500s. Yet at this point in his letter, Mather was seized by an agnotological imperative to cancel out the local Indian fossil knowledge. And he seems to make this decision mid-sentence. Did Mather intuit that articulating alternative, non-biblical ideas about giant bones would undermine his "creation science" argument? Mather's fellow Puritan, Edward Taylor, maintained that the evidence of the huge bones at Claverack *legitimized* native traditions about past giants. In contrast, Mather believed that all pagan mythology was inspired by Satan. Could the seemingly spontaneous interruption in the letter be an artifact of a collision between Mather's faith-based belief system and his scientific impulse to be objective and inclusive by citing Indian giant legends as proof of Christian doctrine?

But Mather was a skilled orator, arguing a case before a learned society, so it is more likely that his digression was a rhetorical strategy. Mather often demonized Indian culture. In this case, however, he needed the long-standing Indian traditions to make his point. Mather brought up the centuries-old tales of giants to prove that huge skeletons were so common in the Americas that the natives had a name for them. Then, having made that point, he cut off further discussion of native accounts with heavy-handed humor. With this decision to cancel out native fossil knowledge, Mather became the first authority on record in North America to deny Indians a role in interpreting fossil evidence. I suggest that Mather modeled his tactic on a similar strategy of the Roman historian Plutarch, whose reports of giant bones Mather cites in his letter. Plutarch described the amazing discovery of a gigantic skeleton in North Africa in the first century BC, but dismissed indigenous explanations as "fantastic legends" and scorned their language as "absolutely unpronounceable."[7]

GEORGES CUVIER'S INTEREST IN ANCIENT AND INDIAN FOSSIL DISCOVERIES, 1796–1821

Over the next century, many more reports of large fossil exposures continued to accumulate from North and South America. Indians familiar with the Pleistocene bone beds guided many English and French naturalists who collected the fossil bones, tusks, and teeth and sent them to Europe for study. In this period of mutual accommodation and exchange, described by Richard White in *The Middle Ground*, scientifically curious Euro-Americans, such as Thomas Jefferson, John Bartram, Mark Catesby, Count Buffon, and Benjamin Smith Barton attempted to learn what native people knew about the mysterious bones.[8]

In Paris, the brilliant naturalist Georges Cuvier (1769–1832; see Figure 7.2) compared mastodon fossils from around the world and gathered every ancient and indigenous tradition about giant bones he could find, drawing on his wide network of American, French, German, Dutch, Italian, Swedish, and Spanish correspondents, who sent him specimens and field reports. In 1796 and more fully in 1799 and 1806, Cuvier published his discovery that mastodons were extinct elephants that once flourished around the world. Part 1 of his three-part monograph "On Living and Fossil Elephants" of 1806 surveyed discoveries of mastodon fossils from fourth-century-BC Greece up to 1802, including mention of native traditions gathered by the Franciscan J. Torrubia in Mexico and Peru. Cuvier

FIGURE 7.2   Georges Cuvier. Engraving in Georges Cuvier,
Recherches sur les ossemens fossiles (Paris, 1825).

continued to amass new reports of fossils from the Americas. His studies
culminated in the great four-volume "Researches on Fossil Bones" (1812,
revised in 1821), proposing worldwide catastrophic extinctions of mastodons. In the 1821 edition, Cuvier devoted some twenty pages to fossil
discoveries and traditions by Native Americans gleaned from his reading
and correspondence.[9]

Beginning with the giant bones at Claverack in 1705, Cuvier turned
to the landmark discovery in 1739 of the famous mastodon site, Big Bone
Lick on the Ohio River in Kentucky, where unnamed "Sauvages" in the
French army collected the first American fossils to be scientifically studied (in a notable example of agnogenesis, the fossils are still prominently
displayed—but mislabeled until 2001—in the Paleontological Museum,
Paris). My historical detective work indicates that the anonymous Indians were Abenakis from Quebec. How they were denied credit for their
discovery for more than 250 years is yet another striking instance of agnogenesis, discussed further below.[10]

Cuvier noted that natives of Canada and the Ohio Valley identified mastodons as the "grandfather or ancestor of the buffalo," and he
combed through reports of British expeditions between 1765 and 1766
along the Ohio, for Iroquois, Huron, Delaware, and Shawnee opinions
about the fossils. In 1795, Cuvier wrote about Iroquois and Delaware

place names in New England that indicated discoveries of mastodon remains (see Figure 7.3).

Cuvier was especially impressed with Shawnee and Delaware legends surrounding the "astonishing abundance" of fossils of mastodons and other mammals in the Ohio Valley. In 1762, five complete mastodon skeletons were described and measured by "les sauvages shawanais." Remarking on Indians' repeated assurances that no living specimens had ever been seen, Cuvier was also struck by the Shawnee observation of "the long nose" on mastodon skulls. He compared this detail to an earlier discovery by Illinois Indians, reported by Swedish naturalist Peter Kalm in 1748–1751, about a well-preserved mastodon skeleton with part of the trunk. Cuvier himself examined a mummified elephant foot discovered by an unnamed tribe in the mountains west of the Missouri River. These finds led Cuvier to wonder whether some mastodons in bogs might be as well preserved as the frozen mammoths of Siberia.[11]

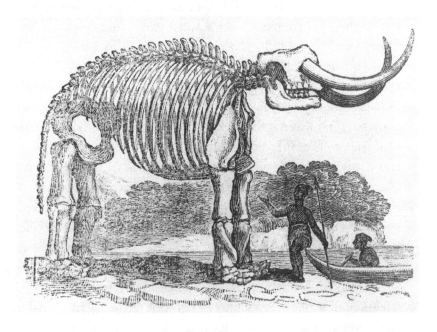

FIGURE 7.3 Indians discovering mastodon skeleton. Engraving by Alexander Anderson, for Thomas Bewick's *General History of Quadrupeds* (New York: G. & R. Waite, 1804).

"Traces of devastation have always been striking to humans," Cuvier remarked. Ancient "traditions of deluges" and giant beings preserved among indigenous people around the world arose from their observations of marine fossils and bones of extinct megafaunas. Moreover, wrote Cuvier, tribes are knowledgeable about all the noteworthy animals in their own lands, and they learn about exotic species through travel and traders. Their insights were not just "vulgar ideas"—even garbled or confused legends could contain scientific truth. Thus, wrote Cuvier, "the sciences, like people, moved from poetry to history."[12]

The details that emerged from indigenous accounts were consistent. The giant beings had lived in the remote past but were wiped out by some violent destruction event before the era of present-day Indians: no one claimed to have seen them alive. These widespread extinction scenarios, from Peru to Canada, helped Cuvier to rule out migration and focus on catastrophic extinctions, and therefore were significant in developing the theories that established the new science of paleontology.

Alluding to Delaware, Shawnee, and other fossil legends, and contradicting Thomas Jefferson's hope that Lewis and Clark would discover live mastodons in the Pacific Northwest, Cuvier wrote: "How can it be believed that the immense mastodons . . . whose bones are found under ground in the two Americas, still live?" Native traditions about their destruction were based on their own discoveries of the bones over generations, wrote Cuvier. If these animals still lived, how could such enormous beasts "escape the knowledge of the nomadic peoples who move ceaselessly around the continent in all directions, and who themselves recognize that the creatures no longer exist?"[13]

Remarkably, no modern historian of paleontology has acknowledged Cuvier's attention to ancient Greek and Native American fossil traditions, or speculated on their influence in his theories. Indeed, only someone who reads Cuvier's original publications would notice the extent of his interest. One modern historian of paleontology who is familiar with all of Cuvier's works is Martin J. S. Rudwick, the modern translator and interpreter of Cuvier. In his extensive writings on Cuvier's correspondence, methods, and theories, Rudwick does not discuss the scientist's interest in indigenous discoveries.[14]

MARTIN RUDWICK'S SELECTIVE SILENCE,
1972–2005

In 1997, Rudwick published the first modern English translations of Cuvier's writings with commentaries. Of the pages Cuvier devoted to Native American fossil knowledge in his 1812/1821 magnum opus, only one passage rated Rudwick's translation: the statement in which Cuvier concluded, citing Native American testimonies, that catastrophic extinctions must have wiped out all American mastodons in an era before human memory. Cuvier's survey of large fossil discoveries and interpretations over the past 2,000 years in Europe, Asia, Africa, and the Americas in his 1806 monograph was dismissed without comment: "The first part . . . on the geographical distribution of finds of fossil elephants" is "not translated here." Cuvier's extensive section on Native American accounts in 1812/1821, summarized above, is not translated or commented on, in the 1997 text or in Rudwick's recent work on Cuvier and his time.[15]

Why did Rudwick ignore Cuvier's interest in ancient and indigenous fossil finds and ideas? Some answers emerge from Rudwick's influential history of paleontological milestones, *The Meaning of Fossils*, first published in 1972. For Rudwick, true paleontological history began in 1565. Before that, he states, fossils may have been "noticed and commented on by men of many different periods and cultures," but "it is only within Western civilization . . . since the Renaissance, that palaeontology has emerged from this diffuse awareness of fossils." According to Rudwick, the use of fossil evidence to understand the history of the earth began in Europe in about 1800. As he acknowledges, modern scholars tend to "devalue" the preceding paleontological investigations of the eighteenth century—the same period of "mutual accommodation" described by Richard White, when Euro-Americans were soliciting native ideas about the "fossil enigma."[16]

Rudwick is a proponent of an "institutional myth" of modern paleontology, that no serious consideration of vertebrate fossils could occur until the scientific theories of evolution and extinction were invented in Europe in the Enlightenment and later. According to this view, meaningful interpretation of fossils as organic remains of the past requires an understanding of natural history that the ancient Greeks and non-Europeans could not have possessed. Of course, as he decided which of Cuvier's words to translate for posterity and which to leave in obscurity, Rudwick was selective (see Chapter 1 in this volume, on selective inquiry). But his neglect of both the ancient Greek and indigenous American evidence, which Cuvier had carefully gathered and cited in his publications, hides the importance that Cuvier and other naturalists of this era placed on traditional information about fossils around the world. Rudwick's omission prevents us from knowing about a time when early scientists respected and actively sought out fossil knowledge from all available sources.[17]

For Rudwick, science progresses by "demythologizing itself"; therefore little of historical or scientific value exists in traditional, often myth-based ideas about fossils, in pre-scientific cultures. Accordingly, Rudwick omitted portions of Cuvier's studies that he judged dated and scientifically uninteresting. Notably, however, Rudwick has written that "each period's interpretation of the meaning of fossils may be an illuminating reflection of that period's view of the natural world." Instead of criticizing the mistakes of the learned European gentlemen who studied fossils, Rudwick suggests that we should "understand them as men of their time, grappling with problems which they rarely had enough evidence to solve, and solving them in terms of their own view of the world." The history of paleontology might be further illuminated by extending the same understanding to ancient and indigenous efforts to comprehend the fossil record.[18]

GEORGE GAYLORD SIMPSON AND "TRUE" FOSSIL DISCOVERIES, 1942–1943

In 1935, the Canadian Edward Kindle was the first modern scientist to suggest that Native Americans should be credited with significant fossil discoveries, in a brief paper in the *Journal of Paleontology*. But in two influential monographs of 1942–1943, the prominent U.S. paleontologist George Gaylord Simpson (1902–1984) strenuously rejected Kindle's suggestion. Simpson declared all Indian fossil discoveries "casual finds without scientific sequel," which deserved no place in the history of "true discovery." With that, Simpson effectively silenced the earlier exchanges between Native Americans and Euro-Americans about the fossil record.

As I have argued elsewhere, Simpson's pronouncements are a major reason why native encounters with fossils are so little known today.[19]

In his official history of vertebrate paleontology in the Western Hemisphere, Simpson maintained that Native Americans contributed nothing to paleontological history, because they only picked up fossils out of "idle curiosity" without ever recognizing their organic nature, and their ideas about fossils were mere superstition. Since there was no record of "continuous consciousness" of fossil knowledge in Indian culture, argued Simpson, their discoveries never resulted in scientific advancement and thus had "no real bearing on paleontological discovery." Why would a towering figure like Simpson go to such lengths to deny Native Americans a role in the early history of paleontology?

Some paleontologists who knew Simpson suggest he was a racist; others describe him as an irascible and arrogant curmudgeon. Léo Laporte, Simpson's biographer, told me Simpson was concerned with defining "science as science. . . . If he did not give them sufficient credit, it was probably because he was not aware of their traditions accounting for fossil remains."[20]

In the 1940s, paleontology was just coming into its own as a scientific field. In 1944, Simpson chaired the new Department of Vertebrate Paleontology at the American Museum of Natural History. His rigid standards of what he called "true discovery" were intended to modernize the new science and define its disciplinary borders. Yet, I think we can glimpse intriguing hints of ambivalence. In a revealing moment, Simpson commented that the "prediscovery finds" by Indians and their knowledge of fossils offered much "sentimental and literary" interest. But, wrote Simpson, "the temptation to consider them in more detail must be resisted," in favor of "true scientific discoveries."[21]

Had Simpson given in to temptation and learned something about Native American fossil accounts, perhaps he would have been impressed by the understanding of Earth's past that can be expressed in mythological language. But, because he so assiduously kept himself and his readers in the dark about native fossil observations, Simpson was led to make some outrageous assertions. He declared, for example, that the "various reported Indian legends of fabulous beasts represented by fossil bones have little ethnological and no paleontological value." The traditions, he said, are "untrustworthy, and carry little conviction of genuine and spontaneous (truly aboriginal) reference to real finds of fossils." He mocked the intellectual capacity of "men who live close to nature." They may be meticulous observers, he wrote, but their "acuteness of physical observation is . . . generally linked with peculiarly dull" understanding. "Men who pass their lives out of doors commonly have a vast store of objective knowledge, but their comprehension of any real interpretations of those facts . . . is usually ludicrously scanty."[22]

Simpson's drive to erase Indians from the story led to convoluted reasoning. In his description of the historic 1739 discovery of mastodon fossils by Abenaki hunters in the French army, Simpson's logic is tortuous: "Even though Indians were probably involved in the real discovery" of the Ohio fossils, "they cannot fairly be called the discoverers." Despite the Indians' "absolute priority," which has been acknowledged by French scientists since 1764, Simpson went so far as to create an ahistorical discovery scenario in order to give credit to the French commander of the expedition. Another important Indian fossil discovery on the Ohio in 1762 led Simpson to mutter, "It is . . . curious to find the Indians as sole authorities in this incident," since surely whites must have known of the fossils.[23]

Simpson stated: "The abundant occurrence of fossil bones in North America was not widely known among Indians and not a common subject of remark by them." Yet Simpson was forced to contradict himself and recount yet another historic fossil discovery by Native Americans, "at the astonishingly early date" of 1519, when Spanish conquistadors recorded that pre-Columbian people in the Aztec Empire had collected mastodon fossils, correctly identified them as belonging to giant mammals, speculated on their behavior, understood mass extinction, and displayed the bones as historical records. Simpson admitted this was a "true find" of "unquestionable priority," but then categorized it as a "casual find," not a "true discovery in the historical sense."[24]

In *Fossil Legends*, I was able to document evidence from more than forty-five Native American cultures, from pre-contact to the present, to prove Simpson wrong on all counts. But for more than half a century, Simpson's calculated assault on Native Americans' role in the history of paleontology has been accepted uncritically by most historians and scientists. Simpson concluded his grand history of American paleontology—which he himself praised as "definitive"—with these words: "Now [that] the thin trickle of fossils collected in America" has become "a flood, . . . the study of the beginnings [of paleontological inquiry] need go no further."[25]

Sioux historian Vine Deloria Jr., in *Red Earth, White Lies*, cited Simpson's official history as a prime example of how "scientists have maintained a stranglehold on the definitions of . . . reliable human experiences." Ironically, a hope expressed by Martin Rudwick in 1972 can be read to refute Simpson. Pointing out that "in every period of its history, palaeontology . . . developed through a series of intricate interactions between philosophical" assumptions and worldviews, theory building, and a "steadily accumulating fund of observed evidence," Rudwick hoped that the next generation of paleontologists would "recover . . . the broad interests and outlook that [the study of fossils] possessed so markedly earlier in its history."[26]

DANGEROUS FOSSIL KNOWLEDGE
AT AGATE SPRINGS, NEBRASKA

As Proctor and Smithson (this volume) point out, some forms of agnogenesis are morally motivated, to limit or control dangerous knowledge. Many Native American groups traditionally believe that fossils contain powerful "medicine" or magical forces for good or ill. Some fossil traditions are sacred, secret knowledge, which should not be made available to the uninitiated or vulnerable or to outsiders. I have participated in maintaining this kind of ignorance: in interviews on reservations, I promised not to publish new oral fossil knowledge unless something similar had already been published.

Some knowledge of fossils is not just withheld from outsiders but within the tribe. Collecting large animal fossils or attempting to obtain power from them is forbidden in some native cultures. For example, many traditional Navajos avoid touching or talking about anything to do with death, including dinosaur fossils in their lands. In the fossiliferous West, many Plains Indian groups traditionally avoid disturbing petrified bones.[27]

The Lakota Sioux feared the awesome powers of fossils eroding out of the badlands of western Nebraska. Agate Springs Fossil Beds on the Niobrara River is a vast graveyard of densely packed, jumbled skeletons of huge, bizarre beasts from the Miocene, 20 million years ago. Long before paleontologists arrived to dig the fossils in 1890s, the Lakotas named the place "Animal Bones Brutally Scattered About." The frightening creatures were thought to be evil Water Monsters slaughtered by Thunder Beings in primeval times. Agate Springs was a sacred place to collect special plants and stones and to make offerings and vision quests, but most Lakotas steered clear of the monster bones spilling out of two hills there.

Agnogenesis by scientists began with their arrival in 1892 to dig up tons of fossils for museums. Had they spoken about the fossils to the Lakotas, who camped every summer at Agate Springs, they might have learned the true identity of the "forest" of six-foot-tall trace fossils, which the mystified scientists named "Devil's Corkscrews." Decades later, the scientists identified the perplexing spiral structures as fossilized burrows made by Miocene beavers, whose skeletons often lay at the bottom (see Figures 7.4 and 7.5). The Lakotas had already figured out the connection between the fossils: their traditional name for the corkscrew was "Beaver's Lodge."[28]

In 2001, the National Park Service (NPS) commissioned a Lakota, Sebastian (Bronco) LeBeau, to create a Cultural Evaluation Report on indigenous knowledge of the fossil beds, now a national monument. After consulting with elders at Pine Ridge, Rosebud, Cheyenne River, and Spirit

FIGURE 7.4 Devil's Corkscrew. Photo courtesy of Agate Springs Fossil Beds National Monument Museum.

FIGURE 7.5 Daemonelix, Beaver's Lodge. Painting on hide calendar by Lakota artist Dawn Little Sky. Courtesy of Agate Springs Fossil Beds, National Monument Museum.

Lake reservations, LeBeau made a pilgrimage to the place called Animal Bones Brutally Scattered About. He mapped archaeological remains of altars and other sites and recounted the traditional story of Thunder Beings Killing Water Monsters.

LeBeau experienced an overwhelming, eerie sensation of danger at the fossil site. He went back to talk with the elders. Reluctantly, they told him more. According to Lakota tradition, when the First People had arrived, an evil spirit used the terrible power of the monster bones to drive a young man crazy. Then the spirit taught the man how to magically "shoot" slivers of fossils into enemies to bewitch or kill them. The first Lakota medicine man had warned the First People to avoid the fossils. Nevertheless, some people undertook vision quests to Agate Springs to learn the evil power of the fossils, known as the Stinging Bones ritual.

Bronco LeBeau returned to Agate Springs. He located old boundary markers warning people away from the bad-medicine fossils and found vision quest sites among the fossils, adding this material to his report. The Park Service allowed me to read LeBeau's detailed field notes and gave permission to cite LeBeau's official evaluation. This was a very rare instance of using fossils for evil instead of for healing, so I wanted to include it in *Fossil Legends*. But I felt anxious about revealing a black-magic fossil ritual, so I searched until I found older published references to similar "shooting" fossil spells among the Sioux when they still lived in the Great Lakes area.[29]

In 2005, the National Park Service hired an experienced non-Indian consultant, Janet Cliff (PhD in folklore), to write an official site bulletin about Lakota traditions at Agate Springs, to be distributed to park visitors. Cliff read the official history of the site, my then-unpublished research about Sioux fossil knowledge, and LeBeau's field notes and report. Noting that the Lakota spiritual leaders and elders "obviously wanted to keep LeBeau ignorant as long as possible" about the malevolent power of the fossils, and respecting their wish to "keep non-Natives ignorant," Cliff produced a watered-down draft of the site bulletin for the public, with a vague allusion to "good and bad medicine" of the fossils.

Cliff explained in an accompanying letter to the NPS that "including anything meaningful about witchcraft can encourage certain individuals to remove fossils . . . and certain individuals would probably find it 'neat' to do their impromptu satanic rituals at midnight," posing a security risk for the park. Indeed, Cliff remarked that she hoped her site bulletin would "never see the light of day."[30]

This latest twist in the shroud of ignorance surrounding Native American fossil knowledge evokes some aspects of the Puritan witch hunter Cotton Mather's anxiety about the satanic influences of Indian fossil legends 300 years ago. Mather deliberately created ignorance as a strategic ploy borrowed from Plutarch. In contrast, Cuvier, 100 years later, sought fossil knowledge from every available source to further science. Then, 200 years after Cuvier, Rudwick's selective "tunnel history" ignored the evidence for eighteenth-century European curiosity about fossils, focusing on the "scientifically interesting" advances of the nineteenth century.[31] Meanwhile, Simpson not only actively suppressed known facts of Indian priority in fossil discoveries and ideas, but he published disinformation to support his Eurocentric history of paleontology. The Agate Springs case differs from the preceding cases, exemplifying "virtuous ignorance," with roots reaching back hundreds of years. For a diverse group of people, Indian and non-Indian, the masses of monstrous bones entombed in the badlands still have the power to evoke fear and tension over how to handle dangerous knowledge, knowledge sincerely believed to pose harm to body or soul.

NOTES

1. On Cusick and Adams, see Adrienne Mayor, *Fossil Legends of the First Americans* (Princeton, NJ: Princeton University Press, 2005), 37–50, 65–67; fossil legends defined, xxix; excavations and revisions, 28–29, 41, 44–45, 67–68, 81, 103, 150, 173, 208.

2. "The fossil enigma" has stimulated curiosity since antiquity: B. Glass, O. Temkin, and W. Straus, *Forerunners of Darwin, 1745–1859* (Baltimore: Johns Hopkins University Press, 1968). Cf. Schiebinger (this volume), on eighteenth-century Europeans' reliance on Native guides in seeking profitable drugs in the West Indies. British and French colonists competed to collect North American mastodon bones and tusks for profit and to advance science. Mayor, *Fossil Legends*, 8–11, 353nn10–13; Claudine Cohen, *The Fate of the Mammoth: Fossils, Myth, and History* (Chicago: University of Chicago Press, 2002), 65–66, 79–80.

3. Adrienne Mayor, *The First Fossil Hunters: Paleontology in Greek and Roman Times* (Princeton, NJ: Princeton University Press, 2000). Typical modern view of ancient fossil knowledge: Glass et al., *Forerunners of Darwin*.

4. Paul Semonin, *American Monster: How the Nation's First Prehistoric Creature Became a Symbol of National Identity* (New York: New York University Press, 2000); Cohen, *Fate*; Mayor, *Fossil Legends*, 33–37.

5. Donald E. Stanford, "The Giant Bones of Claverack, New York, 1705," *New York History* 40 (1959): 47–61; Semonin, *Monster*, 9, 15–40; Mayor, *Fossil Legends*, 33–37; Henry Fairfax Osborn, "Mastodons of the Hudson Highlands," *Natural History* 23 (1923): 3–24, esp. 7.

6. David Levin, "Giants in the Earth: Science and the Occult in Cotton Mather's Letters to the Royal Society," *William & Mary Quarterly*, 3rd ser., 45 (1988): 751–770. *Maughkompos* translates as "giant man," a variant of the Massachusetts Indian name *Maushops*; all based on *mogke* (great) and *wosketomp* (man). John Hammond Trumbull, *Natick Dictionary* (Washington, DC, 1903).

7. Mather cites Plutarch: Levin, "Giants," 765. Plutarch: Mayor, *First Fossil Hunters*, 124, 304n23.

8. Mayor, *Fossil Legends*, xxxv, xxxviii, 13, 21–25, 50–65; Richard White, *The Middle Ground* (Cambridge, UK: Cambridge University Press, 1991).

9. Cuvier's interest in the uniformity of fossil species parallels the eighteenth-century interest in the uniformity of plant species; cf. Schiebinger (this volume). For Cuvier's correspondence, methods, and theories, see Martin Rudwick's *Georges Cuvier, Fossil Bones, and Geological Catastrophes: New Translations & Interpretations of Primary Texts* (Chicago: University of Chicago Press, 1997); *The New Science of Geology: Studies in the Earth Sciences in the Age of Revolution* (Chicago: University of Chicago Press, 2004); and *Bursting the Limits of Time: The Reconstruction of Geohistory in the Age of Revolution* (Chicago: University of Chicago Press, 2005). Cuvier's use of native traditions: Mayor, *Fossil Legends*, 61–64, 93–94.

10. Mayor, *Fossil Legends*, 1–19; fossil mislabeled as gift of Thomas Jefferson: 16–19. Martin Rudwick, *The Meaning of Fossils: Episodes in the History of Paleontology* (Chicago: University of Chicago Press [1972, 1976], 1985), e.g., 107, 115 on Cuvier; 105 on 1739 discovery, with no mention of Indians who collected the fossils.

11. Quotations in this section: Georges Cuvier, "Sur les éléphans vivans et fossiles," *Annales du Museum d'Histoire Naturelle* (Paris) 8 (1806): 3–58, esp. "Article Premier," 4–7, 14, and 54 on ancient Greek and Roman accounts; 54–58, mastodon fossils in North and South America and native traditions. Cuvier, *Discours sur les revolutions de la surface*

du globe, 8th ed. (Paris: Cousin [1812], 1840, and Paris: Bourgeois, rpt. 1985). Cuvier, *Recherches sur les ossemens fossiles* [1812], 2nd rev. ed., 5 vols. (Paris: Belin, 1821), vol. 1, 153–159, 208–224, 266–267, 223; and Cuvier, *Discours* (1812), section 28. See also Rudwick, *Cuvier*, 208, 254–255, 262–263, 464–467.

12. Cuvier's appeal to international amateurs in 1800: Text 6 in Rudwick, *Cuvier*, 46–47; see 178 on Cuvier's belief that legends contain "a kernel of scientific truth" and 208 on tribes' zoological knowledge.

13. Cuvier's 1796 treatise, and Cuvier, *Discours* (1840), 59; *Discours* (1985), 94; see Cohen *Fate*, 111; Rudwick, *Cuvier*, 216.

14. Glass et al.'s history of eighteenth-century forerunners of Darwin has no mention of Native American discoveries. Henry Fairfield Osborn briefly noted Cuvier's interest in ancient Greek fossil finds in his history of prehistoric elephant discoveries, *Proboscidea*, 2 vols. (New York: American Museum of Natural History, 1936–1942), vol. 2, 1147. Rudwick, *Cuvier*, 178, acknowledged Cuvier's "extended review" of fossils described by "writers of classical antiquity." Fleeting allusions to Native American traditions in Semonin, *Monster*, e.g., 309–310; and in Cohen, *Fate*, 86–87. Native American scholar Vine Deloria Jr.'s comparison of indigenous worldviews and Euro-American science cited examples of native paleontological knowledge excluded from orthodox science: *Red Earth, White Lies* (Golden, CO: Fulcrum, 1997).

15. Rudwick, *Cuvier*, 216, 91n1. In both *New Science* (2004) and *Bursting the Limits* (2005), Rudwick omits Native American fossil discoveries or ideas, even in discussions where the topic seems relevant: for example, *New Science* 7: 2–8 on how "geohistory" came to be based on fossils; 8: 2–12 on Cuvier's appeal to "amateurs"; 9: 53–65 on Cuvier's voluminous "paper museum" and archives. See also Rudwick, *Cuvier*, 43.

16. Rudwick, *Meaning of Fossils*, preface to 1976 ed., n.p. (fourth page); preface to 1972 ed., n.p. (first page). Rudwick, *New Science* 7: 2–8. Glass et al., *Forerunners*, completely ignore American fossils. For a critical view of Rudwick's omissions, see Peter Dodson, foreword to Mayor, *First Fossil Hunters*, xiv–xvi. On the value of indigenous geomythology, see Edward Burnet Tylor, Dorothy Vitaliano, Roger Echo-Hawk, and Vine Deloria Jr., cited in Mayor, *Fossil Legends*, e.g., xxix–xxxiv, 195; also K. Krajick, "Tracking Myth to Geological Reality," *Science* 310 (2005): 762–764.

17. Rudwick's selection criteria: *Cuvier*, x–xi. See Naomi Oreskes, "The Humanistic and Religious Foundations of Deep Time" [review of Rudwick's *Bursting the Limits of Time*], *Science* 314 (2006): 596–597.

18. Rudwick, *Meaning of Fossils*, preface to 1972 ed., n.p. (last page).

19. E. M. Kindle, "American Indian Discoveries of Vertebrate Fossils," *Journal of Paleontology* 9, 5 (1935): 449–452; George Gaylord Simpson, "The Beginnings of Vertebrate Paleontology in North America," *Proceedings of the American Philosophical Society* 86 (1942): 130–188; and "The Discovery of Fossil Vertebrates in North America," *Journal of Paleontology* 17, 1 (1943): 26–38, esp. 26–27.

20. Simpson, "Beginnings," 132–135; "Discovery," 26–27; Léo F. Laporte, *George Gaylord Simpson* (New York: Columbia University Press, 2000). Interviews cited in Mayor, *Fossil Legends*, xxvi–xxviii. Simpson also criticized Jefferson's paleontological writings and the notion that "forerunners" anticipated Darwin. Glass et al., *Forerunners*, 414n78.

21. Simpson, "Beginnings," 132–135; "Discovery," 26–27. In *Attending Marvels* (New York: Macmillan, 1934), 110, 161, Simpson credited his uneducated Patagonian guide Justino with the discovery of important fossils now in the American Museum of

Natural History: Justino possessed that "consuming curiosity which is the real reason for any scientific research."

22. Simpson, "Beginnings," 132–135, 139; "Discovery," 26–27; Simpson, *Attending Marvels*, 110.

23. Simpson, "Beginnings," 135–138, 132n2; "Discovery," 28–34. Simpson's biased version of the historic discovery of mastodon fossils on the Ohio in 1739 is accepted by recent historians, such as Cohen, *Fate*, and Semonin, *Monster*, whereas French scientists, from Daubenton in 1764 to Pascal Tassy in 2000, have given the Indians credit. See Mayor, *Fossil Legends*, 4–5.

24. Simpson, "Beginnings," 132–134; "Discovery," 27. Mayor, *Fossil Legends*, 78–79.

25. Anthropologist Loren Eiseley, for example, said Indian "myths" about fossils were inspired by Europeans' leading questions, and cited Simpson with approval in 1945. Ethnologist Robert Lowie famously rejected the historical value of *all* oral traditions in 1915. Mayor, *Fossil Legends*, xxxi; Simpson, "Discovery," 26, 37.

26. Deloria, *Red Earth*, 7, 9; Rudwick, *Meaning of Fossils*, 265–266.

27. Groups who keep fossil knowledge secret or fear fossils' dangerous powers: Mayor, *Fossil Legends*, xxxiv, 117, 129–137, 298–303, 309, 321–323.

28. Lakota name for the site: *A'bekiya Wama'kanskan s'e*; for beaver burrow fossils: *Ca'pa el ti*. Mayor, *Fossil Legends*, 241–254.

29. Sebastian C. [Bronco] LeBeau, "Wico'cajeyate: Traditional Cultural Property Evaluation," Agate Fossil Beds National Monument, Harrison, NE, Department of the Interior, National Park Service, December 2001. Early missionaries reported similar rituals in Minnesota: Mayor, *Fossil Legends*, 387nn31–32.

30. Janet Cliff, "Site Bulletin: Native Americans and Agate Fossil Beds National Monument," draft prepared for NPS Superintendent Ruthann Knudson, Agate Springs Fossil Beds National Monument, Harrison, NE, April 16, 2005. Janet Cliff to Ruthann Knudson, NPS, April 16, 2005. Janet Cliff, pers. corr., March 13, 2005.

31. "Tunnel history" is Rudwick's phrase; *Meaning of Fossils*, preface to 1972 ed. (n.p.), last page.

CHAPTER 8

Mapping Ignorance in Archaeology

The Advantages of Historical Hindsight

ALISON WYLIE

Compared to the pond of knowledge, our ignorance remains atlantic. Indeed the horizon of the unknown recedes as we approach it.

THUS BEGINS *The Encyclopedia of Ignorance,* a collection of fifty-one short essays on "what it is [scientists] would most like to know" that appeared in 1977.[1] Most of the contributors are physicists and biologists, but cognitive neuroscientists and biomedical researchers are also well represented. The social sciences are considered explicitly only by a mathematician who is concerned about understanding why the tools of his discipline had not realized the kind of success in application to these fields that they have in the physical sciences, and by a computer scientist worried about the instability of technical systems that interact with endlessly inventive humans.[2] Psychology is represented by entries on sleep and addiction research that are resolutely biomedical in orientation. There are several essays on evolutionary theory, one on the earth sciences, and one on paleontology, but nothing on archaeology or history—the focus of my interest here.

MAPPING IGNORANCE

In these assembled essays, ignorance emerges as a complex phenomenon. It is not just a lack of knowledge in specific areas but also a matter of uncertainty and incompleteness, of knowledge that degrades from conventional ideals even in fields where we know a great deal. Sometimes ignorance is clearly delimited. It is identified with evidence not yet collected, variables not yet precisely measured, dimensions of a subject domain not yet explored—a well-tempered, prospectively domesticated ignorance. But often ignorance is more unruly. The life scientists and evolutionary theorists allow that the systems they study may be too complex or unbounded, too rapidly evolving or too unstable, to sustain a secure, well-ordered—exact and predictively robust—body of knowledge. Others acknowledge, at a meta-level, that we may not know what it is we do not know. A few link ignorance of this kind to erotetic worries; perhaps the knowledge we have is question specific and our ignorance extends to innumerable domains we will not begin to recognize until we learn to ask different questions.[3]

Although their charge was descriptive—to identify gaps in and limitations of scientific knowledge—a number of contributors, and the author of an "Introduction" that appears midway through *The Encyclopedia of Ignorance*,[4] take up the question of why specific kinds of ignorance have arisen and persist. For the most part their diagnoses are resolutely epistemic, but they also cite ontological constraints inherent in the objects of inquiry, and a few consider contextual factors: sociopolitical, economic, and cultural impediments to research. Consider some of the details of their analyses, as a point of departure for assessing the sources and forms of ignorance that concern archaeologists.

Epistemological Factors

A primary source of ignorance cited by a number of contributors to the *Encyclopedia of Ignorance* is the poverty of the empirical data on which they rely; the relevant evidence has not survived, as in the case of the fossil record of hominid evolution,[5] or the technologies necessary to recover, analyze, and interpret data as evidence had not yet been developed. Brain research is an especially striking case; the cognitive neuroscientists describe a field that, in 1977, was about to be transformed by dramatic developments in neural imaging.[6] But limited evidence was not the only epistemic constraint that concerned these contributors; several cite a lack of adequate theory as well. An astronomer inveighs against a tendency among his colleagues to immerse themselves in the "unimaginative" collection of observations.[7] The "strangely paradoxical nature of science," he says, is that although some observations are a necessary precondition for generating theory, they offer no real understanding until they are embedded in a theory. A molecular biologist expands on this theme: a major source of ignorance in his field is "the lack of a theoretical framework in which to order and interpret the relevant facts."[8] Others report that they are awash in detailed knowledge of form but not function, of correlations but not causal relations, of manifest pattern but not mechanism.[9] Clearly the central tenets of a narrowly conceived positivism were losing their grip, although the language of exactness, causal determinism, prediction, and control, is ubiquitous.[10]

Ontological Constraints

In a complementary vein, a number of contributors to the *Encyclopedia* suggest that the limits of their knowledge are a function of the phenomena they study. Ignorance may be irreducible if complexity is "an intrinsic condition and characteristic of the phenomena," for example, in the life sciences.[11] A psychobiologist considers the implications of ongoing evolution: it "keeps complicating the universe by adding new phenomena that have new properties and new forces."[12] He worries that ignorance may proliferate even as we expand the scope of knowledge. But most daunting for these scientists is any phenomenon that is conditioned by human action and intention. The computer scientist argues that there is an "essential uncertainty" inherent in knowledge of artificial systems that operate in a human environment; as we learn about these systems we change our responses to them and this, in turn, changes the environment to which they adapt in open-ended and unpredictable ways. He worries that anything that touches the human is contaminated by our "unbounded ability to invent new rules, new twists, new objectives" such that exact science becomes impossible.[13] Reading these entries, it comes as no surprise that the social sciences, perhaps especially archaeology and history, are not more prominently represented.

Contextual and Normative Factors

A few contributors break this focus on epistemic and ontological sources of ignorance and consider social, cultural, and economic factors. Some experiments that might resolve long-standing puzzles about brain function cannot be conducted for ethical reasons. The legacy of a Cartesian

mind-body dualism weighs heavily on those intent on developing a scientific understanding of consciousness, pain, and memory. We have such
strong and complex normative responses to drug dependency it is difficult, not just to uncover causes, but even to specify what constitutes the
phenomenon under study: "ignorance begets confidence more surely than
there is knowledge," observes the addiction researcher, quoting Bacon.[14]
The geologist asks why, for want of a systematic drilling program on land
like that already well developed for the oceans, so much ignorance is allowed to "remain below our feet": the technology was available; it would
be comparatively inexpensive; and there is considerable cost attached to
our continued reliance on structural geology for what he describes as
three-dimensional understanding when dealing with a four-dimensional
subject.[15]

Although this is an expansive list of contextual factors, it is striking that
these scientists do not chiefly blame biasing intrusions from outside science
for the failures and limitations of inquiry they describe. In emphasizing
epistemic and ontological factors no doubt they account for ignorance in
roughly the same way as they would the epistemic *successes* of their fields,
attributing these to good reasons and evidence, and limiting contextual,
cultural factors to a walk-on role. In short, they embrace a symmetry thesis,
albeit the inverse of that which has been advocated by sociologists of science as an antidote to the philosophical convention of reserving epistemic
analysis for cases of scientific success and relegating ignorance and error to
the history and sociology of science, as failures of scientific rationality that
require explanation in terms of non-epistemic factors.[16] With the benefit of
hindsight—specifically, thirty years of development in science studies—there
is clearly considerable scope for asking why particular lines of evidence
and theoretical insight had languished while others were avidly pursued,
rebalancing the weight of the factors cited in the direction of the political economy, the institutional structure, and the culture of the sciences in
question, as well as the larger social contexts in which they operate. At the
same time, these reflections on ignorance in the heartland of science make
it clear how recalcitrant empirical evidence can be and how hard won the
theoretical constructs that give it epistemic significance.

In approaching the question of ignorance in archaeology, I am committed to a symmetry thesis: the same range of factors that explain the production of knowledge are relevant for understanding the production (and maintenance) of ignorance. But I would insist that we cannot determine in advance what these will be, what weight each will bear, how they interact. My aim here is not so much to illustrate how ignorance arises in archaeology, a field famous for the incomplete, enigmatic nature of its data and for the complexity and inaccessibility of its (cultural) subject. Rather, it is to identify a set of strategies that archaeologists use to discern and to counteract the particular forms of ignorance that afflict the research traditions in which they work.

IGNORANCE AS SILENCES IN HISTORY

The threat of ignorance in all the forms identified in the *Encyclopedia of Ignorance* is a matter of active concern among practitioners in a range of historical sciences, evident, for example, in the perennial debate among historians about ideals of "objectivity" and its various relativist and constructivist antitheses.[17] Within archaeology anxieties about error and ignorance—and the prospects for detecting and effectively countering it—have issued in crisis debates roughly every thirty years since archaeology began to professionalize in the early twentieth century. The emphasis in analysis of the sources of archaeological ignorance has shifted quite dramatically since the 1960s from a preoccupation with jointly ontological, empirical constraints to concern with the limitations of inadequate theory and, finally, to a focus on sociocultural and political factors.[18] As a framework for understanding these developments and the responses to ignorance they mobilize, Trouillot's analysis of silences in the production of historical knowledge is especially useful. He refuses the oppositional pull of positivist and constructivist impulses in history;[19] there is no prospect, he argues, for eliminating the systematic ambiguities inherent in the way we use the term *history* to refer both to events in the past and to the narratives by which we understand the past in the present. History, the narrative, is produced at innumerable sites, few of them controlled by professional historians and all of them deeply structured by contemporary interests and power relations. What we do not know, as much as what we do know, tracks power as it operates in social contexts both past and present. And yet, Trouillot insists, history is not "infinitely susceptible of invention."[20] To understand how silences arise, Trouillot attends to four moments in historical production, each of which has an archaeological counterpart: the generation of textual traces, the compilation of these traces as an archive, the retrieval of traces as facts to be built into historical narratives, and the construction of narratives that have retrospective significance. The factors symmetrically shaping ignorance and knowledge figure at each of these junctures as they have been engaged by archaeologists in the context of ongoing debate about disciplinary status and standards.

Empirical and Ontological Factors

The convention among archaeologists now identified as engaged in "traditional" forms of practice[21] has been to see the limitations of knowledge and the contours of ignorance as a function of the fragmentary, inscrutable nature of the data with which they work, a jointly epistemic and ontological concern with limitations inherent in the archaeological record. The attrition of material traces begins in Trouillot's first moment and, despite optimism about the egalitarian nature of garbage (that it provides evidence of the lives of many who never figure in historical records), those who peopled the past are by no means equally represented. The production, consumption, circulation, and discard of material culture are as deeply structured by power relations as is the creation of a textual record. This attrition continues, dramatically, with the creation of an archaeological record, a second moment in the production of an archaeological past that is as much a matter of decay, displacement, and destruction as it is of preservation and survival. Here ontological constraints enter: what archaeologists can know (or know reliably) is conditioned by the differential survival of stone tools and metal artifacts, fired ceramics, and architectural features, by contrast, for example, to cordage, wood hafts, straw roofs, and other relatively ephemeral (although by no means archaeologically unrepresented) classes of material. But sociocultural and economic factors of a different order enter as well: the tomb robbers and conquerors of antiquity, centuries of farmers and settlers, as well as modern-day developers, looters, and antiquities dealers, all play a role in determining what aspects of the material record of human activity will survive and what will be erased just as surely as do geological processes of erosion and bioturbation. Finally, these selection processes are amplified at Trouillot's third moment, in the retrieval of facts suitable for making narratives. Here the whole panoply of epistemic and sociopolitical factors is in play. What material archaeologists recover depends not only on what is visible, accessible, and technologically tractable but also on what archaeologists find interesting, puzzling, and relevant to current concerns, academic and popular. The retrieval and constitution of archaeologically usable facts of the record is very largely a function of what questions we know to ask and what material traces we know (how) to look for in attempting to answer them. Then come the vagaries of the curation of the archaeological records and collections generated by third moment retrieval, a contingency to which I return shortly.

The result is an unevenly preserved, fragmentary, and enigmatic data base. For many this has been cause for profound epistemic pessimism. Third moment retrieval can be as systematic and exhaustive as possible, argued M. A. Smith, a British field archaeologist writing in the mid-1950s, but the "Diogenes" problem remains: "the archaeologist may find the tub but altogether miss Diogenes."[22] Archaeologists should respect the (limited) "potentialities of the evidence" she insisted, and recognize that it is folly to elaborate speculative fourth moment narratives about the cultural past that extend beyond the available (limited) evidence. There is no prospect for decisively testing these conjectures given that there is no "logical relation between human activity in some of its aspects and the evidence left for the archaeologist; . . . there are real and insuperable limits to what can be legitimately inferred from archaeological material."[23] On a variant of this argument, known as Hawkes' "ladder of inference,"[24] archaeological interpretations are understood to reflect a hierarchy of credibility. Those aspects of the cultural past that are most closely constrained by material conditions of life may be reconstructed with some reliability (for example, technologies, some aspects of tool function, and some forms of subsistence practice), but the further an archaeologist strays from these and considers, for example, forms of social organization or systems of belief, the more unavoidably they indulge in speculation.

Theoretical Considerations

A sharp reaction against these skeptical arguments was the impetus for an ambitiously scientific research program in archaeology, the New Archaeology of the 1960s and 1970s. The limitations of archaeological understanding are not inherent in the record, the New Archaeologists insisted; they reflect, not the ontological opacity and empirical poverty of the surviving traces, but rather inadequacies in the conceptual resources that archaeologists bring to inquiry.[25] With these arguments the third and fourth moments of archaeological production came sharply into focus; attention turned to the challenge of securing the interpretive inferences necessary to constitute archaeological data as evidence that bears on historical and anthropological narratives. Two strategies of response to skeptical worries were pursued in this connection. The chief architect of the New Archaeology, Lewis Binford, and many of those committed to the program he advocated, put primary emphasis on a reorientation of third moment retrieval practices: all empirical investigation of the archaeological record (excavation, survey, data analysis) should be designed with the aim of recovering data relevant to specific questions—it should be problem oriented, rather than an exercise in open-ended exploration.[26] Here the emphasis was on theory building as a necessary framework for articulating interesting, productive questions, fueled by an impatience with "unimaginative observation" for its own sake, much like that recorded by contributors to *The Encyclopedia of Ignorance*.[27]

Within a decade, however, it became clear that problem-oriented research requires a second strategy: that of building, or borrowing, the substantive background knowledge—"middle range theory," linking or interpretive principles—necessary to secure claims about the significance of archaeological data as evidence of particular past events, conditions of life, patterns of activity, and social relations or beliefs. Here a complex interplay of epistemic and sociopolitical factors comes into play, requiring considerable expansion of Trouillot's account of third moment retrieval practices. The contours of possible knowledge and probable ignorance are shaped by the resources—technical, empirical, theoretical, economic, and social—that archaeologists recruit for the purpose of constituting facts of the past: identifying, recovering, recording material traces, and, crucially, interpreting them as evidence. What facts (of the record and of the past) archaeologists can establish has everything to do with what resources they have internally, or what connections they cultivate with the collateral fields that supply the crucial linking principles, and this is a function of institutional dynamics as much as of internal, problem, and theory-driven judgments of relevance; of conventions of authority and prestige, and the shifting availability of research funds, as well as accidents of personal interest and connection.

The Sociopolitics of Archaeology

Since the early 1980s a powerful reaction against the scientism of the New Archaeology has taken shape and, with it, skepticism about the possibility of knowing the past has resurfaced. In this context, however, the Diogenes problem has been cast in explicitly sociopolitical terms and the focus is resolutely on the vagaries of fourth moment narrative construction. The necessary reliance on linking principles and middle range theory opens space for ignorance that takes the form, not just of incomplete knowledge but of systematic distortion: the projection of contemporary preoccupations and expectations onto past lifeways and cultural formations that may bear little relation to anything familiar from the ethnohistoric present. Critics of the New Archaeology argue pointedly that archaeological narratives about the past are "always already" narratives of contemporary significance; they so radically overreach any available evidence that they cannot but track power in the present.[28] What these critical analyses draw attention to is not just the fact of underdetermination and the insecurity of inference in particular instances of third and fourth moment production, but the cumulative, amplifying effects of error and ignorance once it enters a historically extended research program.

To understand this temporal dynamic, consider an argument developed by Ian Hacking in an essay on weapons research.[29] When scientists focus on particular weapons-related problems, Hacking argues, not only are resources diverted from other currently promising lines of inquiry but the options available for future research are restructured. The decision to channel research energies in these ways reshapes everything from descriptive categories and research techniques to explanatory hypotheses and orienting theories; it changes the science itself and the "world of mind and technique" in which science is transacted.[30] By extension, this canalization of inquiry in any one field has implications for what is or becomes possible in other fields, determining what technologies of investigation, what collateral knowledge, is available for application in the kinds of interdisciplinary exchanges that have enriched archaeology from its inception. The impact and tortuous history of carbon-14 dating in archaeology is a case in point; the difficulty in refining applications of isotope analysis is another.[31]

In the hands of the sharpest critics of the New Archaeologists, these worries have been assumed to entail an uncompromising constructivism according to which there is nothing to archaeological accounts of the past but layered silences: expansive ignorance and exuberant invention. Trouillot both invokes and resists such constructivism as it arises in history; he insists that the line between history and fiction may be transgressed and blurred in innumerable ways, but nonetheless bears epistemic as well as rhetorical weight. An unequivocal constructivism "cannot give a full account of the production of any single narrative"; it undercuts the "cognitive purpose" of history." It is *because* fields like history and archaeology have contemporary significance that we require more than fictionalization: we impose "test[s] of credibility on certain events and narratives" because it matters whether they are "fact or fiction."[32] And in these tests of credibility, Trouillot argues, we exploit the intransigent materiality of the record left by the events that concern us.

What happened leaves traces, some of which are quite concrete—buildings, dead bodies, censuses, monuments, diaries, political boundaries—that limit the range and significance of any historical narrative. This is one of the many reasons why not any fiction can pass for history: the materiality of the socio-historical processes (historicity 1) sets the stage for future historical narratives (historicity 2).[33]

Trouillot identifies three strategies by which historians make use of these resources to identify and counteract silences: repositioning evidence, critical historiography, and the cross-examination of contrasting interpretations. Consider the critical appraisal of ignorance and the constructive responses to it by which such strategies have been used to negotiate the silences inherent in one particularly rich tradition of North American archaeological research.

The earthen mound sites of the Mississippi, Tennessee, Illinois, and Ohio river valleys—sites associated with the prehistoric Hopewell and Mississippian cultures—are among the most intensively studied in North America; they have been mapped, described, excavated, interpreted, and speculated about since the mid-nineteenth century. In a symposium sponsored by the Society for American Archaeology in 2003—"Emblems of American Archaeology's Past: Eminent Mound Sites of the Eastern Woodlands Revisited"—a dozen archaeologists currently working on these sites took stock of the trajectory of research through the 100–150 years they have been investigated.[34] They were concerned, not only to delineate specific loci and patterns of ignorance that mark this long and complicated research tradition, but also to assess the prospects for making effective use of its accumulated records and finds to address new questions and to redress long-standing gaps and distortions. The Hopewell sites consist of earthworks and settlements ranging from 200 BC to AD 400 (Middle Woodland), associated with horticulture based on indigenous domesticates and with assemblages of artifacts characterized by a distinctive design tradition that incorporates material traded from as far away as the Rocky Mountains and the Appalachians, the Gulf Coast and the Great Lakes. The later Mississippian sites date to AD 950–1550 and are characterized by elaborate ceremonial complexes that include earthworks and extensive palisades as well as mounds, a related design tradition—the Southern Ceremonial Complex—and well-established practices of maize agriculture. Everyone discussing the history of research at these sites acknowledged that the body of accumulated knowledge "crafted by the scholars who preceded us" is an exceedingly mixed legacy[35] and, in assessing this legacy, they illustrate how knowledge and ignorance are co-produced in all the ways suggested by contributors to *The Encyclopedia of Ignorance* and at each of the moments in the historical research process identified by Trouillot.

The Vagaries of Evidence

One might think that, at the very least, a century of investigation would deliver contemporary researchers an enviably rich body of empirical data, but, in fact, this is where the trouble starts. Hopewell and Mississippian mound sites were mapped and excavated in widely varying, inconsistent ways throughout the period in which anthropological archaeology professionalized—its goals shifting and its standards of practice changing dramatically in the process. In the nineteenth century, documentation and opportunistic excavation focused on the highly visible, the monumental, the exotic, and was structured by curiosity about who could possibly have built the mounds that were so prominent in the central North American landscape. It was widely assumed that none of the indigenous peoples living in the region at the time of contact were capable of such massive construction, but even so, the mounds stood as a reproach to claims of manifest destiny and the presumption that the rich lands along the interior waterways were uncultivated and unpeopled. A great many earthworks and mounds were destroyed to make way for construction, or were more slowly dispersed by successively deeper and more destructive plowing, as agriculture was increasingly mechanized and industrialized. Large-scale archaeological projects supported by the Works Projects Administration in the 1930s generated vast quantities of archaeological data, but the detail and precision of documentation varied widely and publication was uneven. Sometimes nothing at all was published, as in the case of Marksville,[36] or only the most superficial of summaries appeared, as at Shiloh.[37] Often even the most substantial publications were highly selective; many of the features reported in field notes went unmentioned in published reports, and general descriptions were published without stratigraphic profiles of excavated trenches or detailed-enough coordinates to allow the reidentification of excavation units.[38] This pattern of expansive excavation and selective recording and publication often continued, on a smaller scale and with a focus on typology and chronology, through the 1950s.

In the last forty years archaeologists have developed more sharply focused and technically sophisticated projects designed not only to refine regional chronologies but to document the internal structure, the sequence of construction, and the occupational histories of "Eminent Mound" sites. This is a necessary foundation for answering more ambitious questions about the function of specific sites and features, regional subsistence patterns, shifting interaction spheres, and, most provocatively, the social organization and the meaning of the distinctive symbolic repertoire of pre-contact Hopewell and Mississippian cultures. Many of the surviving mounds are now protected sites at the state or national level, so excavation is strictly limited and there is a strong presumption that any new fieldwork must be informed as comprehensively as possible by the results of previous field projects; old data must be enlisted to answer new questions.

To this end, archaeologists now working on such sites, represented by contributors to the "Eminent Mounds" symposium, routinely undertake what amounts to a secondary retrieval of facts of the record: they reassemble surviving collections and records; they reconstruct architectural and stratigraphic drawings from field notes; and they integrate whatever they can glean from fragmentary records into comprehensive site maps, sometimes with the help of stratigraphic profiles and other data generated by reopening the trenches excavated by earlier generations of archaeologists. In the process, they find not only that the empirical legacy of 150 years of archaeological work is rife with gaps and inconsistencies, a reflection of evolving retrieval and recording practices, but also that it has been badly compromised by poor storage conditions, sometimes lost altogether,[39] or dispersed among institutions in ways that greatly complicate any systematic use of existing records and collections.[40] The tragedy is that often these maps and photographs, field notes, and collections are all that remains of sites that have long since been heavily looted, plowed under, or bulldozed to make way for land development projects. Even when material survives in the collections of sponsoring institutions, it may be presumed unusable by later generations of archaeologists and ignored.[41]

At the same time archaeologists intent on reclaiming what they can from existing collections and records have discovered unexpectedly rich resources in museum basements and warehouses, pieced together from collections and archives that had been ignored or presumed unusable by intervening generations of archaeologists. The process of recovering this material and putting it to work is often highly labor intensive,[42] and sometimes depends on creative use of new computer-based technologies to effect a variant of

Trouillot's first strategy, quite literally repositioning the evidence. For example, archaeologists working on the Mississippian sites of Aztalan in Wisconsin and Jonathan Creek in Kentucky have transposed all existing site maps to a single GIS system, to which they then link the information they have retrieved from surviving field notes and excavated collections.[43] This has generated some startling results, and represents a strategy of reassessment that throws into relief the contours of systematic bias and elisions—forms of ignorance—that reflect deeply entrenched interpretive conventions.

The Legacy of Interpretative Conventions

Ironically, while the material record of the cultural past has proven distressingly vulnerable to attrition, interpretations of this record have demonstrated remarkable staying power; they "haunt our current understanding,"[44] setting "interpretive frameworks . . . that persist in popular and even in scholarly reviews."[45] The play of power traced by Trouillot is clearly evident in the third and fourth moment production of claims about the archaeological past, manifest in structures of evidence and interpretive theory that have been shaped by institutional interests and cultural politics.

The dominant interpretive themes in the archaeology of Hopewell and Mississippian sites reflect a preoccupation with the question of origins and, by extension, the place of the mound builders in a hierarchy of social, cultural forms that were presumed to lie along a linear trajectory of cultural evolution. The mound builder debates of the nineteenth century were resolved, at least in professional contexts, when excavation revealed burial populations whose morphology was well within the frame of that typical of contemporary Native Americans, as avidly documented by nineteenth-century collectors of skulls and skeletal material. But the fascination with burials, with the exotic and ceremonial, and with the savage (especially evidence of warfare and cannibalism) continued to dominate archaeological thinking well into the twentieth century. The legacy of this interpretive tradition is a history of third moment archaeological retrieval in which those working on Hopewell and Mississippian sites have sought out and selectively emphasized forms of evidence that are consonant with the political and cultural interests that animate fourth moment narratives about the cultural past.

This canalization of archaeological thought and action is evident in the entrenched presumption that mounds were all burial sites or cremateoria. At the Middle Woodland earthwork sites of Fort Ancient in Ohio and Poverty Point in Louisiana, the mortuary interpretation sometimes originated in the reports of excavators in the 1890s and 1930s who, it turns out, actually described a puzzling *lack* of skeletal material, or the presence of fragmentary and ambiguous faunal remains that have since disappeared from collections.[46] In cases where mortuary material was recovered, fascination with the exotic dominates; the incidence of disarticulated or dispersed human bones at Aztalan is the basis for attributions of cannibalism that have proven hard to dislodge.[47] In the first case, in which a burial function is inferred in the absence of mortuary remains, ignorance is addressed by recovering the history of the narrative at issue, returning to original sources, and reexamining the archaeological evidence on which these narratives are purportedly based. And in the second, the crucial strategy has been to reassess the background assumptions that inform the interpretation. Attributions of cannibalism are only plausible if interpretation presupposes a narrowly ethnocentric set of assumptions about mortuary practice; if a broader range of ethnohistoric sources are considered, it becomes clear that disarticulated and dispersed skeletal material is the archaeological signature for a variety of mortuary traditions that involve elaborate preparation of the dead and secondary burial, not necessarily (or only) cannibalism.[48] This is an instance of Trouillot's strategy of repositioning evidence that extends to the interpretive sources as well as the surviving material record of archaeological subjects.[49]

These strategies of repositioning evidence and critical historiography, supplemented by Trouillot's third strategy—that of exploiting dissonance among interpretive conventions to identify points at which projective conventions may be operating—all play a role in identifying and countering simplistic models of social organization that have dominated fourth moment interpretive and explanatory theorizing. A limited repertoire of narratives about mound builder cultures both reinforces and is reinforced by a selective focus on the monumental and the exotic. In most general terms, this interpretive tradition reflects the lingering influence of nineteenth-century theories of cultural evolution. The local and regional histories of these sites are routinely read in terms of the conventions of a theory of cultural evolution that posits a linear progression from bands to tribes to chiefdoms to states. Interpretation vacillates between a tendency to identify mound centers either as emergent proto-states or as inherently unstable chiefdoms, exaggerating their social differentiation, internal complexity, hierarchy, and centralization of power, on the one hand, or emphasizing the repetitive structure and relative autonomy of the local polities that periodically coalesced into regional networks, on the other.[50] Neither set of conventions fits these sites well when the complexity of occupational histories is taken into account.

On conventional accounts it was assumed that the major Hopewell and Mississippian sites must have been occupied continuously, showing gradual, sustained growth into their status as regional centers, followed by precipitous collapse. But site chronologies and occupational histories— now refined through reanalysis of existing data and reexcavation of old trenches to establish stratigraphic sequences—demonstrate that many of these sites were periodically abandoned, sometimes for as much as 100 years at a time in occupational histories of 450 years.[51] When they were occupied, they expanded and contracted in size and configuration; their periods of major fluorescence were not necessarily the culmination of a history of successively larger and more visible occupation.[52] It had also been presumed that, where regional commonalities are evident in the style of earthworks, various classes of material culture, and inferred ceremonial practice, these must have diffused from regional centers to smaller sites in the hinterland. There is certainly evidence of a distinctive Hopewell architectural grammar marked by common units of measure,[53] astronomical alignment in the internal structure of Mississippian sites,[54] and widely distributed stylistic conventions (for example, the Southern Ceremonial Complex), but reexamination of regional and site-specific chronologies makes it clear that simple patterns of migration and diffusion are implausible. Sites identified as regional centers prove to have been abandoned during the periods in which their influence was assumed to have been at its height.[55] Sites like Marksville, that had been interpreted as Hopewell outposts, show persistent and puzzling anomalies that suggest they were manifestations of a locally derived tradition onto which some features familiar from Hopewell sites were grafted: a "veneer on a local tradition."[56] Moreover, local traditions are proving to have been highly variable within the regions and periods of their influence. Stylistic diversity within sites (of architecture and of artifacts) had been interpreted as evidence of displacement by or coexistence between distinct cultural groups. At sites like Jonathan Creek, however, reworked chronologies suggest the contemporaneity of styles that had been assumed to mark successive occupations, and the integration of site maps brings into focus intra-site distribution patterns that overwhelm any simplistic model of group affiliation.[57]

These critical insights reinforce a healthy respect for the systematic nature of our ignorance about these cultures. They suggest that what archaeologists are dealing with in these reaches of the cultural past are social, cultural formations that do not conform either to the idealized stages posited by theories of cultural evolution or to the expectations generated by a repertoire of canonical ethnohistoric examples.[58] They throw into relief the effects of a canalization of research by narrative conventions that shape the world of thought in which "Eminent Mounds" are investigated on every level, from fieldwork strategies and descriptive claims about the contents of the record, to culture-specific reconstructions and broad explanatory theory. At the same time, they open up intriguing new possibilities for interpretation. The upshot is an emerging consensus that conventional assumptions about cultural evolution, succession, and interaction must be systematically reassessed. Muller argues against exaggerating vertical hierarchy and the degree of social differentiation in Mississippian societies, and King urges attention to shifting elite strategies at Etowah, while Kelly, Brown, and Machiran argue for recognizing a dynamic tension between the corporate and network strategies of elites at Cahokia. Milner and Schroeder caution, more generally, against the imposition of "restrictive and static cultural categories" derived from evolutionary schemas; when archaeologists attend to a broader range of ethnohistoric sources than is typically considered, the well-documented volatility of chiefdoms calls into question the usefulness of this category for understanding the prehistoric societies associated with Eminent Mound sites.[59]

Ignorance is atlantic, to be sure, but focusing on how it is produced and maintained holds the potential for systematic, empirically and theoretically well-informed calibration of what we know. The greatest challenge lies in resisting the pressure to assume that when comprehensive, definitive knowledge lies out of reach, the result is undifferentiated ignorance.

It seems to be a common defect of human minds that they tend to crave for complete certainty of belief or disbelief.[60]

NOTES

1. Duncan and Weston-Smith, "Editorial Preface," *The Encyclopaedia of Ignorance* (New York: Pergamon Press, 1977), ix.

2. C. W. Kilmister, "Mathematics in the Social Sciences"; M. M. Lehman, "Human Thought and Action as an Ingredient of System Behaviour," *Encyclopaedia of Ignorance*, 175–189, 347–354.

3. O. R. Frisch, "Why," *Encyclopaedia of Ignorance*, 1–4.

4. Sir John Kendrew, "Introduction," *Encyclopaedia of Ignorance*, 205–207.

5. D. C. Johanson, "Rethinking the Origins of the Genus *Homo*," *Encyclopaedia of Ignorance*, 243–250.

6. H. B. Barlow, "The Languages of the Brain"; H. A. Buchtel and G. Berlucchi, "Learning and Memory and the Nervous System"; R. W. Sperry, "Problems Outstanding in the Evolution of Brain Function," *Encyclopaedia of Ignorance*, 250–272, 317–330, 283–298, 423–433.

7. R. A. Lyttleton, "The Nature of Knowledge," *Encyclopaedia of Ignorance*, 12.

8. Kendrew, "Introduction," *Encyclopaedia of Ignorance*, 206.

9. W. B. Webb, "Sleep"; R. L. Gregory, "Consciousness"; Kendrew, "Introduction," *Encyclopaedia of Ignorance*, 374, 276, 206.

10. For example, Sperry, "Problems Outstanding," *Encyclopaedia of Ignorance*, 432–433.

11. Kendrew, "Introduction," *Encyclopaedia of Ignorance*, 206.

12. Sperry, "Problems Outstanding," *Encyclopaedia of Ignorance*, 424.

13. Lehman, "Human Thought and Action," *Encyclopaedia of Ignorance*, 354.

14. J. H. P. Willis, "Drug Addiction," *Encyclopaedia of Ignorance*, 370.

15. N. L. Falcon, "Ignorance beneath Our Feet," *Encyclopaedia of Ignorance*, 420.

16. Barry Barnes and David Bloor, "Relativism, Rationalism and the Sociology of Knowledge," *Rationality and Relativism*, eds. M. Hollis and S. Lukes (Oxford: Basil Blackwell, 1982), 22–23; Bruno Latour, *We Have Never Been Modern* (Hempstead, UK: Harvester Wheatsheaf, 1993), 24, 103.

17. Peter Novick, *That Noble Dream: The "Objectivity Question" and the American Historical Profession* (Cambridge, UK: Cambridge University Press, 1988).

18. Alison Wylie, *Thinking from Things: Essays in the Philosophy of Archaeology* (Berkeley: University of California Press, 2002), esp. "Philosophy from the Ground Up," 1–23.

19. Michel-Rolph Trouillot, *Silencing the Past: Power and the Production of History* (Boston: Beacon, 1995), 4–13.

20. Trouillot, *Silencing the Past*, 8, 26.

21. In the debates that gave rise to the New Archaeology in the 1960s and 1970s, traditional archaeology was identified with culture-historical inquiry, a research program

chiefly concerned with "space-time systematics"—establishing chronological and typological schemes—that was said to have dominated anthropological archaeology in North America up to the 1960s. In fact, antecedents of the New Archaeology are evident well before its appearance, and forms of so-called traditional archaeology continue to characterize research in many contexts. Wylie, "The Conceptual Core of the New Archaeology," *Thinking from Things*, 57–76.

22. Diogenes of Sinope was a philosopher associated with the Cynics of the fourth century BCE who, in renouncing worldly wealth and ambition, was said to have taken up temporary residence in a large tub. M. A. Smith, "The Limitations of Inference in Archaeology," *Archaeological News Letter* 6 (1955): 1–7, esp. 2; Wylie, "How New Is the New Archaeology?" *Thinking from Things*, 5–41.

23. Smith, "Limitations of Inference," 4–5.

24. Christopher Hawkes, "Archaeological Theory and Method: Some Suggestions from the Old World," *American Anthropologist* 56 (1954): 155–168. See also Stuart Piggott, *Approach to Archaeology* (Cambridge, MA: Harvard University Press, 1959); and Bruce G. Trigger, *A History of Archaeological Thought* (Cambridge, UK: Cambridge University Press, 1989), 392–393.

25. Wylie, "Conceptual Core," 61–76.

26. See, for example, Lewis R. Binford, "Archeology as Anthropology," *American Antiquity* 28 (1962): 217–225; "A Consideration of Archeological Research Design," *American Antiquity* 29 (1964): 425–441; "Archaeological Perspectives," *New Perspectives in Archeology*, eds. Lewis R. Binford and Sally R. Binford (Chicago: Aldine, 1968), 5–32. Discussed in Wylie, "Conceptual Core," esp. 63–64, 73–76.

27. Lyttleton, "The Nature of Knowledge," 11.

28. For example, Michael Shanks and Christopher Tilley, *Re-Constructing Archaeology* (Cambridge, UK: Cambridge University Press, 1987), esp. iii, 104. For discussion, see Wylie, "The Interpretive Dilemma" and "'Heavily Decomposing Red Herrings': Middle Ground in the Anti-/Postprocessualism Wars," *Thinking from Things*, 117–126, 171–178.

29. Ian Hacking, "Weapons Research and the Form of Scientific Knowledge," *Canadian Journal of Philosophy* Supplementary vol. 12 (1986): 237–260. Reprinted in *The Social Construction of What?* (Cambridge, MA: Harvard University Press, 1999), 163–185.

30. Hacking, "Weapons Research," 259.

31. In the case of carbon-14 dating, substantial resources were brought to bear to facilitate the development of peacetime applications of nuclear physics immediately after World War II. Archaeological chronologies have been dramatically reframed and extended as a result, although the process of standardization and calibration has been more complex than anticipated. By contrast, the use of stable (nonradioactive) isotope analysis to reconstruct lifetime dietary profiles has been limited by a lack of any comparable support, despite its promise. Alison Wylie, "Rethinking Unity as a Working Hypothesis for Philosophy of Science: How Archaeologists Exploit the Disunity of Science," *Perspectives on Science* 7.3 (2000): 293–317; "Philosophy in Practice: Evidence Stabilizing Technologies in Archaeology," presented in "Methodology in Practice," Philosophy of Science Association Biennial Meeting (Milwaukee, WI, 2002).

32. Trouillot, *Silencing the Past*, 11, 13.

33. Trouillot, *Silencing the Past*, 29.

34. Symposium organized by Sissel Schroeder for the 68th Annual Meeting of the Society

for American Archaeology (Milwaukee, WI, 2003). Wherever possible I cite published versions of the papers presented in this symposium, or related publications on the sites discussed.

35. Lynne Sullivan, "Archaeological Time Constructs and the Construction of the Hiwassee Island Mound," *75 Years of TVA Archaeology*, eds. Todd Ahlman and Erin Pritchard (Knoxville: University of Tennessee Press, forthcoming), 1.

36. Charles R. McGimsey, Katherine M. Roberts, E. Edwin Jackson, Michael L. Hargrave, "Marksville Then and Now: 75 Years of Digging," *Louisiana Archaeological Society Bulletin* 26 (2005): 1, 4. Marksville is identified as a type site for the Middle Woodland in the Lower Mississippi River valley, significant for demonstrating the extent of the Hopewell cultural traditions that had chiefly been identified with sites in Ohio.

37. Paul D. Welch, David G. Anderson, and John E. Cornelison, "A Century of Archaeology at Shiloh Indian Mounds," paper presented at the 68th Annual Meeting of the Society for American Archaeology (Milwaukee, WI, 2003). Welch, Anderson, and Cornelison describe a four-page report that was the only publication on excavations at Shiloh that had opened up thousands of square feet. See also Paul D. Welch, *Archaeology at Shiloh Indian Mounds, 1899–1999* (Tuscaloosa: University of Alabama Press, 2006), 23.

38. Welch, *Shiloh Indian Mounds*, 30, 35–40.

39. Welch describes the difficulty of working with surviving collections from WPA-era excavations at the Museum of Natural History, given fragmentary documentation (*Shiloh Indian Mounds*, 23–24) (see note 41 below). McGimsey et al. observe that the artifact collections generated by extensive excavations at Marksville in the 1930s "are substantial and would have been of great value as the ceramic characteristics and culture history of the Marksville period were being defined" but that many of the original field records had been lost ("Marksville Then and Now," 3). King found that not only had all the documents been lost that might link artifact collections to specific excavation contexts at mound sites in the Etowah Valley, but "a substantial percentage of the artifacts collected [by WPA excavation teams] were discarded after the original analysis was performed"; all that remain are type collections "composed of unique sherds and representative examples of more common types." Adam King, *Etowah: The Political History of a Chiefdom Capital* (Tuscaloosa: University of Alabama Press, 2003), 36.

40. "Working with the Etowah data is made more complex by the fact that four different institutions sponsored excavations at the site, so collections are housed in six locations . . . [each of which] has its own history, organizational system, and procedures for accessing collections." Adam King, "Return to Etowah, Ancient Cult Center," paper presented at the 68th Annual Meeting of the Society for American Archaeology (Milwaukee, WI, 2003), 2. King outlines the history of Etowah Valley archaeology in more detail and describes the surviving collections and records in *Etowah*, 33–36, 50–52.

41. Sometimes, Connolly observes, there is a tendency to dismiss the value of surviving records, and to generate interpretations that do not take into account counterevidence available in the field notes and collections generated by earlier generations of archaeologists (pers. comm., May 18, 2006). He describes, for example, the quality of the field records compiled by some of the excavators who worked at Fort Ancient in the 1940s (e.g., by Morgan, whose records included a video of the excavations as well as detailed profiles and maps), and the useful insights to be derived from records of less systematic work undertaken sixty years earlier (e.g., by Moorehead in 1887). These provided the basis for reassessing Prufer's "defensive fortification/vacant ceremonial center model" of the 1960s. Robert P. Connolly, "The Evidence for Habitation at the Fort Ancient Earthworks, Warrant County, Ohio,"

Ohio Hopewell Community Organization, eds. W. S. Dancy and P. J. Pacheco (Kent, OH: Kent State University Press, 1997), 251–282.

42. Welch describes the groundwork laid by Bruce Smith, who assembled scattered documents related to Shiloh over several decades, and then spent weeks working with the collections held by the National Museum of Natural History collections in order to "piece together what is recorded and to discover what information is truly missing." *Shiloh Indian Mounds*, 28, 23–24.

43. Sissel Schroeder, "Reclaiming New Deal–Era Civic Archaeology: Exploring the Legacy of William S. Webb and the Jonathan Creek Site," *CRM: The Journal of Heritage Stewardship* 2.1 (2005): 53–71, esp. 57–59; Lynne Goldstein and Donald H. Gaff, "Recasting the Past: Examining Assumptions about Aztalan," *The Wisconsin Archaeologist* 83.2 (2002): 98–110, esp. 107–108.

44. Peter Cunningham, Lynne Goldstein, and Donald H. Gaff, "Reexamining and Reinterpreting Aztalan: Making Old Data Useful by Integrating It with New Approaches," paper presented at the 68th Annual Meeting of the Society for American Archaeology (Milwaukee, WI, 2003), 1.

45. Jon Muller, "Kincaid Mx1, Pp1," paper presented at the 68th Annual Meeting of the Society for American Archaeology (Milwaukee, WI, 2003), 1. See also Jon Muller, "The History of Archaeology in West Virginia," *Histories of Southeastern Archaeology*, eds. Shannon Tushingham, Jane Hill, and Charles H. McNutt (Tuscaloosa: University of Alabama Press, 2002), 99–114.

46. Robert P. Connolly, "From Authority to Guide: The Archaeologist in Public Interpretation," paper presented at the 68th Annual Meeting of the Society for American Archaeology (Milwaukee, WI, 2003), Fort Ancient, 3–4; Poverty Point, 6–9. See also Robert P. Connolly and Bradley T. Lepper, eds., *The Fort Ancient Earthworks: Prehistoric Lifeways of the Hopewell Culture in Southwestern Ohio* (Columbus: Ohio History Society, 2004), 85–113.

47. Cunningham, Goldstein, and Gaff, "Aztalan," 2.

48. Goldstein makes a general argument for recognizing the diversity of mortuary practice; "context is everything," and simplistic interpretive assumptions about the practices associated with particular types of skeletal treatment or biophysical attributes are largely untenable. Lynne Goldstein, "Mortuary Analysis and Bioarchaeology," *Bioarchaeology: The Contextual Analysis of Human Remains*, eds. L. A. Beck and J. E. Buikstra (Burlington, MA: Elsevier, 2006), 375–388. Reassessment of the assumptions that underpin attributions of cannibalism appear in Gordon F. M. Rakita, Jane Buikstra, Lane Beck, eds., *Interacting with the Dead: Perspectives on Mortuary Archaeology for the New Millennium* (Gainesville: University Press of Florida, 2005); see especially Estella Weiss-Krejci, "Excarnation, Evisceration, and Exhumation in Medieval and Post-Medieval Europe," *Interacting with the Dead*, 155, 170–172.

49. For a more detailed account of these strategies for deploying evidence drawn both from archaeological subjects and from interpretive sources, see Wylie, "The Reaction against Analogy" and "The Constitution of Archaeological Evidence," *Thinking from Things*, 136–153, 185–199.

50. This dynamic of debate is described in a number of contexts. See, for example, George R. Milner and Sissel Schroeder, "Mississippian Sociopolitical Systems," *Great Towns and Regional Polities in the Prehistoric American Southwest and Southeast*, ed. Jill E. Neitzel (Albuquerque: University of New Mexico Press, 1999), 95–107, esp. 96–99.

51. Sullivan, "Hiwasee," 7–8.

52. King, *Etowah*, 60–64, 73, 81–83, 140–143.

53. Robert P. Connolly, "Architectural Grammar Rules at the Fort Ancient Hilltop Enclosure," *Ancient Earthen Enclosures of the Eastern Woodlands*, eds. Robert C. Mainfort and Lynne P. Sullivan (Gainesville: University Press of Florida, 1998), 85–113.

54. John E. Kelly, "Redefining Cahokia: Principles and Elements of Community Organization," *The Ancient Skies and Sky Watchers of Cahokia: Woodhenges, Eclipses, and Cahokian Cosmology*, ed. Melvin L. Fowler, Special Issue: *The Wisconsin Archaeologist* 77 (1996): 97–119.

55. Sullivan, "Hiwassee," 8.

56. McGimsey et al., "Marksville Then and Now," 11.

57. For example, Schroeder observes that "as was common in the mid-twentieth century, Webb assumed that similar material traits between archaeological contexts and ethnohistoric and ethnographic descriptions reflected 'common origins, history, and ethnicity,' failing to recognize, as we do today, that evolutionary convergence and independent invention can produce material similarities." Schroeder, "Jonathan Creek," 64.

58. Reflecting on the ways in which prehistoric societies of the U.S. Southeast violate the expectations of these categories, Yoffee, Fisch, and Milner argue that "not all prehistoric societies [can be assumed to] lie on a single evolutionary trajectory that leads to statehood"; the regional polities of the Mississippian era are interesting precisely because they may be examples of "alternative evolutionary trajectories" (Norman Yoffee, Suzanne K. Fish, and George R. Milner, "Comunidades, Ritualities, Chiefdoms: Social Evolution in the American Southwest and Southeast," *Great Towns and Regional Polities*, ed. Neitzel, 261). In a similar vein, Goldstein argues against a tendency to equate cultural complexity with stratification. See Lynne Goldstein, "Ancient Southwest Mortuary Practices: Perspectives from Outside the Southwest," *Ancient Burial Practices in the American Southwest: Archaeology, Physical Anthropology, and Native American Perspectives*, eds. Douglas R. Mitchell and Judy L. Brunson-Hadley (Albuquerque: University of New Mexico Press, 2001), 249–253.

59. Muller, "Kincaid," 20; for a more detailed discussion, see Muller's arguments against state or proto-state attributions: Jon Muller, "Southeastern Interaction and Integration," *Great Towns and Regional Polities*, ed. Neitzel, 143–158, esp. 157–158; "Regional Interaction in the Later Southeast," *Native American Interactions: Multiscalar Analyses and Interpretations in the Eastern Woodlands*, eds. Michael S. Nassaney and Kenneth E. Sassaman (Knoxville: University of Tennessee Press, 1995), 317–340, esp. 321–324, 335–336. King provides an overview of debate about how the political structures of chiefdoms have been characterized, with particular attention to the distinction between network and corporate strategies employed by elites in the exercise and maintenance of political authority (*Etowah*, 7). He and Kelly, Brown, and Machiran make use of these categories in analysis of the complexity of Etowah and of Cahokia, respectively: King, *Etowah*, 140–143; Kelly, Brown, and Machiran, "Cahokia," 7, 10. See also Charles R. Cobb and Adam King, "Re-Inventing Mississippian Tradition at Etowa, Georgia," *Journal of Archaeological Method and Theory* 12 (2005): 167–192. Schroeder calls into question the assumptions of cultural stability that informed WPA-era interpretations of Mississippian sites ("Jonathan Creek," 64–66). In developing their argument against the use of cultural categories derived from conventional evolutionary schemes, Milner and Schroeder argue that, although "Mississippian societies are generally called chiefdoms," some show evidence of "a structure more closely approximating sociopolitical formations commonly referred to as tribes," and those that

do seem appropriately described as chiefdoms manifest patterns of "cycling"—"periods of formation, florescence, and fragmentation"—that undermine any expectation that they are on a trajectory of development toward "truly stratified socio-political systems" (Milner and Schroeder, "Mississippian Sociopolitical Systems," 96, 103).

60. Lyttleton, "The Nature of Knowledge," 14.

PART III

Theorizing Ignorance

CHAPTER 9

Social Theories of Ignorance

MICHAEL J. SMITHSON

DESPITE THE THREAT of insoluble problems and paradoxes, it is possible to attain useful knowledge about ignorance. For Western intellectuals, four characterizations can clear a path to initial insights:

1. Ignorance is socially constructed but this realization neither necessitates relativism nor a denial of "real world" influences.
2. Ignorance is not always a negative aspect of human affairs. In fact, it is an essential component in social relations, organizations, and culture. People are motivated to create and maintain ignorance, often systematically.
3. Ignorance is not invariably a disadvantage for the ignoramus.
4. Ignorance is neither marginal nor aberrant in its impact. It is a pervasive and fundamental influence in human cognition, emotion, action, social relations, and culture.

Most of this chapter is devoted to elaborating these four points in hopes of advancing our understanding how ignorance is constructed, the work it does, and the impacts it has. First, however, we must attend to two preliminary issues: terminology and what constitutes a genuinely social theory of ignorance.

A CONFUSION OF DEFINITIONS AND TERMINOLOGY

One difficulty plaguing "ignorance" is that the scattered literature on the topic lacks an agreed-on nomenclature. Let us begin by considering terms for the overarching concept in this domain. Böschen and Wehling use the term *nichtwissen*, whose English equivalent is "nonknowledge."[1] This usage echoes earlier proposals for a "sociology of nonknowledge."[2] A related, if less common, term is *nescience* (total ignorance). Alternative usages have referred to a social theory of *ignorance*.[3] Knorr-Cetina introduces the term *negative knowledge*, that is, knowledge of the limits of knowing, mistakes in attempts to know, things that interfere with knowing, and what people do not want to know.[4] This concept is quite similar to *closed ignorance* in Faber and Proops.[5] Outside the social sciences, the most popular general term seems to be *uncertainty*. For example, this is so in artificial intelligence.[6]

Knorr-Cetina and I have accurately identified the main problem here, namely that anyone referring to ignorance cannot avoid making claims to know something about who is ignorant of what.[7] It probably does not matter greatly what term we choose so long as our definition of it recognizes this point. In this chapter I will use *ignorance* as the generic term.

The intuition that there might be different kinds of ignorance has motivated a number of scholars to propose various distinctions and taxonomies.[8] One of the most popular distinctions is absence or neglect versus distortion.[9] Another popular distinction is reducible versus irreducible ignorance, as suggested in the negative-knowledge concepts articulated by Knorr-Cetina and Faber and Proops.[10] A third, often implicit, distinction is between that which can be known versus that which must not be known (for example, the pioneering work by Douglas on taboo).[11] Taking a cue from Unger, I distinguish the active voice (ignoring) from the passive voice (being ignorant).[12] Brown echoes this when he observes that "in science, we may be missing useful knowledge either because: (1) we intentionally close a problem (act of ignoring) or (2) we are unaware of alternative views of the world, or their potential utility (ignorance)."[13] In a similar vein in this book, Proctor distinguishes among ignorance as a native state (or resource), ignorance as a lost realm (or selective choice), and ignorance as a deliberate and strategic ploy (active construct).[14]

Some taxonomies of ignorance have emphasized distinctions that operate at a meta-level rather than describing the nature of different kinds of ignorance per se. The most popular distinction is between knowing that we don't know and not knowing that we don't know.[15] I prefer the terms *conscious ignorance* and *meta-ignorance*.

Several disciplines have produced relatively sophisticated and productive distinctions among special kinds of ignorance and uncertainty. In addition to at least three major schools of probability theory, several different kinds of mathematical uncertainty measures have been proposed, in the setting of alternative mathematical uncertainty frameworks such as fuzzy set theory and belief functions.[16] Scholars of ignorance could benefit from these developments in two ways: as conceptual suggestions for their own theories and as exemplars of distinctions-in-use by a particular linguistic community.

Should we even attempt a definition or taxonomy of ignorance? Brown and Rogers eschew taxonomies in their study of miscommunication on the grounds that classification uncouples phenomena from their contexts, thereby sacrificing interpretive richness.[17] But it is not difficult to come up with definitional criteria that are sensitive to both context and viewpoint.

My definition seems to handle these problems reasonably well: "A is ignorant from B's viewpoint if A fails to agree with or show awareness of ideas which B defines as actually or potentially valid."[18] This definition allows B to define what she or he means by ignorance. It also permits self-attributed ignorance, since A and B may be the same person. Most importantly, it incorporates anything B thinks A could or should know (but doesn't) and anything that B thinks A must not know (and doesn't). B's notions about ignorance may be as context dependent and subjective as required.

Two aforementioned distinctions, also generally helpful, are not always clearly made in writings about ignorance. The meta- versus primary-level distinction is crucial; we must specify whether meta-knowledge or meta-ignorance is our focus as opposed to knowledge and ignorance themselves. Likewise, a ubiquitous and important distinction is between ignorance that people think is reducible and ignorance that is irreducible.

How can we assess what other typological distinctions are worth making? I suggest four criteria, namely whether candidate kinds of ignorance:

1. Are consistently distinguished from other kinds when referred to in communication by members of the same linguistic community
2. Are accorded statuses or roles distinct from other kinds in the same situations or for the same purposes in social interaction

3. Produce different social consequences for those to whom they are attributed
4. Are (dis)preferred to other kinds of ignorance

An example fulfilling the first criterion is Hacking's observations of how the term *probability* changed meaning with the advent of modern probability theory.[19] The second and third criteria are exemplified by the belief that the consequences of being found out uttering a falsehood will be worse than being found out omitting part of a truth (for example, Burgoon, Callister, and Hunsaker's investigation of equivocation or omission versus falsification in doctor-patient interviews in which about 85 percent of the participants admitted to omission but only 34 percent admitted to falsification).[20] Finally, an example of the fourth criterion is evidence that for many people probabilistic uncertainty is preferred to ambiguity, which in turn is preferred to conflict.[21]

Although I am among those who have proposed all-weather taxonomies of ignorance, I regard it as clearly advisable for researchers to use criteria such as the four suggested above to guide their choices of terms and definitions.[22] For instance, if we wish to understand how artists in the Dada movement used "uncertainty" and "chance" in art making then we should start by understanding what they meant by these terms and how they used them before imposing our own terms or definitions.

CONSTRUCTIVISM AND IGNORANCE

Whereas it is very difficult to know anything directly about our own or anyone else's ignorance, it is not as hard to find out about people's representations and accounts of ignorance. Ignorance, like knowledge, is largely socially constructed. The study of how people represent, explain, justify, and use ignorance also has plenty of room for debates among constructivist positions ranging from relativism to realism.

Most of the literature on uncertainty in disciplines such as economics, psychology, and (to a lesser extent) communications presupposes agreement among all stakeholders on what constitutes knowledge and ignorance. Yet it seems obvious that the behavior of a dugong in waters off Cape York, Australia, will convey rather different "information" to a marine biologist and a Torres Strait Island fisherman. Accordingly, an in-depth understanding of how ignorance is construed and constituted requires attention to the following particulars. First, what claims are made regarding who is ignorant about what? Second, how do these claims match on aspects of what knowledge and ignorance are, and what can and cannot be known? Third, how are stakeholders using and responding to their own and others' claims about ignorance? What are the consequences of these notions about ignorance in social interaction?

Conversely, constructivist theories have tended to be biologically, psychologically, and economically blind. This error should be avoided in social theories of ignorance, which, after all, concern attributions about mental states and processes. Material from cognitive psychology, ethnology, communications studies, and behavioral economics can help establish connections between ignorance and relevant phenomena, such as selective attention, denial, forgetting, miscommunication, privacy, and trust.

CULTURAL SOURCES

Where, in our cultural stock, do our ideas about ignorance come from? I propose two principal, though not exhaustive, sources: *commonsense realism* and *commonsense sociality*. Commonsense realism encompasses everything we believe or think about how the nonsocial world works, including sacred as well as profane domains (to invoke the Durkheimian distinction). Commonsense sociality refers to our beliefs about the social world and includes our theories of mind. Both kinds of common sense are essentially realist. Regardless of the ontological or epistemological positions adopted by scholars and researchers, as Rosa points out, "realism—the idea that a world exists independent of percipient human observers . . . is the bedrock of our commonsense ideas of the world around us," and, more pointedly, many laypersons are ontological realists.[23]

Although ignorance may be socially constructed, we should be open-minded about the origins of our primary metaphors for ignorance. After all, some of them appear to be shared with other species and may have been selected in evolutionary processes. The examples for which we have the best evidence of this are the temporal and spatial analogues of uncertainty. Many species (including ours) behave as if events or influences that are nearby or in the near future are more certain than those farther away or further into the future (see Rachlin for an excellent overview of the research on delay).[24] The underlying metaphor is that certainties are here and now. Uncertainties are later and farther away. Delay is uncertainty. Distance is uncertainty.

Even the hallmark of a "theory of mind," namely the ability to infer a state of ignorance or false belief in another organism, may not be unique to humans. In humans, it emerges almost ubiquitously in early childhood at about 3–4 years of age, but the extent to which it manifests itself in culturally specific ways is an open question.[25]

WHAT IS AND WHAT IS NOT A "SOCIAL" THEORY OF "IGNORANCE"?

Put simply, a social theory of ignorance should be about ignorance and it should focus on ignorance with sociocultural origins. The literature on uncertainty and ignorance frequently conflates theoretical concerns. This is an attempt to provide some elementary but helpful clarifications by distinguishing among four different kinds of accounts that focus on ignorance.

1. *Ignorance as encountered in the external world*: Accounts of how ignorance and uncertainty arise in the nonsocial world. These include science (and scientific accounts of the limits of science; compare Horgan), as well as epistemological and religious frameworks that make claims about nonknowledge.[26] These accounts make strong claims about meta-knowledge and explain ignorance in exogenous (and usually nonsocial) terms.

2. *Ignorance as emergent, constructed, and imposed*: Accounts of how ignorance and uncertainty are constructed, imposed, and manipulated by agents. These accounts treat ignorance as at least partly socially constructed. In some cases, ignorance is deliberately or intentionally constructed, whereas in others it emerges as a by-product of some social process. Either way, these can be genuinely social theories of ignorance.

3. *Managing under ignorance*: Accounts of how people think and act in uncertain environments. Some of these accounts may invoke or refer

to ignorance and uncertainty, but they are not necessarily theories about those topics.

4. *Managing ignorance*: Accounts of how people think about ignorance or uncertainty and how they act on it. The distinction between this kind of account and (2) is admittedly fuzzy. Accounts in (2) tend to emphasize the notion that the construction and distribution of knowledge and ignorance are implicated in power relations. Accounts that fall in this fourth category place greater emphasis on individual agency, the micro-level, focusing on how people conceptualize, represent, negotiate, and respond to ignorance.

Only theories in the second and fourth categories can become fully fledged social theories of ignorance. Much of the recent sociological literature on risk falls into the third category and therefore cannot form the basis for a social theory of ignorance. Both Beck and Giddens claim that an upsurge of ignorance, indicated by unpredictability, lack of control, and unintended outcomes, is a major driving force of contemporary modern societies.[27] But their accounts neglect the issues that would need to be addressed by a social theory of ignorance. Neither fleshes out any theory of how people might come to believe that ignorance has increased (to say nothing of whether their own or someone else's has increased), what kinds of ignorance people think have increased, or even how people conceptualize their own and other people's ignorance.

In contrast, much of the work in the present volume and other work by its contributors falls squarely in the second category. Robert Proctor's account of efforts by the tobacco industry to obfuscate the link between smoking and lung cancer is an exemplar of ignorance strategically created or imposed.[28] Likewise, Michaels and Monforton explicate a strategy whereby opponents of health and environmental regulations "manufacture uncertainty" by calling into question the validity of the science on which the regulations are based.[29] In another vein, Schiebinger provides thoroughgoing examples of how colonial-period European scientific and social priorities were oriented to pursue some kinds of knowledge and neglect others.[30]

Theory and research in categories (2) and (4) can fruitfully exchange ideas and findings with those in category (3). For example, in line with the aforementioned doctor-patient interview study by Burgoon, Callister, and Hunsaker, Brown and Levinson's work on politeness suggests that people intending to be polite to one another will resort to what they consider to be ambiguity or vagueness more than outright distortion or deception.[31]

THE NEGATIVE BIAS TOWARD IGNORANCE

Western intellectual culture is predominantly about banishing or reducing ignorance, and negative associations with ignorance are the default, even though this is manifestly not so in quotidian social life. Common metaphors for ignorance are negative.[32] For example, ignorance is blindness; to know is to see. Or knowledge is power; ignorance is helplessness and impotence. Some of the best illustrations of the overwhelmingly negative bias toward uncertainty and ignorance in the human sciences occur in the psychology and communications literature. However, both of these disciplines also yield valuable concepts and insights for agnotology. I will briefly examine the views of uncertainty and ignorance in psychology and communications studies.

There are, broadly speaking, three traditional normative orientations regarding how people deal with the unknown in psychology. Perhaps the oldest is the "Knowledge Seeker," contained in the psychoanalytic canons for the well-adjusted individual and found in most branches of ego psychology. This view champions the person who seeks novel information and experience, is open to full and honest communication, can tolerate uncertainty and even ignorance in the short run in order to gain knowledge, and who is not defensive about prior beliefs.[33]

The second tradition, the "Certainty Maximizer," concerns the debilitating consequences of uncertainty, unpredictability, and uncontrollability for the affective, cognitive, and physiological capabilities of the affected organism. Most of the evidence for this viewpoint originates from research concerning learning and adaptation. But an entire set of emotion-based theories also proposes that anxiety is a consequence of uncertainty.[34] Thus, there is a natural tension between this tradition and that of the "Knowledge Seeker."

The third tradition, the "Intuitive Statistician-Economist," originates from psychophysics, perception, and cognitive psychology, and reflects information-processing models of cognition. It is primarily concerned with criteria for rationality in judgment and choice, and the dominant normative viewpoints have been Bayesian probability and a view of humans as hedonic (seeking pleasure and avoiding pain). This view has a lot in common with neo-classical economics.[35]

Despite the obvious tensions among these three perspectives, they are underpinned by the assumption that ignorance is to be reduced (by gaining knowledge or applying logical systems of rules to quantifying and managing it) or banished altogether. There is a potentially interesting but largely unexplored set of linkages between ignorance (and knowledge), emotional responses, moral assessments, and thereby legitimation. For example, ignorance can be used by the ignoramus as a justification for evading culpability or responsibility. In many cultures, education and other forms of knowledge transmission are moralizing projects; so too are ignorance arrangements such as secrecy, privacy, and the protection of innocence. While the exploration of these linkages should not be limited to psychology, that discipline is well equipped to undertake certain parts of this task.

Scholars in the domain of communications have a long-standing interest in misunderstanding and miscommunication, two topics clearly related to ignorance. Until about fifteen years ago communications studies were severely hobbled by what Coupland, Wiemann, and Giles call a "Pollyanna" perspective, in which the default assumption was that miscommunication or misunderstanding was "aberrant behavior which should be eliminated."[36] The negative connotations of terms for these phenomena (for example, "miscommunication," "breakdown," or "failure") were also built into communication theories and research programs (for example, the overwhelming emphasis on studying how to detect deception rather than studying how it is constituted and the often essential roles it plays in social interaction).

The literature on self-disclosure provides a good case in point. A pioneer of this research, Jourard, claimed that people's psychological health is indicated by an ability to make themselves "fully known to at least one other significant human being."[37] Self-disclosure thereby is identified with intimacy, which in turn is privileged as an ideal kind of relationship. McCall and Simmons, and Goffman were early dissidents from the view

that complete communication would solve all problems in human relations.[38] As McCall and Simmons pointed out and as Goffman illustrated
numerous times, many important kinds of social interactions and arrangements would be impossible without some unshared perceptions, secrecy,
and even deception by the participants.

As in psychology, most communications researchers assume that people
are motivated to reduce or banish ignorance and uncertainty.[39] Exceptions
include Babrow, and Afifi and Weiner.[40] Afifi and Weiner's perspective is
noteworthy because it attempts to incorporate aspects of interpersonal
exchange and competing motives to seek or avoid information.

A minority literature in communications and organizations studies
brings attention to the idea that shared communication or meanings are
not necessary for effectively coordinated action. Weick observes that the
coordination of action is more important than the coordination of meanings or beliefs for organizational functioning.[41]

A more radical stance is that unshared understanding actually is essential for some pervasive forms of social life, as in Goffman's work. Eisenberg is among the few communications scholars to have gone so far as to
suggest that lack of shared understandings can enable more effective collaboration than shared understandings would.[42] Likewise, Conrad points
out that many organizations demand and reward people for closed rather
than open communication.[43]

TOWARD A BALANCED VIEW OF IGNORANCE: MIXED MOTIVES AND INTERESTS, BOUNDED RATIONALITY, AND CONFIRMATION BIAS

Contrary to the view of ignorance and uncertainty as primarily negative, human engagement with ignorance or uncertainty is almost always
a mixed-motive enterprise. People sometimes are motivated to discover
or create, maintain, and use ignorance (their own as well as others'). The
very concept of research, for example, presupposes conscious ignorance
about the object of research at the outset; otherwise there is nothing to
research. Numerous social relations depend on systematic ignorance arrangements. Trust and politeness are obvious examples. The cohesion
and smooth operation of many organizations and institutions hinge on

ignorance arrangements, and not only (or even typically) for maintaining power differentials.

It is not difficult to find examples of motives for people to remain ignorant about information directly relevant to themselves even when that information is readily available. The uptake rate on genetic marker tests for individuals with a hereditary risk of a life-threatening disease such as Huntington's chorea or colon cancer is notoriously low, and the same is true regarding the diagnosis of carrier status for such conditions.[44] More "positive" examples include the majority of parents-to-be not wanting to know the gender of their unborn child, social arrangements such as surprise gift giving, entertainment (for example, spoiling the ending of a novel or movie), and games.[45] These examples highlight the cultural and motivational stock from which people fashion decisions about when to know and when not to.

Two strands of empirical and theoretical work in cognitive psychology invoke the idea of generalized and pervasive tendencies to avoid information that do not seem entirely reducible to hedonic motivations. One is the "bounded rationality" view of how people make decisions under uncertainty. The other is the literature on "confirmation bias." Both are important because, although they take ignorance and uncertainty as unproblematic, they highlight universal tendencies that militate against the notion that people indiscriminately seek information.

The *bounded rationality* approach was first articulated by Simon, partly in reaction against the rational-hedonic model in neo-classical economics.[46] Humans and other animals make judgments and decisions not only under uncertainty but also under limitations in cognitive capacity and time. The result is that people use mental shortcuts called *heuristics* that are fast and cognitively frugal but also adapted to environmental structures.[47]

Confirmation bias, on the other hand, refers to an information processing wherein "one selectively gathers, or gives undue weight to, evidence that supports one's position while neglecting to gather, or discounting, evidence that would tell against it."[48] More specifically, there is widespread evidence that this bias can operate unconsciously.

Most explanations for confirmation bias point to how it reduces cognitive load. A crucial mistake in many perspectives that privilege knowledge over ignorance is the failure to realize that knowledge seeking and possession are not costless. The early literature on foraging behavior is pioneering in this regard, taking into account energy and time costs in search strategies. There are also social costs in seeking information. Directly interrogating someone, for example, is socially inappropriate or costly in many circumstances.

IS IGNORANCE ALWAYS A COGNITIVE DEFICIT?

Ignoramuses are not always worse off than knowledgeable folk; in fact there are plenty of contexts in which it can be demonstrated that they are better off. Imagine for a moment that humans were endowed with the ability and a compulsion to indiscriminately absorb all information that came their way and retain all of it for a lifetime. As Luria concluded in his study of just such a person, higher cognitive functions such as abstraction or even mere classification would be extremely difficult.[49] Information acquired decades ago would be as vividly recalled as information acquired seconds ago, so older memories would interfere with more recent and usually more relevant recollections.

William James proposed that forgetting is just as important as remembering and linked with selectivity of information processing.[50] A more elaborate version of this functionalist argument is offered by Schooler and Hertwig: "the memory system (a) meets the informational demands stemming from environmental stimuli by retrieving memory traces associated with the stimuli and (b) acts on the expectation that environmental stimuli tend to recur in predictable ways."[51]

Schooler and Hertwig address another relevant connection, namely, how forgetting facilitates the use of inferential heuristics that also trade on environmental structures.[52] These are the recognition and fluency heuristics, both of which require partial ignorance. To understand the *recognition heuristic*, consider this question: "Which city has the larger population, Pasadena (California) or Pasadena (Maryland)?"[53] If we do not know the populations of those two cities, the recognition heuristic says that if we recognize one city (say, Pasadena, California) and not the other then we choose the recognized city. Recognition of a city is correlated with its population (as I am writing this, Pasadena, California, has about 145,000 people, whereas Pasadena, Maryland, has about 12,000). The *fluency heuristic* (see, for example, Kelley and Jacoby) is quite similar, stipulating that the city that is more fluently or rapidly recalled will be the one selected.[54]

Goldstein and Gigerenzer demonstrated that a greater number of correct choices (for example, which of a pair of German cities has the greater population) can be made by ignorant decision makers (for example, American university students) than by more knowledgeable decision makers (for example, German citizens).[55] Ignoramuses are not always at a disadvantage.

SPECIALIZATION, PRIVACY, TRUST, POLITENESS, AND LEGITIMATION

Now let us move to a more social (or at least interpersonal) level and explore the adaptive interests and functions served by negotiated ignorance arrangements. I will briefly survey five of these here: specialized knowledge, privacy, trust, politeness, and legitimation. The first two exemplify truly social ignorance arrangements as opposed to unilateral ones such as secrecy or deceit. The second pair, trust and politeness, are examples of social relations and modes of social conduct that mandate or even require ignorance. Finally, legitimation concerns the uses of ignorance to justify actions and choices.

Specialization is a social ignorance arrangement. The stereotypical explanation for specialization is that it arises when there is too much for any one person to learn everything. But viewed from an adaptational standpoint, specialization is an example of spreading risk in three respects. First, the risks of direct learning (versus vicarious learning, which is less risky) are spread across the population by diversifying learning. Second, the risk of being ignorant about crucial matters is spread by diversifying ignorance. Third, the risks associated with bearing knowledge also are diversified. As with any kind of risk spreading, specialization requires various forms of social cooperation to yield these benefits.

Privacy is an example of another kind of social ignorance arrangement. Privacy often has been construed as control over access by others to information, mainly about the self. As Warren and Laslett point out, privacy involves a consensual and essentially cooperative ignorance arrangement, whereas secrecy is unilaterally imposed.[56]

Organized specialization and privacy, along with other consensual social ignorance arrangements, are entwined with trust. For instance, effectively functioning expertise requires that nonexperts trust experts to warrant only the knowledge they possess and not to falsify evidence or conclusions within the scope of their expertise.

Despite long-running debates about the nature of trust, there is widespread agreement among scholars that trust "entails a state of perceived vulnerability or risk."[57] A primary source of that risk is a requirement that the truster remain partially ignorant about the trustee. Trust is not about concealing information from others, but trust relationships (for example, friendships) do entail a kind of privacy. If people believe that someone is monitoring them or insisting that they self-disclose or account for their actions, they will infer that the other person does not trust them.

Yamagishi and his colleagues argue that trust and "commitment formation" are alternative ways of reducing the risk of being exploited in social interactions.[58] Commitment formation involves the development of mutual monitoring and powers to sanction and reward each other's behavior. However, the reduction of transaction costs in commitment formation via uncertainty reduction comes at a price, namely the difficulty and costliness in exiting from the relationship and foregoing opportunities to form other relationships. Trust, on the other hand, entails running the risk of being exploited but increases opportunities by rendering the truster more mobile and able to establish cooperative relations more quickly. Trust, therefore, is both an example of a social relation that requires tolerance of ignorance and also trades undesired uncertainty (the risk of being exploited) against desired uncertainty (freedom to seize opportunities for new relations).

Polite social interaction is another important example of how social relations trade on ignorance. In polite conversation, conversationalists do not expect to deal in the truth, the whole truth, and nothing but the truth. Brown and Levinson elaborate various strategic requirements of politeness.[59] As I have pointed out, those strategies often are achieved via disinformation (for example, promoting a false impression of approval), or by referential abbreviation (particularly vagueness and ambiguity, as in tactful utterances).[60]

The employment of vagueness and ambiguity in communication serves many of the same purposes in polite conversation as it does in other settings where participants want to promote cooperative goodwill, even if some clarity is sacrificed for it. Eisenberg claimed ambiguity is used strategically in organizational communications for several purposes.[61] One is to achieve "unified diversity," whereby a diversity of interpretations of such things as mission statements or organizational goals are permitted to exist and dysfunctional conflicts are avoided. Another is to enable deniability, for example, the ability to claim that a face-threatening interpretation was not the intended meaning of what was said. A third is increasing capacity for organizational change and adaptability by permitting diverse possible interpretations of organizational goals and rules while still appearing consistent. Eisenberg's main insight is that fully clear communication is not always as effective as ambiguous communication and ambiguity often is highly functional.

Finally, let us consider ignorance as a legitimating influence. Ignorance is used in various guises to justify inaction, maintenance of the status quo, opportunism, evasion of responsibility or culpability, and risk management policies. For example, Western legal traditions distinguish between civil cases in which a guilty verdict may be returned on the "balance of probabilities" and criminal cases wherein guilt must be established "beyond reasonable doubt."

However, justifications for actions and choices on the basis of ignorance abound in mundane life as well. Johnson-Hanks's ethnographic research on Southern Cameroonian women's intentions and actions regarding marriage and childbearing is a striking case in point. Life under the twenty-year economic crisis in Cameroon encompasses not only economic hardship but a "generalized state of distrust."[62] The extreme uncertainty associated with the crisis accounts for "incompetence, graft, sexual infidelity, school failure, and even witchcraft." It also legitimates the rejection of planning and ascription of intentionality to acts, various kinds of opportunism, and a type of fatalistic retrospective assent to whatever unfolds in life's course.

In recent times perhaps the premier example of ignorance and uncertainty being used to justify and legitimize high-level policy change in

Western countries is the precautionary principle.[63] The precautionary principle essentially stipulates that the burden of proof must not be placed on the environment to show harm in decisions about whether to moderate or halt potentially environmentally damaging activities. Different kinds of ignorance play distinctive roles in both debates and legitimation regarding this principle. For example, Dovers, Norton, and Handmer emphasize the relevance of elements in my typology of ignorance, especially forms such as taboo, distortion, and irrelevance, all of which are prevalent features of sustainability debates.[64]

CAN AGNOTOLOGY BE INTERDISCIPLINARY?

In this chapter I have attempted a survey of several problems that face any would-be social theory of ignorance. Ignorance is inherently a multidisciplinary topic. But to what extent can it become interdisciplinary? What are the prospects for collaboration and integration across disciplines and domains on this difficult, multifarious, important topic?

At first glance, the prospects seem quite daunting. The problems with nomenclature, "blind spots," and "negative bias" are bad enough, but some relevant disciplines pay only limited attention to ignorance or rule it out altogether (for example, some areas in law, engineering, and medicine). Nonetheless, plenty of examples exist of fruitful interdisciplinary collaboration on difficult topics. The key to this collaboration seems to be negotiating a working consensus about the basic nature of the field of inquiry. As Wagner and Berger expressed it, any topic regarded as a "field" in the social sciences usually contains a core of "orienting strategies" that incorporate widely agreed-on core concerns, goals, metatheoretical concepts and presuppositions, research standards, and methodological prescriptions.[65] The usual price to be paid by participants in multi- or interdisciplinary fields of inquiry is, as Foddy and I observed about the study of social dilemmas, that such agreements are looser, less stable, and continually debated and reassessed.[66] In a new area such as agnotology, this kind of contestability would have to be a sign of good health.

The topics covered in this chapter indicate several candidates for "orienting strategies" and "core concerns" in agnotology. A primary orienting strategy suggested here (and elsewhere) is, broadly speaking, a constructivist approach to understanding how people conceptualize ignorance, communicate about it, cope with it, and utilize it. A second strategic possibility is reflexivity, again in a broad sense of the term. All research domains have orientations, practices, norms, and methods for dealing with ignorance in the process of inquiry. A third strategy is participatory inclusiveness, that is, an exchange of views and understandings of how each discipline construes those issues. I will end this chapter by mentioning three core concerns that could be added to the mix: privileged viewpoints, prescriptive frameworks, and dilemmas.

A problem shared by nearly all attempts to theorize about ignorance is privileging some viewpoints above others. "Privileging" is a crude term but it will have to do for the time being. Simplistic solutions such as thoroughgoing relativism hold too many pitfalls and limitations to be viable. The problem is important because it dramatically affects the nature of the questions that can be addressed in studying ignorance. Most disciplines privilege the viewpoints of the researcher, theorist, or critic in various ways. There is nothing necessarily misguided or wrong in doing this, but the issue does need to be systematically assessed and debated.

The study of ignorance almost inevitably confronts us with prescriptive questions, that is, how people "should" deal with ignorance. As has already been the case in debates about rationality, it is very likely that cross-disciplinary debates about the study of ignorance will also encompass debates about prescriptions for dealing with it. Nor should the consideration of prescriptions be limited to the "rational." They should encompass moral philosophy as well. When is ignorance "virtuous" and why?

The roles played by knowledge and ignorance are not merely mirror images of one another. In fact, the interplay between knowledge and ignorance involves as yet largely unexplored trade-offs and dilemmas. In earlier work, I have presented several examples of both. In "Collingridge's Dilemma," the less well-entrenched a system is and the shorter the time it has been operating, the more easily and inexpensively it can be changed; but the greater is our ignorance of the likely effects or problems.[67] By the time ignorance of those effects has been reduced, it is too expensive and difficult to change the system. In this trade-off, time is both knowledge and money.

"Mattera's Dilemma" is an example of a conundrum in social regulation that has both trade-off and dilemmatic components.[68] The trade-off arises from the fact that a climate favoring creativity and entrepreneurship requires the toleration of ignorance in the service of freedom. Insistence on full knowledge and control eliminates the latitude needed for creativity. The dilemmatic component arises from the fact that the greater the attempts to regulate behavior, the more reactive people become and the more they attempt to generate ignorance in the would-be controllers by withholding information or giving false information. If both parties pursue their self-interests, then the end result is a system of constraints and controls built on disinformation.

My book on ignorance and uncertainty concluded with a plea for interdisciplinary, boundary-spanning work on ignorance.[69] In the years since then, real progress does seem to have been made along these lines, even if falling far short of forming a coherent field of inquiry. Nevertheless, that progress leaves little doubt that many disciplines can benefit from one another in studying ignorance, as long as specialists attempt to understand other disciplines' viewpoints with a certain amount of Quine-like charity. Perhaps that is where we must leave the matter for now.

NOTES

1. S. Böschen and P. Wehling, *Wissenschaft zwischen Folgenverantwortung und Nichtwissen* (Wiesbaden: Verlag für Sozialwissenschaften, 2004).

2. D. Weinstein and M. A. Weinstein, "The Sociology of Nonknowledge: A Paradigm," *Research in Sociology of Knowledge, Sciences & Art* 1 (1978): 151–166.

3. W. E. Moore and M. M. Tumin, "Some Social Functions of Ignorance," *American Sociological Review* 14 (1949): 787–795; M. Smithson, "Toward a Social Theory of Ignorance," *Journal for the Theory of Social Behaviour* 15 (1985): 151–172; Robert K. Merton, "Three Fragments from a Sociologist's Notebooks: Establishing the Phenomenon, Specified Ignorance, and Strategic Research Materials," *Annual Review of Sociology* 13 (1987): 1–28.

4. Karin Knorr-Cetina, *Epistemic Cultures: How the Sciences Make Knowledge* (Cambridge, MA: Harvard University Press, 1999).

5. M. Faber and J. L. R. Proops, *Evolution, Time, Production and the Environment* (Berlin: Springer, 1998), 117.

6. P. Krause and D. Clark, *Representing Uncertain Knowledge: An Artificial Intelligence Approach* (Norwell, MA: Kluwer Academic Publishers, 1993).

7. Knorr-Cetina, *Epistemic Cultures*; M. Smithson, *Ignorance and Uncertainty: Emerging Paradigms* (New York: Springer, 1989).

8. Smithson, *Ignorance and Uncertainty*; Faber and Proops, *Evolution*.

9. Moore and Tumin, *Some Social Functions of Ignorance*; Smithson, *Toward a Social*

Theory of Ignorance; Weinstein and Weinstein, *The Sociology of Nonknowledge*.

10. Knorr-Cetina, *Epistemic Cultures*; Faber and Proops, *Evolution*.

11. M. Douglas, *Purity and Danger* (London: Routledge and Kegan Paul, 1966).

12. P. Unger, *Ignorance: A Case for Scepticism* (Oxford: Clarendon, 1975); Smithson, *Ignorance and Uncertainty*.

13. J. D. Brown, "Knowledge, Uncertainty, and Physical Geography: Towards the Development of Methodologies for Questioning Belief," *Transactions of the Institute of British Geographers* 29 (2004): 272.

14. Robert N. Proctor, "Agnotology: A Missing Term to Describe the Cultural Production of Ignorance (and Its Study)," this volume.

15. Smithson, *Ignorance and Uncertainty*; J. Ravetz, "The Sin of Science: Ignorance of Ignorance," *Knowledge: Creation, Diffusion, Utilization*, 15 (1993): 157–165; Ann Kerwin, "None Too Solid: Medical Ignorance," *Knowledge: Creation, Diffusion, Utilization* 15 (1993): 166–185.

16. T. L. Fine, *Theories of Probability* (New York: Academic Press, 1973); G. A. Klir and B. Yuan, *Fuzzy Sets and Fuzzy Logic* (Englewood Cliffs, NJ: Prentice-Hall, 1995); Smithson, *Ignorance and Uncertainty*.

17. J. R. Brown and L. E. Rogers, "Openness, Uncertainty and Intimacy: An Epistemological Reformulation," *"Miscommunication" and Problematic Talk*, eds. N. Coupland, H. Giles, and J. M. Wiemann (Newbury Park, CA: Sage, 1991), 150.

18. Smithson, *Ignorance and Uncertainty*.

19. I. Hacking, *The Emergence of Probability* (Cambridge, UK: Cambridge University Press, 1975).

20. M. Burgoon, M. Callister, and F. G. Hunsaker, "Patients Who Deceive," *Journal of Language and Social Psychology* 13 (1994): 443–468.

21. D. Ellsberg, "Risk, Ambiguity and the Savage Axioms," *Quarterly Journal of Economics*, 75 (1961): 643–669; M. Smithson, "Conflict Aversion: Preference for Ambiguity vs. Conflict in Sources and Evidence," *Organizational Behavior and Human Decision Processes* 79 (1999): 179–198.

22. Smithson, *Ignorance and Uncertainty*.

23. E. A. Rosa, "Metatheoretical Foundations for Post-Normal Risk," *Journal of Risk Research* 1 (1998): 15–44, esp. 18.

24. H. Rachlin, *Judgment, Decision, and Choice* (New York: Freeman, 1989).

25. H. Wimmer and J. Perner, "Beliefs about Beliefs: Representation and Constraining Function of Wrong Beliefs in Young Children's Understanding of Deception," *Cognition* 13 (1983): 103–128.

26. J. Horgan, *The End of Science: Facing the Limits of Knowledge in the Twilight of the Scientific Age* (London: Little, Brown, 1996).

27. Ulrich Beck, *World Risk Society* (Oxford: Polity, 1999); Anthony Giddens, *The Consequences of Modernity* (Stanford: Stanford University Press, 1990).

28. Proctor, "Agnotology," this volume; Robert Proctor, *Cancer Wars: How Politics Shapes What We Know and Don't Know about Cancer* (New York: Basic Books, 1995).

29. D. Michaels and C. Monforton, "Manufacturing Uncertainty: Contested Science and the Protection of the Public's Health and Environment," *American Journal of Public Health Supplement* 95 (2005): S39–S48.

30. Londa Schiebinger, "West Indian Abortifacients and the Cultural Production of Ignorance," this volume.

31. Burgoon, Callister, and Hunsaker, "Patients Who Deceive"; P. Brown and S. C. Levinson, *Universals in Language Usage: Politeness Phenomena* (Cambridge, UK: Cambridge University Press, 1987).

32. G. Lakoff and M. Johnson, *Metaphors We Live By* (Chicago: University of Chicago Press, 1980).

33. M. Rokeach, *The Open and Closed Mind* (New York: Basic Books, 1960).

34. C. E. Izard, *The Psychology of Emotions* (New York: Plenum, 1991); W. Gudykunst and T. Nishida, "Anxiety, Uncertainty, and Perceived Effectiveness of Communication across Relationships and Cultures," *International Journal of Intercultural Relations* 25 (2001): 55–71.

35. D. Kahneman and A. Tversky, "Prospect Theory: An Analysis of Decision under Risk," *Econometrica* 47 (1979): 263–291; D. Kahneman and A. Tversky, "On the Study of Statistical Intuitions," *Cognition* 11 (1982): 123–141; H. Jungermann, "The Two Camps on Rationality," *Decision Making under Uncertainty*, ed. R. W. Scholz (Amsterdam: Elsevier, 1983).

36. N. Coupland, J. M. Wiemann, and H. Giles, "Talk as 'Problem' and Communication as 'Miscommunication': An Integrative Analysis," *"Miscommunication,"* eds. Coupland, Giles, and Wiemann, 1.

37. S. Jourard, *The Transparent Self*, 2nd ed. (New York: Van Nostrand Reinhold, 1971), 32.

38. M. McCall and T. Simmons, *Identities and Interactions*, 2nd ed. (New York: Free Press, 1978); E. Goffman, *The Presentation of Self in Everyday Life* (Garden City, NY: Doubleday, 1959).

39. C. R. Berger and R. J. Calabrese, "Some Explorations in Initial Interaction and Beyond: Toward a Developmental Theory of Interpersonal Communication," *Human Communication Research* 1 (1975): 99–112.

40. A. S. Babrow, "Uncertainty, Value, Communication, and Problematic Integration," *Journal of Communication* 51 (2001): 553–573; W. A. Afifi and J. L. Weiner, "Toward a Theory of Motivated Information Management," *Communication Theory* 14 (2004): 167–190.

41. K. E. Weick, *The Social Psychology of Organizing*, 2nd ed. (New York: Random House, 1979).

42. E. M. Eisenberg, "Jamming: Transcendence through Organizing," *Communication Research* 17 (1990): 139–164.

43. C. Conrad, *Strategic Organizational Communication* (New York: Holt, Rinehart and Winston, 1985).

44. C. Lerman, C. Hughes, B. J. Trock, R. E. Myers, D. Main, A. Bonney, M. R. Abbaszadegan, A. E. Harty, B. A. Franklin, J. F. Lynch, and H. T. Lynch, "Genetic Testing in Families with Hereditary Nonpolyposis Colon Cancer," *Journal of American Medical Association* 281 (1999): 1618–1622; J. H. Fanos and J. P. Johnson, "Barriers to Carrier Testing for Adult Cystic Fibrosis Sibs: The Importance of Not Knowing," *American Journal of Medical Genetics* 59 (1995): 85–91.

45. T. D. Wilson, D. B. Centerbar, D. T. Gilbert, and D. A. Kermer, "The Pleasures of Uncertainty: Prolonging Positive Moods in Ways People Do Not Anticipate," *Journal of Personality and Social Psychology* 88 (2005): 5–21.

46. H. A. Simon, "Rational Choice and the Structure of Environments," *Psychological Review* 63 (1956): 129–138; H. A. Simon, *Models of Bounded Rationality* (Cambridge, MA: MIT Press, 1982).

47. G. Gigerenzer, P. M. Todd, and the ABC Research Group, *Simple Heuristics That Make Us Smart* (London: Oxford University Press, 1999).

48. R. S. Nickerson, "Confirmation Bias: A Ubiquitous Phenomenon in Many Guises," *Review of General Psychology* 2 (1998): 175.

49. A. R. Luria, *The Mind of a Mnemonist* (New York: Basic Books, 1968).

50. W. James, *The Principles of Psychology*, vol. 1 (New York: Holt, 1890).

51. L. Schooler and R. Hertwig, "How Forgetting Aids Heuristic Inference," *Psychological Review* 112 (2005): 610–611.

52. Schooler and Hertwig, "How Forgetting Aids Heuristic Inference."

53. D. G. Goldstein and G. Gigerenzer, "Models of Ecological Rationality: The Recognition Heuristic," *Psychological Review* 109 (2002): 75–90.

54. C. M. Kelley and L. L. Jacoby, "Subjective Reports and Process Dissociation: Fluency, Knowing, and Feeling," *Acta Psychologica* 98 (1998): 127–140.

55. Goldstein and Gigerenzer, "Models of Ecological Rationality."

56. C. Warren and B. Laslett, "Privacy and Secrecy: A Conceptual Comparison," *Journal of Social Issues* 33 (1977): 43–51.

57. R. M. Kramer, "Trust and Distrust in Organizations: Emerging Perspectives, Enduring Questions," *Annual Review of Psychology* 50 (1999): 571.

58. T. Yamagishi, K. S. Cook, and M. Watanabe, "Uncertainty, Trust and Commitment Formation in the United States and Japan," *American Journal of Sociology* 104 (1998): 165–194.

59. Brown and Levinson, *Universals in Language Usage*.

60. Smithson, *Ignorance and Uncertainty*.

61. E. M. Eisenberg, "Ambiguity as Strategy in Organizational Communication," *Communication Monographs* 51 (1984): 227–241.

62. J. Johnson-Hanks, "When the Future Decides: Uncertainty and Intentional Action in Contemporary Cameroon," *Current Anthropology* 46 (2005): 366.

63. C. Raffensperger and J. Tickner, eds. *Protecting Public Health and the Environment: Implementing the Precautionary Principle* (Washington, DC: Island Press, 1999).

64. S. Dovers, T. W. Norton, and J. W. Handmer, "Ignorance, Uncertainty and Ecology: Key Themes," *Ecology, Uncertainty and Policy: Managing Ecosystems for Sustainability*, eds. J. W. Handmer, T. W. Norton, and S. R. Dovers (London: Prentice-Hall, 2001), 1–25; Smithson, *Ignorance and Uncertainty*.

65. D. G. Wagner and J. Berger, "Do Sociological Theories Grow?" *American Journal of Sociology* 90 (1985): 697–728.

66. M. Smithson and M. Foddy, "Theories and Strategies for Studying Social Dilemmas," *Resolving Social Dilemmas: Dynamic, Structural, and Intergroup Aspects*, eds. M. Foddy, M. Smithson, S. Schneider, and M. Hogg (Philadelphia: Psychology Press, 1999), 1–14.

67. Smithson, *Ignorance and Uncertainty*.

68. Smithson, *Ignorance and Uncertainty*.

69. Smithson, *Ignorance and Uncertainty*.

CHAPTER 10

White Ignorance

CHARLES W. MILLS

EPISTEMOLOGY is one of the oldest and most central areas of Western philosophy, as famously illustrated by Plato and his unknowing cave dwellers. So if any subject should have a special expertise in agnotology, it is epistemology. After all, surely studying how and why we know should also illuminate how and why we don't? Yet, ironically, it could be argued that mainstream epistemology has itself been part of the problem rather than part of the solution, generating its own distinctive ignorances. Classically individualist, indeed sometimes self-parodically to the verge of solipsism, modern Anglo-American epistemology has for hundreds of years from its Cartesian origins been profoundly inimical terrain for the development of any concept of structural group-based miscognition, group ignorance. The paradigm exemplars studied of phenomena likely to foster mistaken belief—optical illusions, hallucinations, phantom limbs, dreams—were by their very banality universal to the human condition.

But W. V. Quine's 1969 naturalizing of epistemology would initiate a sequence of events with unexpectedly subversive long-term theoretical repercussions for the field.[1] If articulating the norms for *ideal* cognition required taking into account (in some way) the practices of *actual* cognition, if the prescriptive needed to pay attention (in some way) to the descriptive, then on what principled basis could cognitive realities of a *supra*-individual kind continue to be excluded from the ambit of epistemology? For it then meant that the cognitive agent needed to be located in his specificity—as a member of certain social groups, within a given social milieu, in a society at a particular time period. Whatever Quine's own sympathies (or lack thereof), his work had opened Pandora's box. A naturalized epistemology had, perforce, also to be a socialized epistemology; this was "a straightforward extension of the naturalistic approach."[2]

What had originally been a specifically Marxist concept, "standpoint theory," was adopted and developed to its most sophisticated form in the work of feminist theorists, and it became possible for books with titles like *Social Epistemology* and *Socializing Epistemology*, and journals called *Social Epistemology*, to be published, and seen (at least by some) as a legitimate part of philosophy.[3]

Obviously, then, for those interested in pursuing such questions this is a far more welcoming environment than that of a few decades ago. Nonetheless, I think it is equally obvious that the *potential* of these developments for transforming mainstream epistemology and elucidating the mechanisms of social ignorance is far from being fully realized. And at least one major reason for this failure is that the conceptions of society in the literature too often presuppose a degree of consent and inclusion that does not exist outside the imagination of mainstream scholars—in a sense a societal population essentially generated by simple iteration of that originally solitary Cartesian cognizer. As Linda Martín Alcoff has ironically observed, the "society" these philosophers are writing about often seems to be composed exclusively of white males, so that one wonders how it reproduces itself.[4] The Marxist critique is seemingly discredited, the feminist critique is marginalized, the racial critique does not even exist. The concepts of domination, hegemony, ideology, mystification, exploitation, and so on that are part of the lingua franca of radicals find little or no place here. In particular, the analysis of the implications for social cognition and social ignorance of the legacy of white supremacy has barely been initiated.

What I want to do in this chapter is to sketch out some of the features and the dynamic of what I see as a particularly pervasive—though hardly theorized—form of ignorance, what could be called white ignorance, which is linked with white supremacy. (This article is an elaboration of one of the key themes of my 1997 book, *The Racial Contract*.[5]) The meta-theoretical approach I find most congenial is that recently outlined by Alvin Goldman in his book *Knowledge in a Social World*. Goldman describes his project as "an essay in social veritistic epistemology," oriented "toward truth determination," as against contemporary poststructuralist or Kuhn/Feyerabend/Bloor/Barnes-inspired approaches that relativize truth. So though the focus is social rather than individual, the traditional concerns and assumptions of mainstream epistemology have been retained:

Traditional epistemology, especially in the Cartesian tradition, was highly individualistic, focusing on mental operations of cognitive agents in isolation or abstraction from other persons. . . . [This] individual epistemology needs a social counterpart: *social epistemology*. . . . In what respects is social epistemology social? First, it focuses on social paths or routes to knowledge. That is, considering believers taken one at a time, it looks at the many routes to belief that feature interactions with other agents, as contrasted with private or asocial routes to belief acquisition. . . . Second, social epistemology does not restrict itself to believers taken singly. It often focuses on some sort of group entity . . . and examines the spread of information or misinformation across that group's membership. Rather than concentrate on a single knower, as did Cartesian epistemology, it addresses the distribution of knowledge or error within the larger social cluster. . . . Veritistic epistemology (whether individual or social) is concerned with the production of knowledge, where knowledge is here understood in the "weak" sense of *true belief*. More precisely, it is concerned with both knowledge and its contraries: *error* (false belief) and *ignorance* (the absence of true belief). The main question for veritistic epistemology is: Which practices have a comparatively favorable impact on knowledge as contrasted with error and ignorance? Individual veritistic epistemology asks this question for nonsocial practices; social veritistic epistemology asks it for social practices.[6]

Unlike Goldman, I will use *ignorance* to cover both false belief and absence of true belief. But with this minor terminological variation, this is basically the project I am trying to undertake: looking at the "spread of misinformation," the "distribution of error" (including the possibility of "massive error"[7]), within the "larger social cluster," the "group entity" of whites, and the "social practices" (some "wholly pernicious"[8]) that encourage it. Goldman makes glancing reference to some of the feminist and race literature (there is a grand total of a single index entry for *racism*), but in general, the implications of systemic social oppression for his project are not addressed. Thus, his account offers the equivalent in social epistemology of the mainstream theorizing in political science that frames American sexism and racism as "anomalies": U.S. political culture is conceptualized as *essentially* egalitarian and inclusive, with the long actual history of systemic gender and racial subordination being relegated to the status of a minor "deviation" from the norm.[9] Obviously, such a starting point crucially handicaps any realistic social epistemology since in effect it turns things upside down. Sexism and racism, patriarchy and white supremacy, have not been the *exception* but the *norm*. So though his book is valuable in terms of conceptual clarification, and some illuminating discussions of particular topics, the basic framework is flawed insofar as it marginalizes domination and its cognitive consequences. A less naive understanding of how society actually works requires drawing on the radical tradition of social theory, in which various factors he does not consider play a pivotal role in obstructing the mission of veritistic epistemology.

WHAT I WANT TO PIN DOWN, then, is the idea of an ignorance, a non-knowing, that is not contingent, but in which race—white racism or white racial domination and their ramifications—is central to its origins. So let me begin by trying to clarify and demarcate more precisely the phenomenon I am addressing, as well as answering some possible objections.

To begin with, *white ignorance* as a cognitive phenomenon has to be clearly historicized. I am taking for granted the truth of some variant of social constructivism, which denies that race is biological. So the causality in the mechanisms for generating and sustaining white ignorance on the macro-level is social-structural rather than physico-biological, though it will of course operate through the physico-biological. Assuming the growing consensus in critical race theory to be correct—that race in general, and whiteness in particular, is a product of the modern period—then you could not have had white ignorance in this technical, term-of-art sense in, say, the ancient world, because whites did not exist then.[10]

Second, one would obviously need to distinguish what I am calling white ignorance from general patterns of ignorance prevalent among people who are white, but in whose doxastic states race has played no determining role. For example, at all times (such as right now) there will be many facts about the natural and social worlds on which people, including white people, have no opinion, or a mistaken opinion, but race is not directly or indirectly responsible (the exact temperature in the earth's crust twenty miles down, the precise income distribution in the United States, and so forth). But we would not want to call this white ignorance, because race has not been the cause for these non-knowings, but other factors.

Third (complicating the foregoing), it needs to be realized that once indirect causation and diminishing degrees of influence are admitted, it will sometimes be very difficult to adjudicate when specific kinds of non-know-ings are appropriately categorizable as white ignorance or not. Recourse to counterfactuals of greater or lesser distance from the actual situation may be necessary ("what they should and would have known if . . ."), whose evaluation may be too complex to be resolvable. Suppose, for example, that a particular true scientific generalization about human beings, P, would be easily discoverable in a society were it not for widespread white racism, and that with additional research in the appropriate areas, P could be shown to have further implications, Q, and beyond that, R. Should these related principles and these factual findings all be included as examples of white ignorance also? How far onward up the chain? And so forth.

Fourth, the racialized causality I am invoking needs to be expansive enough to include both straightforward racist motivation and more im-personal social-structural causation, which may be operative even if the cognizer in question is not racist. For in both cases, racialized causality can give rise to what I am calling white ignorance, straightforwardly for a racist cognizer, indirectly for a non-racist cognizer.

Fifth, the "white" in "white ignorance" does not mean that it has to be confined *to* white people. Indeed, it will often be shared by nonwhites to a greater or lesser extent because of the power relations and patterns of ideological hegemony involved. Providing the causal route is appropriate, nonwhites can manifest white ignorance also.

Sixth, and somewhat different, *white* racial ignorance can produce a doxastic environment in which particular varieties of *nonwhite*, such as black, racial ignorance flourish—so that racial causality is involved—but which one would hesitate to subsume under the category of white igno-rance itself, at least without significant qualification. Think, for example, of "oppositional" African American varieties of biological and theological determinism: whites as melanin deficient and therefore inherently physiologically and psychologically flawed, or whites as "blue-eyed devils" created by the evil scientist Yacub (as in early Black Muslim theology). These theories invert claims of white racial superiority, though obviously they have been shaped by key assumptions of "scientific" and theological white racism.

Seventh, though the examples I have given so far have all been factual ones, I want a concept of white ignorance broad enough to include moral ignorance—not merely ignorance of facts *with* moral implications, but moral non-knowings, incorrect judgments about the rights and wrongs of moral situations themselves. For me, the epistemic desideratum is that the naturalizing and socializing of epistemology should have, as a component, the naturalizing and socializing of *moral* epistemology also, and the study of pervasive social patterns of mistaken *moral* cognition, *moral* ignorance.[11]

Eighth, it presumably does not need to be emphasized that white ignorance is not the only kind of privileged group ignorance. Male ignorance could be analyzed similarly, and clearly has a far more ancient history and arguably a more deep-rooted ancestry in human interrelations, insofar as it goes back to the origins of patriarchy.

Ninth, speaking generally about white ignorance does not commit one to the claim that it is uniform across the white population. Whites are not a monolith, and if the analysis of white ignorance is to be part of a social epistemology and agnotology, the obvious needs to be remembered—that people have other identities beside racial ones, so that whites will be divisible by class, gender, nationality, religion, and so forth, and these factors will modify, by differential socialization and experience, the bodies of belief and the cognitive patterns of the subpopulations concerned. But this is, of course, true for all sociological generalizations, which has never been a reason for abandoning them, but of employing them cautiously.

Tenth, and finally, the point of trying to understand white ignorance is, of course, *normative* and not merely sociological: the goal of trying to reduce or eliminate it. For a social epistemology, where the focus is on supra-individual processes, and the individual's interaction with them, the aim is to understand how certain social structures and group memberships tend to promote these crucially flawed patterns of cognition. So, the idea is that there are typical ways of getting things wrong and one has a better chance of getting things right through a self-conscious recognition of their existence, and corresponding self-distancing from them.

LET US TURN NOW TO THE PROCESSES OF COGNITION, individual and social, and the examination of the ways in which race may affect some of their crucial components. As examples, I will look at perception, conception, memory, testimony, and motivational group interest (in a longer treatment, differential group experience should also be included). Separating out these various components is difficult because of the fact that they are all constantly in complex interaction with one another, involving multiple intricate feedback loops of various kinds. So an analytic separating out of elements for purposes of conceptual isolation and clarification will necessarily be artificial, and in a sense each element so extracted bears a ghostly trail of all the others in its wake.

Start with perception. A central theme of the epistemology of the past few decades has been the discrediting of the idea of a raw perceptual "given," completely unmediated by concepts. Perceptions are in general simultaneously conceptions, if only at a very low level. Moreover, the social dimension of epistemology is obviously most salient here, since individuals do not in general make up these categories themselves, but inherit them from their cultural milieu. "The influence of social factors begins at birth, for language is not reinvented by each individual in social isolation, nor could it be. Because language acquisition is socially mediated, the concepts we acquire are themselves socially mediated from the very beginning."[12] But this means that the conceptual array with which the cognizer approaches the world needs itself to be scrutinized for its adequacy to the world, for how well it maps the reality it claims to be describing. If the society is one structured by relations of domination and subordination (as of course most societies in recent human history have been), then in certain areas this conceptual apparatus is likely going to be shaped and inflected in various ways by the biases of the ruling groups. So crucial concepts may well be misleading in their inner makeup and their external relation to a larger doxastic architecture.

Now apply this to race: consider the epistemic principle of what has come to be called "white normativity," the centering of the Euro-, and later Euro-American, reference group as constitutive norm. Ethnocentrism is, of course, a negative cognitive tendency common to all peoples, not just Europeans. But with Europe's gradual rise to global domination, the European variant becomes entrenched as an overarching, virtually unassailable framework, a conviction of exceptionalism and superiority that seems vindicated by the facts, and thenceforth, circularly, shapes perception of the facts. We rule the world because we are superior; we are superior because we rule the world. In his pioneering essays of the 1950s against Eurocentrism, the world historian Marshall G. S. Hodgson invokes Saul Steinberg's famous March 29, 1976, *New Yorker* cover cartoon depiction of the "View of the World from 9th Avenue," the bizarrely foreshortened view of the United States afforded from the Upper East Side, and argues that the standard geographical representations of Europe by Europeans, as in the Mercator projection world map, are not really that radically different:

It would be a significant story in itself to trace how modern Westerners have managed to preserve some of the most characteristic features of their ethnocentric medieval image of the world. Recast in modern scientific and scholarly language, the image is still with us. . . . The point of any ethnocentric world image is to divide the world into moieties, ourselves and the others, ourselves forming the more important of the two. . . . We divide the world into what we call "continents." . . . Why is Europe one of the continents but not India?. . . . Europe is still ranked as one of the "continents" because our cultural ancestors lived there. By making it a "continent," we give it a rank disproportionate to its natural size, as a subordinate part of no larger unit, but in itself one of the major component parts of the world. . . . (I call such a world map the "Jim Crow projection" because it shows Europe as larger than Africa.) . . . [Mercator] confirms our predispositions.[13]

And this geographical misrepresentation and regional inflation have gone in tandem with a corresponding historical misrepresentation and inflation. Criticizing the standard historical categories of Western historians, Hodgson suggests that "the very terms we allow ourselves to use foster distortion." The "convenient result" is that Europe, an originally peripheral region of what Hodgson calls the "Afro-Eurasian historical complex," is lifted out of its context and elevated into a self-creating entity unto itself, "an independent division of the whole world, with a history that need not be integrated with that of the rest of mankind save on the terms posed by European history itself."[14]

From this fatally skewed optic, of course, stem all those theories of innate European superiority to the rest of the world that are still with us in modified and subtler versions today. Whiteness is originally coextensive with full humanity, so that the nonwhite Other is grasped through a historic array of concepts whose common denominator is their subjects' location on a lower ontological and moral rung.

Consider, for example, the category of the "savage," and its conceptual role in the justification of imperialism. As Francis Jennings points out, the word was "created for the purposes of conquest rather than the purposes of knowledge." "Savagery" and "civilization" were "reciprocals," and were "both independent of any necessary correlation with empirical reality." The conceptual outcome was a "conjoined myth" that "greatly distorted [white] Americans' perceptions of reality," necessarily involving "the suppression of facts."[15] In effect,

the Englishman devised the savage's form to fit his function. The word *savage* thus underwent considerable alteration of meaning as different colonists pursued their varied ends. One aspect of the term remained constant, however: the savage was always inferior to civilized men. . . . The constant of Indian inferiority implied the rejection of his humanity and determined the limits permitted for his participation in the mixing of cultures. The savage was prey, cattle, pet, or vermin—he was never citizen. Upholders of the myth denied that either savage tyranny or savage anarchy could rightfully be called government, and therefore there could be no justification for Indian resistance to European invasion.[16]

When Thomas Jefferson excoriates the "merciless Indian Savages" in the Declaration of Independence, then, neither he nor his readers experience any cognitive dissonance with the earlier claims about the equality of all "men," since savages are not "men" in the full sense. Locked in a different temporality, incapable of self-regulation by morality and law, they are humanoid but not human. To speak of the "equality" of the savage would then be oxymoronic, since one's very location in these categories is an indication of one's inequality. Even a cognizer with no antipathy or prejudice toward Native Americans will thus be cognitively disabled in trying to establish truths about them insofar as such a category and its associated presuppositions will tend to force his conclusions in a certain direction, will constrain what he can objectively see. It is not a matter of seeing the phenomenon with the concept discretely attached, but rather of seeing things *through* the concept itself. In the classic period of European expansionism, it then becomes possible to speak with no sense of absurdity of "empty" lands that are actually teeming with millions of people, of "discovering" countries whose inhabitants already exist, because the nonwhite Other is so located in the guiding conceptual array that different rules apply to them. Even seemingly straightforward empirical perception will be affected—the myth of a nation of hunters in contradiction to widespread Native American agriculture that saved the Jamestown colonists' lives, the myth of stateless savages in contradiction to forms of government from which the white Founders arguably learned, the myth of a pristine wilderness in contradiction to a humanized landscape transformed by thousands of years of labor.[17] In all these cases, *the concept is driving the perception, with whites aprioristically intent on denying what is before them.* So if Kant famously said that perceptions without concepts are blind, here it is the blindness of the concept itself that is blocking vision.

Originally, then, foundational concepts of racialized difference, and their ramifications in all sociopolitical spheres, preclude veridical perception of nonwhites and serve as a categorical barrier against their equitable moral treatment. The transition away from old-fashioned racism of this kind has not, however, put an end to white normativity but transformed its character. If previously whites were color demarcated as biologically or culturally unequal and superior, now through a strategic "color-blindness" nonwhites are assimilated as putative equals to the status and situation of whites on terms that negate the need for any measures to repair the inequities of the past. So white normativity now manifests itself in a white refusal to recognize the long history of structural discrimination that has left them with the superior resources they have today and all the consequent advantages they provide for negotiating opportunity structures. Woody Doane suggests that:

"Color-blind" ideology plays an important role in the maintenance of white hegemony. . . . Because whites tend not to see themselves in racial terms and not to recognize the existence of the advantages that whites enjoy in American society, this promotes a worldview that emphasizes *individualistic* explanations for social and economic achievement, as if the individualism of white privilege was a universal attribute. Whites also exhibit a general inability to perceive the persistence of discrimination and the effects of more subtle forms of institutional discrimination. In the context of color-blind racial ideology, whites are more likely to see the opportunity structure as open and institutions as impartial or objective in their functioning. . . . This combination supports an interpretative framework in which whites' explanations for inequality focus upon the cultural characteristics (e.g., motivation, values) of subordinate groups. . . . Politically, this blaming of subordinate groups for their lower economic position serves to neutralize demands for antidiscrimination initiatives or for a redistribution of resources.[18]

What makes such denial possible, of course, is the management of memory. Memory is not a subject one usually finds in epistemology texts, but for social epistemology it is obviously pivotal. The French sociologist Maurice Halbwachs was one of the pioneers of the concept of a collective, social memory, which provided the framework for individual memories.[19] But if we need to understand collective memory, we also need to understand collective amnesia. Indeed, they go together insofar as memory is necessarily selective—out of the infinite sequence of events, some trivial, some momentous, we extract what we see as the crucial ones and organize them into an overall narrative. Social memory is then inscribed in textbooks, generated and regenerated in ceremonies and official holidays, concretized in statues, parks, monuments. Historian John Gillis argues that "the notion of identity depends on the idea of memory, and vice versa. . . . [But] memories and identities are not fixed things, but representations or constructions of reality. . . . '[M]emory work' is . . . embedded in complex class, gender and power relations that determine what is remembered (or forgotten), by whom, and for what end. If memory has its politics, so too does identity."[20] Thus, there will be both official and counter-memory, generating, in the case of race, an intimate relationship between white identity, white memory, and white amnesia, especially about nonwhite victims.

Hitler is supposed to have reassured his generals, apprehensive about the launching of World War II, by asking them: "Who now remembers the Armenians?" Because the Third Reich lost, the genocide of the Jews (though far less the Romani) is remembered. But who now remembers the Hereros, the Nama, the Beothuks, the Tasmanians? (For that matter, who does remember the Armenians, except the Armenians themselves?) Who remembers the Congolese? In Adam Hochschild's chilling book on King Leopold II's regime of rubber and extermination, which resulted in the deaths of 10 million people in the Belgian Congo in the 1890s–1900s, the final chapter is titled "The Great Forgetting." Through the systematic destruction of state archives in Brussels—"the furnaces burned for eight days"—and the deliberate noncommemoration of the African victims— "in none of the [Brussels Royal Museum of Central Africa]'s twenty large exhibition galleries is there the slightest hint that millions of Congolese met unnatural deaths"—a "deliberate forgetting" as an "active deed" was achieved, a purging of official memory so thorough and efficient that a Belgian ambassador to West Africa in the 1970s was astonished by the "slander" on his country in a Liberian newspaper's passing reference to the genocide: "I learned that there had been this huge campaign, in the international press, from 1900 to 1910; millions of people had died, but we Belgians knew absolutely nothing about it."[21] Similarly, and closer to home, James Loewen's critical study of the silences and misrepresentations of standard American history textbooks points out that "The Indian-white wars that dominated our history from 1622 to 1815 and were of considerable importance until 1890 have disappeared from our national memory," encouraging a "feel-good history for whites": "By downplaying Indian wars, textbooks help us forget that we wrested the continent from Native Americans."[22]

Moreover, the misrepresentations of national textbooks have their counterpart in monuments and statuary: social memory made marble and concrete, national mnemonics of the landscape itself. In his study of Civil

War monuments, Kirk Savage argues that "monuments served to anchor collective remembering," fostering "a shared and standardized program of memory," so that "local memory earned credibility by its assimilation to a visible national memory."[23] The postbellum decision to rehabilitate Robert E. Lee, commander in chief of the Confederate Army, thereby "eras[ing] his status as traitor," signified a national white reconciliation that required the repudiation of an alternative black memory:

The commemoration of Lee rested on a suppression of black memory, black truth. . . . [U.S. statesman Charles Francis] Adams could not justify a monument to Lee without denying the postwar reality of racial injustice and its congruence with the Confederate cause. "Sectional reconciliation" of this kind was founded on the nonconciliation of African-Americans, and on their exclusion from the legitimate arenas of cultural representation. Black Americans did not have their own monuments, despite the critical role they had played in swinging the balance of power—both moral and military—to the North. . . . The commemoration of the Civil War in physical memorials is ultimately a story of systematic cultural repression. . . . Public monuments . . . impose a permanent memory on the very landscape within which we order our lives. Inasmuch as the monuments make credible particular collectivities, they must erase others.[24]

At the level of symbolism and national self-representation, then, the denial of the extent of Native American and black victimization contributes to the airbrushed white narrative of discovery, settlement, and building of a shining city on the hill. But the editing of white memory has more concrete and practical consequences also: it enables a personal self-representation in which differential white privilege, and the need to correct for it, does not exist. In other words, the mystification of the past underwrites a mystification of the present. The erasure of the history of Jim Crow makes it possible to depict the playing field as historically level, so that current black poverty just proves black unwillingness to work. As individual memory is assisted through a larger social memory, so individual amnesia is then assisted by a larger collective amnesia.

In his research on the continuing, indeed deepening, wealth gap between white and black Americans, Thomas Shapiro remarks on how often white interviewees seemed to "forget" what they had just told him about the extensive parental assistance they received, claiming instead that they had worked for it: "[X's] memory seems accurate as she catalogues all sorts of parental wealthfare with matching dollar figures. . . . However, as soon as the conversation turns to how she and her husband acquired assets like their home, cars, and savings account, her attitude changes dramatically. . . . The [Xs] describe themselves as self-made, conveniently forgetting that they inherited much of what they own." Thus, the "taken-for-granted sense of [white] entitlement" erases the fact that "*transformative assets*," "inherited wealth lifting a family beyond their own achievements," have been crucial to their white success, and that blacks do not in general have such advantages because of the history of discrimination against them.[25]

But forgetting, whether individual or social, will not even be necessary if there is nothing to remember in the first place. C. A. J. Coady's now classic book on testimony has made it irrefutably clear how dependent we are on others for so much of what we know, so that testimony must be crucial to the elaboration of a social epistemology.[26] Yet if one group, or specific groups, of potential witnesses are discredited in advance as epistemically suspect, reports from them will tend to be dismissed, or never solicited to begin with. Kant's infamous line about a "Negro carpenter's" views has often been quoted, but never stales: "And it might be, that there were something in this which perhaps deserved to be considered; but in short, this fellow was *quite black* from head to foot, a clear proof that what he said was stupid."[27] Nonwhite inferiority necessarily has cognitive ramifications, undermining nonwhite claims to knowledge that are not backed up by European epistemic authority. During slavery, blacks were generally denied the right to testify against whites, because they were not seen as credible witnesses, so when the only (willing) witnesses to white crimes were black, these crimes would not be brought to light.

Moreover, in many cases, even if witnesses would have been given some kind of grudging hearing, they were terrorized into silence by the fear of white retaliation. A black woman recalls the world of Jim Crow and the dangers of describing it for what it was: "My problems started when I began to comment on what I saw. . . . I insisted on being accurate. But the world I was born into didn't want that. Indeed, its very survival depended on not knowing, not seeing—and certainly, not saying anything at all about what it was really like."[28] If black testimony could be aprioristically rejected because it was likely to be false, it could also be aprioristically rejected because it was likely to be true. Testimony about white atrocities—lynchings, police killings, race riots—would often have to be passed down through segregated informational channels, black to black, too explosive to be allowed exposure to white cognition. The memory of the 1921 Tulsa race riot, the worst American race riot of the twentieth century, with a possible death toll of 300 people, was kept alive for decades in the black community long after whites had erased it from the official record. Ed Wheeler, a white researcher trying in 1970 to locate documentation on the riot, found that the official Tulsa records had mysteriously vanished, and was only able with great difficulty to persuade black survivors to come forward with their photographs of the event: "The blacks allowed Wheeler to take the pictures only if he promised not to reveal their names, and they all spoke only on the condition of anonymity. Though fifty years had passed, they still feared retribution if they spoke out."[29]

And even when such fears are not a factor, and blacks do feel free to speak, the epistemic presumption against their credibility remains in a way that it does not for white witnesses. Black counter-testimony against white mythology has always existed, but would originally have been handicapped by the lack of material and cultural capital investment available for its production—oral testimony from illiterate slaves, ephemeral pamphlets with small print runs, self-published works like those by the autodidact J. A. Rogers laboriously documenting the achievements of men and women of color to contest the white lie of black inferiority.[30] But even when propagated in more respectable venues—for example, the Negro scholarly journals founded in the early twentieth century—they were epistemically ghettoized by the Jim Crow intellectual practices of the white academy. As Stephen Steinberg points out, the United States and its white social sciences have "played ostrich" on the issues of race and racial division,[31] so that—in W. E. B. Du Bois's famous image of blacks in a cave trying desperately to communicate to white passersby, before despairingly realizing that they are silenced behind "some thick sheet of invisible but horribly tangible plate glass"—"[black critics] of whatever political stripe . . . were simply met with a deaf ear." The testimony of Negro scholars saying the wrong thing (almost an analytic statement!) would not be registered. "[T]he marginalization of black voices in academia was facilitated by an 'invisible but horribly tangible' color line that relegated all but a few black scholars to teach in black colleges far removed from the academic mainstream."[32] Consider, for example, an anthropology founded on the "obvious" truth of racial hierarchy. Or a sociology failing to confront the central social fact of structural white domination. Or a history sanitizing the record of aboriginal conquest and black exploitation. Or a political science representing racism as an anomaly to a basically inclusive and egalitarian polity. Or a political philosophy thriving for thirty years and supposedly dedicated to the elucidation of justice that makes next to no mention of the centrality of racial *injustice* to the "basic structure" of the United States, and assumes instead that it will be more theoretically appropriate to start from the "ideal theory" assumption that society is the product of a mutually agreed-on, nonexploitative enterprise to divide benefits and burdens in an equitable way—and that this is somehow going to illuminate the distinctive moral problems of a society based on exploitative white settlement! In whatever discipline that is affected by race, the "testimony" of the black perspective and its distinctive conceptual and theoretical insights will tend to be whited out. Whites will cite other whites, in a closed circuit of epistemic authority that reproduces white delusions.

Finally, the dynamic role of *white group interests* needs to be recognized and acknowledged as a central causal factor in generating and sustaining white ignorance. Cognitive psychologists standardly distinguish between "cold" and "hot" mechanisms of cognitive distortion, those attributable to intrinsic processing difficulties and those involving motivational factors, and in analytic philosophy of mind and philosophical psychology there is a large and well-established body of work on self-deception and motivated irrationality, though located within an individualistic framework.[33] So claiming a link between interest and cognition is not at all unheard of in this field. But because of its framing individualism, and of course the aprioristic exclusion in any case of the realities of *white* group domination, the generalization to racial interests has not been carried out.

What needs to be done, I suggest, is to extrapolate some of this literature to a social context—one informed by the realities of race. Because of its marginalization of social oppression, the existing social epistemology literature tends to ignore or downplay such factors. By contrast, in the left tradition this was precisely the classic thesis: (class) domination and exploitation were the foundation of the social order, and as such they produced not merely material differentials of wealth in the economic sphere, but deleterious cognitive consequences in the ideational sphere. Marxism's particular analysis of exploitation, resting as it does on the labor theory of value, has proven to be fatally vulnerable. But obviously this does not negate the value of the concept itself, suitably refurbished, nor undercut the prima facie plausibility of the claim that if exploitative socioeconomic relations are indeed foundational to the social order, this is likely to have a fundamental shaping effect on social ideation. So vested white group interest in the racial status quo—the "wages of whiteness" in David Roediger's adaptation of Du Bois's famous phrase from *Black Reconstruction*—needs to be recognized as a major factor in encouraging white cognitive distortions of various kinds.[34]

Nor is such "motivated irrationality" confined to the period of overt racism and de jure segregation. Recent attitudinal research by Donald Kinder and Lynn Sanders on public policy matters linked to race reveals "a deep and perhaps widening racial divide [that] makes the discovery of commonality and agreement between the races a dim prospect," and central to the shaping of white opinion, it turns out, is their perception of their group interests: "the threats blacks appear to pose to whites' collective well-being, not their personal welfare."[35] These two political scientists conclude that race is the primary social division in the United States, and that whites generally see black interests as opposed to their own. Inevitably, then, this will affect white social cognition—the concepts favored (for example, today's "color-blindness"), the refusal to perceive systemic discrimination, the convenient amnesia about the past and its legacy in the present, the hostility to black testimony on continuing white privilege and the need to eliminate it so as to achieve racial justice. As emphasized at the start, then, these analytically distinguishable cognitive components are in reality all interlocked with and reciprocally determining one another, jointly contributing to the blindness of the white eye.

In his wonderfully titled *States of Denial*, Stanley Cohen argues that "[w]hole societies may slip into collective modes of denial":

> Besides collective denials of the past (such as brutalities against indigenous peoples), people may be encouraged to act as if they don't know about the present. Whole societies are based on forms of cruelty, discrimination, repression or exclusion which are "known" about but never openly acknowledged. . . . Indeed, distortions and self-delusions are most often synchronized. . . . Whole societies have mentioned and unmentionable rules about what should not be openly talked about. You are subject to a rule about obeying these rules, but bound also by a meta-rule which dictates that you deny your knowledge of the original rule.[36]

White ignorance has been able to flourish all these years because a white epistemology of ignorance has safeguarded it against the dangers of an illuminating blackness or redness, protecting those who for "racial" reasons have needed not to know. Only by starting to break these rules and meta-rules can we begin the long process that will lead to the eventual overcoming of this white darkness and the achievement of an enlightenment that is genuinely multiracial.

NOTES

1. W. V. Quine, "Epistemology Naturalized," *Ontological Relativity, and Other Essays* (New York: Columbia University Press, 1969); Hilary Kornblith, *Naturalizing Epistemology*, 2nd ed. (Cambridge, MA: MIT Press, 1994), orig. ed. 1985.

2. Hilary Kornblith, "A Conservative Approach to Social Epistemology," *Socializing Epistemology: The Social Dimension of Knowledge*, ed. Frederick F. Schmitt (Lanham, MD: Rowman & Littlefield, 1994), 93.

3. Sandra Harding, ed., *The Feminist Standpoint Theory Reader: Intellectual and Political Controversies* (New York: Routledge, 2004); Steve Fuller, *Social Epistemology*, 2nd ed. (Bloomington: University of Indiana Press, 2002), orig. ed. 1988; Schmitt, *Socializing Epistemology*.

4. Linda Martín Alcoff, *Real Knowing: New Versions of the Coherence Theory* (Ithaca, NY: Cornell University Press, 1996), 2n1.

5. Charles W. Mills, *The Racial Contract* (Ithaca, NY: Cornell University Press, 1997).

6. Alvin I. Goldman, *Knowledge in a Social World* (New York: Oxford University Press, 1999), 4–5.

7. Kornblith, "Conservative Approach," 97.

8. Ibid.

9. Rogers M. Smith, *Civic Ideals: Conflicting Visions of Citizenship in U.S. History* (New Haven, CT: Yale University Press, 1997).

10. George M. Fredrickson, *Racism: A Short History* (Princeton, NJ: Princeton University Press, 2002).

11. Richmond Campbell and Bruce Hunter, eds., *Moral Epistemology Naturalized, Canadian Journal of Philosophy* supp. vol. 26 (Calgary, AB: University of Calgary Press, 2000).

12. Kornblith, "Conservative Approach," 97.

13. Marshall G. S. Hodgson, "Interrelations of Societies in History," *Rethinking World History: Essays on Europe, Islam, and World History*, ed. Edmund Burke, III (New York: Cambridge University Press, 1993), 3–5.

14. Hodgson, "Interrelations," 9.

15. Francis Jennings, *The Invasion of America: Indians, Colonialism, and the Cant of Conquest* (New York: W. W. Norton, 1976 [1975]), 12, 10.

16. Jennings, *Invasion*, 59.

17. Jennings, *Invasion*.

18. Woody Doane, "Rethinking Whiteness Studies," *White Out: The Continuing Significance of Racism*, ed. Ashley W. Doane and Eduardo Bonilla-Silva (New York: Routledge, 2003), 13–14.

19. Maurice Halbwachs, *On Collective Memory*, ed. and trans. Lewis A. Coser (Chicago: University of Chicago Press, 1992).

20. John R. Gillis, "Memory and Identity: The History of a Relationship," *Commemorations: The Politics of National Identity*, ed. John R. Gillis (Princeton, NJ: Princeton University Press, 1994), 3.

21. Adam Hochschild, *King Leopold's Ghost: A Story of Greed, Terror, and Heroism in Colonial Africa* (New York: Houghton Mifflin, 1998), 293–295, 297. However, Hochschild's book initiated a debate in Belgium that has now led to a Royal Museum of Central Africa show on the issue: "Memory of Congo: The Colonial Era." Belgian historians dispute his figures and reject the charge of genocide: *New York Times*, February 9, 2005, B3.

22. James W. Loewen, *Lies My Teacher Told Me: Everything Your American History Textbook Got Wrong* (New York: Touchstone/Simon & Schuster, 1996), 133.

23. Kirk Savage, "The Politics of Memory: Black Emancipation and the Civil War Monument," *Commemorations: The Politics of National Identity*, ed. John R. Gillis (Princeton, NJ: Princeton University Press, 1994), 130–131.

24. Savage, "Politics of Memory," 134–135, 143.

25. Thomas M. Shapiro, *The Hidden Cost of Being African American: How Wealth Perpetuates Inequality* (New York: Oxford University Press, 2004), 75–76, 10.

26. C. A. J. Coady, *Testimony: A Philosophical Study* (Oxford: Clarendon, 1994 [1992]).

27. Immanuel Kant, *Observations on the Feeling of the Beautiful and Sublime*, trans. John T. Goldthwait (Berkeley: University of California Press, 1960), 113.

28. Cited in Leon F. Litwack, *Trouble in Mind: Black Southerners in the Age of Jim Crow* (New York: Alfred A. Knopf, 1998), 34.

29. James S. Hirsch, *Riot and Remembrance: The Tulsa Race War and Its Legacy* (New York: Houghton Mifflin, 2002), 201.

30. J. A. Rogers, *100 Amazing Facts about the Negro with Complete Proof: A Short Cut to the World History of the Negro* (St. Petersburg, FL: Helga M. Rogers, 1985 [1952]).

31. Stephen Steinberg, *Turning Back: The Retreat from Racial Justice in America*, 3rd ed. (Boston: Beacon, 2001 [1995]), ix.

32. Ibid., 51.

33. Brian P. McLaughlin and Amelie Oksenberg Rorty, eds., *Perspectives on Self-Deception* (Berkeley: University of California Press, 1988); Alfred R. Mele, *Self-Deception Unmasked* (Princeton, NJ: Princeton University Press, 2001).

34. David R. Roediger, *The Wages of Whiteness: Race and the Making of the American Working Class*, rev. ed. (New York: Verso, 1999), orig. ed. 1991; W. E. B. Du Bois, *Black Reconstruction in America, 1860–1880* (New York: Free Press, 1998 [1935]); Charles W. Mills, "Racial Exploitation and the Wages of Whiteness," *The Changing Terrain of Race and Ethnicity*, ed. Maria Krysan and Amanda E. Lewis (New York: Russell Sage, 2004), 235–262.

35. Donald R. Kinder and Lynn M. Sanders, *Divided by Color: Racial Politics and Democratic Ideals* (Chicago: University of Chicago Press, 1996), 33, 85.

36. Stanley Cohen, *States of Denial: Knowing about Atrocities and Suffering* (Malden, MA: Polity, 2001), 10–11, 45.

CHAPTER II

Risk Management versus the Precautionary Principle

Agnotology as a Strategy in the Debate over Genetically Engineered Organisms

DAVID MAGNUS

AGNOTOLOGY IS THE CONSTRUCTION OF IGNORANCE. But it is also often a strategy that can be utilized to bring about specific ends, such as avoiding regulation or liability. Indeed several chapters presented here illustrate how companies and other entities willfully create uncertainty to avoid unwanted regulation. In "Doubt Is Their Product," David Michaels argues that this has become a common response when industries find their interests threatened:

Uncertainty is an inherent problem of science, but manufacturing uncertainty is another matter entirely. Over the past three decades, industry groups have frequently become involved in the investigative process when their interests are threatened. . . . The business typically responds by hiring its own researchers to cast doubt on . . . studies.[1]

Chris Mooney, in *The Republican War on Science*, argues that this strategy has become a mainstay of conservatives in their political battles with science:

In political science debates, one specific form of misrepresentation occurs so frequently that it needs its own category. And that is the hyping and exaggerating of scientific uncertainty, frequently with the goal of preventing political action. . . . Since scientific uncertainty can never be fully dispelled, it hardly provides a good excuse for ducking political action. If it did, nothing would ever get done. Yet in policy fights with a strong scientific component, conservatives have touted uncertainty to precisely this end. Moreover, they have strategically magnified uncertainty itself, effectively misrepresenting what scientists actually know. Some industry groups have even gone so far as to "manufacture" uncertainty by strategically attempting to sow doubt about mainstream conclusions.[2]

This story has now become so common that we know it by heart: industry and its politically conservative allies oppose science-based regulation and support the creation of uncertainty to protect their interests. Examples range from the tobacco industry fighting the idea that smoking has a negative impact on health to combating the growing consensus on global warming.[3] Following Proctor, I will refer to this strategy of focusing on and magnifying uncertainty to avoid the introduction of something seen as undesirable (for example, regulations) as "construct agnotology."

In environmental regulation, this agnogenesis eventually led to a strategy by regulators that would enable them to move forward, even in the face of uncertainty, through the use of what would become known as "the precautionary principle." Ironically, this principle evolved from a tool employed by industry to aid risk management into a new agnotological strategy used by anti-industry non-governmental organizations (NGOs) to oppose the creation of genetically engineered organisms (GEOs).

RISK ASSESSMENT AND MANAGEMENT:
THE CREATION OF THE PRECAUTIONARY PRINCIPLE

In the realm of environmental policy, risk assessment and management determine whether an activity is safe and are seen as "scientific" and systematic approaches to risk evaluation. For government regulators trying to decide, for example, whether they should allow ships to discharge their ballast in their ports, the starting point would be systematic review of the environmental impact of such activities on the port. This is only a starting point, as a value-based assessment of whether the degree of risk is worth the potential benefit of an action involves weighing many factors, including economic and public benefits against risks. The general goal is to reduce risks and to find ways of eliminating any harm that occurs once risks are identified.

This approach to risk management might be characterized as "we know what we know and we ignore what we don't know." Taking this approach is difficult in the absence of good information about risks, and, in a sense, it invites agnogenesis since creating uncertainty about the existence of risks reduces the role risks play in the assessment and therefore limits the impetus to manage those risks. Risk management, as it is currently practiced, is essentially an invitation to move forward with an activity in the face of a great deal of uncertainty in the hope that serious environmental problems do not emerge.

The precautionary principle, or the precautionary approach to regulation, is a response to this problem. It has a long history. In 1854, John Snow, a British anesthesiologist who did pioneering work on epidemiology, found evidence to support his hypothesis that polluted water was the source of cholera in London. Prior to publishing his research in 1855, and at a time when there was a great deal of uncertainty over whether water bred cholera, Snow took action, removing the handle of a water pump on Broad Street in London to prevent a cholera outbreak.[4] In the 1970s, German environmental law introduced the concept of *Vorsorgeprinzip*, as the nation sought to allow preventive measures to protect forests from acid rain and other environmental harms even if the science behind the connection, for example, between power plant emissions and acid rain, had not been established.[5]

In the 1980s, the precautionary principle became part of international law. In 1982, the World Charter for Nature was adopted by the UN General Assembly. It included the following:

Activities which are likely to cause irreversible damage to nature shall be avoided (11. a) and Activities which are likely to pose a significant risk to nature shall be preceded by an exhaustive examination; their proponents shall demonstrate that expected benefits outweigh potential damage to nature, and where potential adverse effects are not fully understood, the activities should not proceed (11 b).[6]

The 1984 International Conference on the Protection of the North Sea gave rise to a 1987 declaration that stated in part that "in order to protect the North Sea from possibly damaging effects of the most dangerous substances, a precautionary approach is necessary which may require action to control inputs of such substances even before a causal link has been established by absolutely clear scientific evidence."[7]

The most prominent early formulation of the precautionary principle was the outcome of the 1992 United Nations Conference on Environment and Development, also known as the Earth Summit. The Rio Declaration on Environment and Development included a clear articulation of a precautionary approach that would avoid agnogenesis as a way of preventing adequate environmental regulation. The key provision is Article 15 of the Rio Declaration:

In order to protect the environment, the precautionary approach shall be widely applied by States according to their capabilities. Where there are threats of serious or irreversible damage, lack of full scientific certainty shall not be used as a reason for postponing cost-effective measures to prevent environmental degradation.[8]

There are several key features of the initial versions of the precautionary principle. The Rio Declaration, like the 1987 North Sea Declaration, was an explicit response to construct agnotology. No longer would efforts to establish uncertainty stand as a reason to avoid prudent regulation or risk management. Uncertainty would not be a bar to action.

Second, the precautionary principle primarily treated the obligations of nations or regulatory bodies. It was developed as part of law and especially international agreements and treaties as those responsible for regulation sought ways of understanding how they should manage risks in the face of uncertainty (but where devastating consequences could result from failure to act). Further, it dealt with the shared obligations of different nations where environmental impact crossed national boundaries.

Third, the precautionary principle became an important tool for risk management. Ignoring uncertainty was simply not sufficient for adequate risk management. The precautionary principle provided managers or regulators with a new tool that would allow them to reasonably move forward when there was clearly sufficient evidence to warrant concern, but not sufficient evidence to establish risks with a high degree of certainty. Sometimes we know what we don't know—and the precautionary principle turned ignorance into knowledge.

THE EVOLUTION OF THE
PRECAUTIONARY PRINCIPLE

The precautionary principle has come to have a number of different meanings and uses. David Vanderzwaag has identified fourteen different formulations of the principle in various treaties and declarations.[9] Though there has been and continues to be variation and hence ambiguity in the meaning of the precautionary principle or a precautionary approach to regulation, its evolution and expansion would eventually transpose agnotological strategy.

The precautionary approach to regulation expanded from strictly environmental concerns and came to play a major role in the framing of issues in genetically engineered organisms. In January 2000, the Conference of the Parties to the Convention on Biological Diversity issued a Protocol on Biosafety, the Cartegena Protocol that applied the precautionary principle to the products of bioengineering.

Lack of scientific certainty due to insufficient relevant scientific information . . . shall not prevent the Party of import, in order to avoid or minimize such potential adverse effects, from taking a decision, as appropriate, with regard to the import of the living modified organism in question.[10]

While the precautionary principle continued to play a role in various conventions, treaties, and agreements, and covered a broader range of topics, it was in the hands of NGOs that the most significant expansion of the concept took place.

In 1998, the Science and Environmental Health Network convened a meeting at Wingspread in which a group of activists and academics issued a statement on the precautionary principle. The Wingspread Statement condemned existing risk management–based policy for failing adequately to protect human health, the environment, and "the larger system of which humans are but a part." They argued that a new paradigm was needed and a new set of principles adopted to address the serious environmental harms that human activity produced. Indeed, they claimed, "there is compelling evidence" that damage had occurred on a large scale.

The Wingspread Statement did not merely apply the precautionary principle to states or regulatory bodies, but identified an obligation on the part of a much broader group of institutions and actors. These included "corporations, government entities, organizations, communities, scientists and other individuals" who all were obligated to "adopt a precautionary approach to all human endeavors."

The Wingspread Statement urged caution and adopted similar language to the Rio Declaration, namely, signaling the importance of not allowing scientific uncertainty about the magnitude of risk to circumvent action to prevent harm. The Wingspread definition of the precautionary principle stated:

Where an activity raises threats of harm to the environment or human health, precautionary measures should be taken even if some cause and effect relationships are not fully established scientifically.[11]

But, Wingspread went far beyond previous statements by shifting the burden of proof to "proponents of an activity rather than the public."

Following Wingspread, many NGOs have taken up the precautionary principle as a critical underpinning of their opposition to genetic engineering. Greenpeace's statement on the precautionary principle, for example, states that "when (on the basis of available evidence) an activity may harm human health or the environment, a cautious approach should be taken in advance—even if the full extent of harm has not yet been fully established scientifically. It recognizes that such proof of harm may never be possible, at least until it is too late to avoid or reverse the damage done."[12]

This statement creates an incentive for opponents of biotechnology to emphasize uncertainty and openly embraces the idea that certainty may be unachievable—leaving strict regulations without scientific rationale.

The Institute of Science in Society (ISIS) has tirelessly addressed the precautionary principle. Peter Saunders, one of the cofounders of ISIS has claimed at various times that

In fact, the precautionary principle is very simple. All it actually amounts to is a piece of common sense: if we are embarking on something new, we should think very carefully about whether it is safe or not, and we should not go ahead until we are convinced it is. . . . The Precautionary Principle states that if there are reasonable scientific grounds for believing that a new process or product may not be safe, it should not be introduced until we have convincing evidence that the risks are small and are outweighed by the benefits.[13]

Saunders defends the precautionary principle from charges that it creates an impossibly high burden of proof, that the uncertainty that is inherent in all science would mean no new technology could ever be safely introduced. He argues instead that what the precautionary principle implies is that the burden of proof is on those introducing a new technology (such as GEOs) and that the standard that must be met is the legally familiar one of "proof beyond a reasonable doubt" rather than certainty:

The precautionary principle does not deal with absolute certainty. On the contrary, it is specifically intended for circumstances in which there is no absolute certainty. It simply puts the burden of proof where it belongs, with the innovator. The requirement is to demonstrate, not absolutely but beyond reasonable doubt, that what is being proposed is safe.

When it comes to GEOs, there are a number of ways in which ISIS and other NGOs argue that introducing these organisms could turn out to be unsafe, even if there is no (or not sufficient) evidence of any harm.

In their report of April 2003 (report no. 4), "The Precautionary Principle Is Science-Based," ISIS argued that GEOs pose a grave risk to the environment. Transgenes may spread from the introduced organism to other, related organisms through out-crossing or horizontal gene transfer may occur through action of bacteria that spread genes from the GEOs to other organisms. There are also risks associated with the impact of GEOs on non-target organisms, as when Bt crops harm butterfly populations in addition to the pest they are designed to target. In addition to environmental harm, ISIS raises worries about food safety. They worry that there may be food allergies that are triggered by the expression of transgenes and even speculate that GEOs could lead to cancer (though no possible mechanism is suggested for how eating a GEO could cause cancer as opposed to the risks of human genetic engineering which has known cancer risks).[14]

The Science and Environmental Health Network (SEHN) that helped organize Wingspread raised similar concerns:

Waiting to take action before a substance or technology is proven harmful, or even until plausible cause-and-effect relationships can be established, may mean allowing irreversible harm to occur—deaths, extinctions, poisoning, and the like. Humans and the environment become the unwitting testing grounds for these technologies. Precaution advocates say this is no longer acceptable. Moreover, science should serve society, not vice versa. Any decision to take action—before or after scientific proof—is a decision of society, not science.[15]

Significantly, this statement introduces an element of hostility to science-based regulation that is a hallmark of the NGO use of the precautionary principle. Nancy Myers of the SEHN claims explicitly that "standard risk assessment . . . is only useful in conditions of relatively high certainty."[16] Opponents of GEOs argue, however, that the nature of biological entities makes genetic engineering inherently dangerous and intrinsically uncertain (and hence, presumably never safe to be introduced). Ted Schettler, also of SEHN, sees biological systems as potentially unknowable in principle. "We're talking about enormously complex interactions among a number of systems. Now we're starting to think that some of these things are probably unknowable and indeterminate."[17]

Similarly, ISIS's Saunders contrasts biological organisms from the relatively clearer nonbiological realm, where a great deal more certainty can be achieved:

We have to appreciate the difference between biological and other kinds of scientific evidence. Most experiments in physics and chemistry are relatively clear cut. If we want to know what will happen if we mix copper and sulphuric acid, we really only have to try it once. We may repeat the experiment to make sure it worked properly, but we expect to get the same result, even to the amount of hydrogen that is produced from a given amount of copper and acid. Organisms, however, vary considerably and don't behave in closely predictable ways.

Moreover, the kind of science that would be needed to understand the products of genetic engineering is not the kind of science that now exists.

SEHN's Carolyn Raffensperger claims that "science has been commodified. What we've created in the last 10 or 15 years is a science that has a goal of global economic competitiveness." Presumably this means introduction of GEOs would have to wait until science has been transformed from its current corporate-dominated approach.

A number of features of this new version of the precautionary principle are significant. First, the concept has been extended from environmental regulation to include a much broader range of concerns, including food safety and health risks. Second, while the precautionary principle was developed initially as a tool to aid risk managers in their attempts at a science-based risk assessment, the new version of the precautionary principle largely rejects risk management and the very idea of a science-based regulatory policy. Indeed, there is a growing sense of unease about science (which is often seen as influenced by corporate interests and goals). Evolving from a tool for risk managers that focused on the obligations of states and regulators, the precautionary principle has become an obligation for multiple actors, including individuals, corporations, and even whole industries. Above all, there was a shift in the nature of the principle from a reason to allow regulation (in the face of uncertainty) to a reason to prohibit or delay introduction of new organisms or new technology. We (sometimes) don't know what we don't know.

The shift in the meaning of the precautionary principle resulted in a shift in strategy. Ironically, this has resulted in an NGO strategy that mirrors the more typical corporate strategy. Some scientists continue to raise concerns about the safety and environmental impact of GEOs. However, the mainstream view (expressed by leading scientific bodies such as the National Research Council of the National Academies of Science) is that most GEOs are safe and that, in principle, the technology can be safely utilized. However, opponents of biotechnology appeal to the fact that there are minority scientific views and to the inherently unknowable nature of biological entities as grounds for claiming that GEOs have not been proved safe "beyond a reasonable doubt." At this point, continued creation of uncertainty becomes a viable strategy to avoid introduction of biotechnology.

RELIGIOUS AGNOTOLOGY

It is unsurprising that religious values would become interwoven into the debate over GEOs. Indeed, many opponents of biotechnology ground their views firmly in religious language. While there are some religiously based arguments in favor of biotechnology, I will focus here on the (largely Christian) opposition. A number of Christian groups have raised theologically and morally grounded objections to genetic engineering, ranging from concern to active opposition. The language used in these debates is quite revealing. The concept of "playing God" looms large and is featured in advertising NGOs use to oppose biotechnology. Promethean imagery and language highlight these concerns as opponents describe "frankenfoods" or "frankenfish."

In this context it was predictable that religiously based opponents of biotechnology would emerge who furthered the NGO agnotological strategy described above. Their response built on the agnogenesis expressed by groups like ISIS: they emphasized the difficulties of achieving full knowledge of the biological world. But, for religious opponents (or even more open-minded skeptics), there was also a moral dimension to attempts to "engineer" organisms. Genetic engineering represented a view of the natural world that is too instrumental, that commodified nature and the organisms in it. This view is seen as inconsistent with good stewardship, which requires balancing obligations to improve the world with obligations to preserve nature. In attempting to control and re-create the natural world, scientists exhibit a dangerous hubris—and pride goes before a fall. Religious-based opponents of biotechnology advocate instead a central role for humility, an embracing of ignorance.

A number of religious groups that work on genetic engineering have expressed this concern, both with respect to biotechnology itself and the practice of patenting the GEOs that are produced. Donald Bruce heads up the Church of Scotland's program on Society, Religion and Technology (SRT). Under Bruce, SRT explored many of the arguments in favor of and against various aspects of genetic engineering, summarized in his and his wife's *Engineering Genesis*. Here a religious agnotology is advocated in which we are urged to recognize our ignorance as a fundamental limitation on human experience, and we are urged not to intervene in matters where only God has knowledge.

There is a wisdom in the natural order of things which reflects the goodness and purposiveness of the creator. For humans to mix aspects of different organisms by genetic engineering would go beyond God's wise ordering of life. . . . It is . . . suggested that genetic engineering is an act of hubris on the part of human beings, in thinking we can alter the very fundamentals of what God has made. In our human pride we are tampering with something which we do not have the knowledge or wisdom to handle.[18]

In New Zealand, the Interchurch Commission on Genetic Engineering made a detailed submission to the Royal Commission on Genetic Modification in November 2000. This group represented the nation's Anglican, Methodist, and Presbyterian churches. In their report, the group identified a number of concerns about GEOs, emphasizing "the need to curb our natural hubris in this area" and instead to "think of the awe with which we should approach a delicate balance which has been slowly evolving to its present state before recorded time."[19]

This group emphasized the difficulty of the possibility of knowledge and how that might entail a "cautious" approach to the new technology.

There is a strong awareness that our knowledge is partial and our ability to predict the future is also partial. We see in a glass darkly and sometimes miss the interconnectedness of all things. Sometimes this makes a mockery of our sense of what is good to do and what should be approached with doubt and caution.[20]

The report also raised a common theme: that both the interconnected nature of biology and the length of time it took to produce the world are far too complex to allow casual engineering.

Calvin DeWitt, president of Au Sable Institute for Environmental Studies (a group that designs curricula for Christian universities) has claimed that "what you discover as you study biotic communities and the ecosystems of which they're a part is that this whole assemblage of different species has historically worked together through time" and criticized biotechnology for its "abuse of our knowledge of genetics, generally driven not by respect for how creation operates or how biological systems operate, but strictly driven by questions of greed or hubris."[21]

In a 2003 report, the Rural Life Committee of the North Dakota Council of Churches claimed that:

While "genetic engineering" implies a scientific precision comparable to the construction of a building or other inanimate tool or article, we recognize that plant and animal life is the result of a biological, not a manufacturing process. "Genetic engineering" seeks to establish specific and uniform genetic traits to achieve particular goals. In essence, it is an effort to industrialize biological processes to produce particular traits in agricultural commodities.

In this context, the precautionary principle can be seen as a moral and religious expression of appropriate humility in the face of human ignorance. The Rural Life Committee goes on to claim that:

We are now involved in the manipulation of life at its most elemental level. Therefore the potentials for both benefit and advancement, and catastrophe and chaos are great. Out of respect for life and creation, we must proceed with disciplines of great caution, intentionality, and patience as we enter this era. Therefore, we endorse the "Precautionary Principle" as a primary guide in the development, application and expansion of GMO biotechnology.

In summary, religious agnotology expresses the view that life is too complex for humans to fully understand and that science and technology will lead to disaster because of the hubris involved in attempting to improve on God's creation. Moreover, biotechnology represents an attempt to understand nature for the purpose of control (on behalf of corporate interests) and leads to the commodification of the natural world, which is inconsistent with good stewardship. The precautionary principle becomes a tool for curbing both hubris and the commodification of nature.

THE INDUSTRY RESPONSE: VALUE AGNOTOLOGY

There are several ways that industry has responded to the use of the precautionary principle against their interests. One part of the response has been to characterize the precautionary principle as implausible by exaggerating the claims that are made in its name. It is clearly true that many opponents of GEOs have transformed the precautionary principle into a tool for constructing uncertainty as a way of opposing new technology. John Hathcock, for example, from the Council for Responsible Nutrition (a pro-GEO group that represents the dietary supplement industry) has been a tireless critic of the precautionary principle and characterized it as requiring an "impossible burden of proof" through an unachievable "zero-risk" assessment.[22] Julian Morris, formerly of the conservative Institute of Economic Affairs, characterized Greenpeace as defining the precautionary principle as not allowing any substance until there is proof that it will "do no harm to the environment."[23] It is worth noting the contrast between this and the definition offered on their website, quoted above, "when (on the basis of available evidence) an activity may harm human health or the environment, a cautious approach should be taken in advance—even if the full extent of harm has not yet been fully established scientifically. It recognizes that such proof of harm may never be possible, at least until it is too late to avoid or reverse the damage done."

Within the United States, regulators, with the backing of industry, have largely rejected the precautionary principle. Unlike the European Union, the United States regulates the products of genetic engineering, but not the process. This means that GEOs can largely be treated as substantially equivalent to their nonengineered counterparts as long as they contain similar substances. In other words, GEOs are presumed to be safe unless there is evidence against them.[24] In this way, uncertainty becomes an ally of industry rather than its opponent. As a result, the biotech industry has largely ignored the strategy that many other industries have taken to actively construct doubt.

Internationally, industry has had a strong ally in the World Trade Organization, which has helped lighten the regulatory burden that the precautionary principle might present. The biotechnology industry and its allies have portrayed the precautionary principle as a trade barrier, claiming that only science-based, established risks can legitimize regulation that effectively prohibits the introduction of a new product (such as a GEO) into a country. For example, the European Union decision to refuse the importation of North American beef that was enhanced by Bovine Growth Hormone (BGH) on the basis of the precautionary principle was challenged by both the United States and Canada. In 1998, the WTO Appellate Body ruled that the ban was not sufficiently scientific. When the EU refused to lift its import ban, the WTO imposed a $124 million penalty and allowed punitive tariffs on some EU goods.[25] Thus, in practice, industry has been able to shield itself somewhat from the precautionary principle.

Much of the industry response to the debate has been to valorize science and to portray the precautionary principle as unscientific. While not all NGOs or regulators reject the earlier approach to the principle as a tool for risk managers, industry has successfully attacked the versions of the precautionary principle that NGOs have developed as the antithesis of science-based regulation. Interestingly, the language that is often used to defend this approach is the concept of "sound science," which is associated with both the tobacco industry and opponents of regulation.[26]

If industry has largely rejected the agnogenesis strategy, it has introduced a new kind of agnotology, which I will call "values agnotology." This constructs ignorance in the realm of values—by denying the existence or relevance of anything seen as "nonscientific"—into the regulatory risk assessment process. However, this way of framing risks bears no relationship to how most people assess risk.[27] Risk is a construction. Science-based risk assessment offers one way of constructing it. However, it is an approach that is alien to the psychology and lived experience of most people. In the realm of biotechnology, Marion Nestle has argued that risk assessment must be values based, not just science based. Instead of simply counting up costs and benefits and balancing these, other dimensions matter, such as whether risks are voluntary or imposed, whether they are familiar or foreign, whether they are natural or technological, and whether they are fairly or unfairly distributed.[28]

Industry's skepticism toward nonscience-based values leads to a fairly crude form of utilitarianism that poorly captures most of the values that are actually at stake in the debate.[29] To the extent that regulators in the United States adopt a similar agnotological stance toward values, they will fail to accord with public values, which may lead to a loss of public confidence in regulatory bodies.

CONCLUSION

The precautionary principle originated as a tool to assist in science-based risk assessment, one that would allow regulation in the face of uncertainty. In the hands of some NGOs, it became an epistemological hurdle that led to an agnotological strategy that ironically mirrored the agnogenesis strategy on the part of industry that had necessitated the creation of the precautionary principle. In response, industry has reinforced its appeal to science and developed a strategy that valorizes science-based risk as real to the exclusion of all value-based considerations. This construction of ignorance in the realm of values has led to a clash between the ways in which regulators assess and the public experiences risk. Whether this clash will lead to a politically effective challenge to the dominant regulatory approach remains to be seen.

NOTES

1. David Michaels, "Doubt Is Their Product," *Scientific American* 292, no. 6 (June 2005): 96–101.

2. Chris Mooney, *The Republican War on Science* (New York: Basic Books, 2005).

3. See Oreskes, Proctor, Michaels, this volume.

4. Kenneth Foster, Paolo Vechia, and Michael Repacholi, "Risk Management: Science and the Precautionary Principle," *Science* 288 (2000): 979–981.

5. P. Saradhi Puttagunta, "The Precautionary Principle in the Regulation of Genetically Modified Organisms," *Health Law Review* 9, no. 2 (2001): 10–17.

6. United Nations, *World Charter for Nature* (1982), http://www.un.org/documents/ga/res/37/a37r007.htm [accessed March 23, 2006].

7. *North Sea Declaration, Ministerial Declaration Calling for Reduction of Pollution* (November 25, 1987): 27 ILM 835.

8. United Nations, *Report of the United Nations Conference on Environment and Development, Rio Declaration on Environment and Development* (1992), http://www.un.org/documents/ga/conf151/aconf15126-1annex1.htm [accessed March 23, 2006].

9. David Vanderzwaag, "The Precautionary Principle in Environmental Law and Policy: Elusive Rhetoric and First Embraces," *Journal of Environmental Law Practice* 8 (1999): 355.

10. Conference of the Parties to the Convention on Biological Diversity, *Cartagena Protocol on Biosafety to the Convention of Biological Diversity* (2000), http://www.cbd.int/biosafety/protocol.shtml [accessed November 16, 2007].

11. See http://www.sehn.org/wing.html [accessed March 23, 2006].

12. See http://www.greenpeace.org/international/campaigns/trade-and-the-environment/the-precautionary-principle [accessed March 23, 2006].

13. Peter Saunders, "Use and Abuse of the Precautionary Principle," *ISIS News* no. 6 (2000), http://www.ratical.org/co-globalize/MaeWanHo/i-sisnews6.html#usea [accessed March 23, 2006].

14. ISIS submission to U.S. Advisory Committee on International Economic Policy (ACIEP) Biotech. Working Group, July 13, 2000.

15. Nancy Myers, "Debating the Precautionary Principle," *Science and Environmental Health Network* (2000), http://www.sehn.org/ppdebate.html [accessed March 23, 2006]. See also Myers, "The Precautionary Principle Puts Values First," *Bulletin of Science, Technology, and Society* 22 (2002): 210–219.

16. Myers, "Debating the Precautionary Principle."

17. Quoted in David Appell, "The New Uncertainty Principle," *Scientific American* 284 (January 2001): 18–19.

18. Donald and Ann Bruce, *Engineering Genesis* (Sterling, VA: Earthscan, 1999).

19. Interchurch Commission on Genetic Engineering, to Royal Commission on Genetic Modification, Section B.(j)(v)ii.

20. ICC report, B.(j)(v)iv.

21. Trey Popp, "God and the New Foodstuffs," *Science and Spirit* 17 (2006): 15–17. See http://www.science-spirit.org/new_detail.php?news_id=573 [accessed March 23, 2006].

22. John N. Hathcock, "The Precautionary Principle: An Impossible Burden of Proof for New Products," *AGBIOFORUM* 3 (2000): 255–259. It is worth noting that many academics share this characterization. Thus, Soren Holm and John Harris claim that "the precautionary principle will block the development of any technology if there is the slightest theoretical possibility of harm." Holm and Harris, "Precautionary Principle Stifles Discovery," *Nature* 400 (1999): 398.

23. Julian Morris, *Rethinking Risk and the Precautionary Principle* (Woburn, MA: Elsevier, 2000).

24. Volker Lehman, "From Rio to Johannesburg and Beyond: Globalizing Precaution for Genetically Modified Organisms," *Report for Heinrich Böll Foundation* (April 2002), 15. See http://www.worldsummit2002.org/texts/PrecautionGMO.pdf [accessed March 23, 2006].

25. Lehman, "From Rio to Johannesburg," 18; Bernard Goldstein, "Precautionary Principle and Endocrine Active Substances," *Pure Applied Chemistry* 75 (2003): 2515–2519.

26. Lehman, "From Rio to Johannesburg," 13.

27. Paul Slovic, *The Perception of Risk* (Sterling, VA: Earthscan, 2000).

28. Marion Nestle, *Safe Food: Bacteria, Biotechnology and Bioterrorism* (Berkeley: University of California Press, 2003).

29. David Magnus and Arthur Caplan, "The Primacy of the Moral in the GEO Debate," *Genetically Modified Foods: Debating Biotechnology*, eds. Michael Ruse and David Castle (New York: Prometheus, 2002), 80–87.

CHAPTER 12

Smoking Out Objectivity

Journalistic Gears in the Agnogenesis Machine

JON CHRISTENSEN

Historically, it would seem that the 1954 emergency was handled effectively.
From the experience there arose a realization by the tobacco industry of a public
relations problem that must be solved for the self-preservation of the industry.
Memorandum from James M. Brady to Clarence Cook Little, Subject:
Tobacco Industry Research Committee Program, April 9, 1962.[1]

MODERN CORPORATE CRISIS MANAGEMENT came of age on December 15, 1953, when the presidents of six major cigarette companies convened a secret meeting with public relations mastermind John W. Hill in New York to plan a response to alarming scientific evidence that smoking caused cancer. This was not just an acute crisis that could be dealt with in a few news cycles or even a few years. It was a chronic crisis that would have to be managed forever if an industry that caused death was to defy death. The strategies and tactics developed and lessons learned in the aftermath of that meeting came to define how corporate public relations could use journalistic values to fatally undermine public understanding and encourage ignorance in even the most clear-cut of public health cases.

Robert Proctor has used the tobacco industry as a primary case study in agnotology. He has analyzed many of the industry's strategies and tactics of agnogenesis, in science, court cases, advertising, and public relations. But the role of communications media and journalism, in particular, in agnotology has remained something of a black box. Agnogenesis goes in. Ignorance comes out.

My aim here is to propose an analytical framework for understanding how journalistic values of objectivity, fairness, balance, and facts—values that form the center of journalism's epistemology—make journalism vulnerable to being enlisted as an accomplice, even if unwilling or unwitting, in the deliberate cultural production of ignorance. I have investigated the history of the tobacco industry's use of public relations and journalism in order to complement Proctor's efforts and the growing body of research on the tobacco industry's agnogenesis. I believe that the framework could prove useful for understanding other cases in which journalism is implicated in agnotology. As a journalist myself, I also hope that this research might contribute to rectifying ignorance and reinforcing self-critical perspectives as well as values and strategies that can arm journalists against deliberate campaigns of agnogenesis.

A caveat is in order, however. This research is based on a fairly comprehensive search of the massive online tobacco industry archives pertaining to public relations, journalism, and science writing. From those documents, I have constructed a chronological and analytical narrative of the industry's shifting strategies and a typology of its tactics for involving journalists in the tobacco industry's project of creating ignorance. This research does not include an investigation of how journalists perceived the industry campaigns, except as reflected through documents in industry files and changes in industry strategies and tactics. This research also does not include an investigation of how consumers of journalism perceived the result, again except as reflected in industry sources. Both of those investigations could prove fruitful in future research to flesh out this framework for understanding the role of journalism in agnogenesis. In the meantime, I believe that this framework could be tested in other cases of agnotology involving journalism. The rather long time frame in which this history played out in the tobacco wars during the second half of the twentieth century may be truncated in other cases, in no small measure because the production of science and news has increased in volume and speed. The shifts in the tobacco industry's strategy, however, seem to be homologous to other more recent controversies that arguably involve agnogenesis, such as the attack on evolution by proponents of intelligent design and the massive industrial, political, and think tank resistance to regulations for reducing global warming.

In broad outline, the strategic shifts in the tobacco industry's development of agnogenesis through public relations and journalism went through four broad phases:

Fighting Science with Science: This first phase involved finding and funding scientific research that could be fed to journalists to argue that the industry was seriously studying the problem, on the one hand, and that there was evidence that factors other than cigarette smoking caused cancer, on the other. In this phase, the industry's stance was positivist and empiricist. It relied on journalism's esteem for facts and awe of science. This phase lasted roughly until the first Surgeon General's report in 1964, which provided public evidence coincident with internal evidence from the industry's own research that cigarette smoke contained carcinogens and smoking was the major factor associated with lung cancer.

"Doubt Is Our Product. . . . Truth Is Our Message": This second phase evolved out of the first phase when the scientific counterevidence was no longer sufficient to balance mounting evidence that smoking was the primary factor in lung cancer and a major factor in other diseases. After the Surgeon General's first report and the first warning labels mandated for cigarettes, the industry settled in for the long haul. In this phase, the industry sought to continue to sow doubt about particular facts while relying on self-evident truths, including, most significantly for this analysis, journalistic principles and values including objectivity, balance, fairness, and free speech. A June 23, 1973, handwritten note in industry files reads: "main point—keep controversy alive."[2]

Undermining Science: This third phase evolved out of the second phase in the early 1980s. When it was no longer efficacious to cast doubt on particular scientific research, the public relations front was broadened to attack entire fields and methods of science, such as epidemiology, risk analysis, statistics, modeling, and forecasting. This period was defined by the extended battles over "environmental tobacco smoke" (aka "secondhand smoke") in the early 1980s through the mid-1990s.

It's Not News: This final phase, spanning the past decade or so, could be seen as a capitulation by the industry to overwhelming evidence. It is not news that cigarette smoking causes cancer, heart disease, other illnesses, and death. There is no more controversy. This phase, however, represents the ultimate strategic triumph of an industry fighting for its survival at any cost. This "New Day," as Philip Morris executives called it, dawned when Philip Morris, along with other major tobacco companies, began to reposition the industry strategically as a "responsible manufacturer of a risky product."[3]

Like most periodizations, these are not precisely demarcated epochs. Aspects of each of these strategies can be seen in each period, which made it possible for the industry to slip from one to the other without major shifts. And in the end the industry got what it wanted in the beginning: to make it not news that smoking causes cancer. In fact, the industry would have preferred to make it not news from the beginning, but that was not possible. The tobacco industry made history, but it had to be made under conditions not entirely of its own choosing.

In the half-century-long, high-profile public health war over smoking, the ultimate result of these strategic shifts has been that cigarette manufacturers can continue to market a product that newly addicts 4,000 teenagers each day in the United States alone and kills millions of people every year around the world. A theoretical-historical concern with agnotology pales beside this human tragedy. As an accomplice to the killing, however, agnogenesis must be investigated and understood, especially as the lessons of the tobacco industry are increasingly being used in other campaigns. As early as 1962, Hill and Knowlton realized that the lessons learned in the "tobacco account" gave the company "experience and personnel for dealing with scientific and medical problems in far better fashion than we had been previously able to do. This has been of considerable help to us in being prepared to deal with similar problems of other clients."[4]

In this long, still-ongoing public relations war, science and public health have been undermined, and journalistic notions of objectivity and balance have been shown to be not just ineffective strengths, but weaknesses. The long-term effects of these trends, along with structural economic problems in the news business, are cause for great concern.

There is hope, however. Public trust in scientists and doctors remains higher than for most other professions. Journalists have other techniques they can use—investigative reporting and narratives—which complicate naive objectivity and routine balance. And there are moments in this history that demonstrate strategies and tactics for journalism and public health campaigns to work together to counter the social construction of ignorance.

HOW JOURNALISM'S HISTORICAL
STRENGTHS BECAME WEAKNESSES

It is one of the ironies of this history that objectivity, a professional code meant, in part, to free journalists from the manipulations of the new field of public relations in the early twentieth century, would in the end prove one of the most useful tools for the professional manipulators of news. Another irony is that a code of balance, meant to create a space for newspapers outside of the confines of the partisan politics of parties, which developed at the same time as an emerging trust in the empiricism of science, would leave journalists ill equipped when scientific evidence itself was politicized.

Most scholars of journalism and the history of journalism agree that objectivity in journalism is a peculiarly American invention, with British-American roots, to be sure, but born and bred in the United States. Some scholars read the roots of objectivity back to the idea of "the reliable witness" of Puritanism. Others see the roots of disinterestedness in republican ideals espoused during the colonial and revolutionary era, although ample evidence shows that the newspapers of that era were partisan and often closely tied to particular interests and emerging parties through patronage. Indeed, the ideas, concepts, and values that would eventually coalesce explicitly in objectivity in the early twentieth century seemed to have first formed clearly in reaction to the rabidly partisan press of early nineteenth-century America. David T. Z. Mindich summarizes the views of many scholars who see in "the first years of the 'penny press' in the Jacksonian era (1828–1836), the primordial soup of journalistic 'objectivity.'" Mindich writes that "the pennies were the first newspapers to formally break from political parties, and this break caused the first step toward journalistic 'objectivity': detachment." This detachment from party politics led to explicit valuing of "nonpartisan-ship," which was typically situated in the center, balanced between the poles of two-party politics.[5]

The professionalization of journalism occurred in roughly the same period, the late nineteenth and early twentieth centuries, as profession-alization in other fields, including medicine, natural sciences, and social sciences, Mindich and other scholars agree. Along with other professions that "were shifting from a paradigm of religion and philosophy to one of science," Mindich writes, "journalism was changing too, moving toward a more empirical and 'fact-based' paradigm." Mindich traces newspaper coverage of nineteenth-century cholera epidemics as an index of this shift. During this period, the medical response evolved from such horrific treat-ments as "tobacco smoke enemas" in the 1832 epidemic to "an efficient and scientific response in the 1866 epidemic" using data gathering and statistical analysis to locate and isolate outbreaks. Over the same period, Mindich writes, journalistic coverage exhibited a parallel abandonment of "atmosphere" as an explanation for cholera and a growing reverence instead for "'facts' and scientific method." Mindich calls this the era of "facticity" and "naive empiricism."[6] One is nevertheless left with admi-ration for a time when the new tools of epidemiology, statistics, and jour-nalistic investigation and reporting worked in tandem to stanch a deadly public health threat.

This journalistic ideology, however, proved vulnerable to the politi-cization of science. A stubborn and sometimes naive discourse of objec-tivity and balance—first enshrined in journalism textbooks in the early twentieth century, in part as an antidote to the rise of public relations professionals—ultimately plays into the hands of those who would ex-ploit its weaknesses, especially when coupled with another characteristic of journalism: an understandable attraction to what is new and contro-versial. In the case of cigarette smoking, this fatal attraction to what is new and controversial favored keeping controversy alive when it served the interests of the tobacco industry, while objectivity and balance always ensured room for the industry's point of view. Later, and on into the pres-ent period, the valuation of the new and controversial has made it possible to quietly bury the news of the industry's ongoing death toll. The terrible irony is that just when the industry's long history of lies was beginning to be revealed fully and there was no longer any doubt about the danger of cigarettes, it was no longer news.

A TACTICAL TOOLBOX FOR AGNOGENESIS

Public Relations Science

The tobacco industry's strategic problem was clear from the beginning in a memo written immediately after the December 1953 meeting between tobacco executives and Hill and Knowlton. "We have one essential job— which can be simply said: Stop public panic," wrote Edward DeHart, an account executive for the public relations firm, in a memo to his staff after the meeting. "There is only one problem—confidence and how to establish it; public assurance and how to create it," he added. "And, most important, how to free millions of Americans from the guilty fear that is going to arise deep in their biological depths—regardless of any pooh-poohing logic—every time they light a cigarette."[7]

Hill and Knowlton executives knew they had a public relations challenge because that was how they defined it. They were not scientists. They were public relations men. "The public relations problem of the cigarette industry is complicated because the health issue is more emotional than scientific," declared a briefing for Hill and Knowlton executives in 1962. "And it is newsworthy. It's hard to think of a news item that could interest more people than one which combines tobacco use—some 70 million smokers and a good many nonsmokers feel intensively about tobacco— and unsolved health problems—which interest almost everyone. Combine smoking and health, and you've got news for the masses."[8]

DeHart's memo is frank—more frank than the "Frank Statement" that the tobacco companies were soon persuaded to have printed in newspapers around the country committing themselves to an open scientific investigation of the health effects of smoking. "At the moment, these men feel thrown for a loop," DeHart wrote about the tobacco executives. "They've competed for years—not in price, not in any real difference of quality—but just in ability to conjure up hypnotic claims and brighter assurances for what their own brand might do for a smoker, compared to another brand. And now, suddenly, they feel all out of bounds because the old claims became unimportant overnight; they suddenly are challenged to produce just one, simple fact."[9]

The Tail of the Kite

From the beginning, science and public relations would be twisted together, and the public relations professionals, not being scientists themselves, would deliver over their professional services to the tobacco industry's version of science.[10] John W. Hill, a principal in the firm that bore his name, insisted that the tobacco companies had to pursue scientific answers to the question of whether cigarette smoking caused cancer, but this was first and foremost a public relations move. And it worked. As Waldemar Keempffert, at the time the "dean of the country's scientific writers," according to Hill and Knowlton, wrote in the *New York Times*: "The case for and against tobacco consumption as a cause of cancer may be settled by the Tobacco Industry's Research Committee of which Dr. C. C. Little, former director of the American Cancer Society, is head. Many will argue that an impartial investigation can hardly be expected from a body of experts paid by the tobacco industry. Dr. Little is an eminent geneticist, a type of scientist who has the courage to face facts and to state them."[11]

Keempffert wasn't the only one to give the tobacco research a favorable pass based on Little's reputation as a scientist. "News handling of the announcement story was nearly 100 per cent favorable," a Hill and Knowlton memo reported. Moreover, 65 percent of the newspapers that published editorials on the committee were favorable. Only 9 percent were unfavorable. "In 1953, no voice was being raised in behalf of industry," reported a confidential Hill and Knowlton memo on the first six months of public relations activities on behalf of the research council. "The bulk of editorial comment now appearing approves and, at times, applauds the action of the industry."[12]

In the summer of 1954, when the *New York Times* reported on a study showing that "cigarette smokers from 50 to 70 years of age have a higher death rate, from all disease, as much as 75 percent higher than that of non-smokers," Little was able to garner a story in the paper the very next day characterizing the study as "preliminary" and "statistical." Senator

Maurine Neuberger, who later sponsored the first warning label legislation for cigarettes and wrote a book about the industry entitled *Smoke Screen*, described this strategy as being like "a tail of a kite, no story about the risk of smoking goes anywhere without a tobacco industry rebuttal trailing along behind." Even more important were stories that never appeared because Hill and Knowlton got wind of them and managed to persuade producers not to air them, such as "one negatively-aimed program (WNBT) which was being scheduled on the cigarette controversy [and] was postponed after a discussion of TIRC facts." This took a personal touch and inside information.[13]

The Personal Touch

Carl Thompson, a Hill and Knowlton account executive, told a staff gathering in 1962: "What we do for tobacco has been said to resemble an iceberg—only one-ninth of it can be seen—the rest is submerged and unseen but important." At that meeting, Thompson introduced Leonard Zahn, the man responsible for much of the invisible work of Hill and Knowlton on behalf of the tobacco industry for most of the 1950s and 1960s. He went on to flack for the industry for nearly three more decades. Zahn worked for Hill and Knowlton on the tobacco account from January 1954 until the company let the contract expire in the mid-1960s. Zahn then went to work for the Tobacco Research Council as an independent public relations consultant. He occasionally wrote stories for two obscure medical newsletters, one in Germany the other in the United States, so that he could qualify to join the National Association of Science Writers and volunteer for many activities essential to the volunteer professional organization over the years, and Hill and Knowlton boasted of having a founding member of the science writers association on staff.[14]

"Len has been trouble-shooting at scientific meetings, conventions, panels of scientists and science writers, press conferences—anywhere that tobacco has come under attack," Thompson boasted at the 1962 "Inside H&K" staff meeting. "Len Zahn has often been the Daniel in the Lions Den. As the man on the spot at a meeting where an adverse attack is being made, Len goes right into the press room with the T.I.R.C. answer and sees that the correspondents working on the stories have our side to go right into their first stories. This takes some doing. And it takes good contacts with the science writers."[15]

David Zimmerman, a science writer who later exposed Zahn's duplicity to the National Association of Science Writers, remembered that many of Zahn's most productive contacts were inclined to see smoking as a personal risk, knowingly taken. "His memos and reports do not say that many, if not most of his press contacts were, as we recall, smokers," Zimmerman wrote. "This minority of smokers among the science press was, in effect, Zahn's potent secret weapon." Over the years, the industry continued to keep close track of reporters, whenever possible noting whether they smoked or not. A 1988 memo notes that Jerry Bishop, a reporter for the *Wall Street Journal*, was given a carton of Premiers—"he likes them," noted a Hill and Knowlton memo. Some reporters, such as Irv Molotsky of the *New York Times*, were deemed "objective" about smoking. On the other hand, Marlene Cimons, a reporter from the *Los Angeles Times* was considered "a foe." According to the memo, "This lady could be trouble."[16]

THE BALANCE ROUTINE

Within the first few years of the tobacco industry campaign, a pattern of tactics was established for exploiting journalistic values of balance, fairness, and objectivity to keep bad news about cigarettes out of the media as much as possible, and when that was not possible to ensure that the industry's point of view was represented in any story that appeared or in a balancing story that followed. This was done by attending scientific meetings, where results were announced to journalists, issuing anticipatory press announcements about tobacco industry research to counterbalance research announcements about smoking and cancer, and vigilantly complaining to editors and publishers when reports were published that did not sufficiently represent the industry's position, and when any doubt could be cast on reporting. The industry complained early and often. In one of the earliest instances, a telegram was sent to Henry Luce, following a June 11, 1956, article in *Life* complaining of a "one-sided discussion of the cigarette–lung cancer issue."[17]

These tactics were remarkably consistent through the years, though over the years they were ratcheted up in scale and became more formal as the industry public relations effort moved from the personal era exemplified by Leonard Zahn to the professional era personified by Chris Cory, a former editor of *Psychology Today* who joined the Corporate Affairs Department of Philip Morris in the mid-1980s. Cory designed an "objectivity index" meant to provide a standard for measuring reporters based on the code of ethics of Sigma Delta Chi, the professional journalism society. The industry was still centrally concerned with using principles of balance to get its own arguments in the media, but under the direction of Cory and others, it was coming to believe that a more aggressive approach would be needed to continue to carve out this space. Philip Morris would "constantly remind the press that there continues to be two sides to all of the controversies surrounding cigarettes." Over the years, this campaign focused on what one letter to the *Newport Daily News* called "the canons of journalism we at Philip Morris thought still applied . . . that news articles should incorporate balance, accuracy and fairness." In a letter to the *Milwaukee Sentinel*, another rule was cited: "The one iron-clad rule of journalism which we at Philip Morris thought still applied was that the subject of an attack is given the chance to respond (or at least the attempt is made) before the story airs."[18]

As the news cycle accelerated in the late 1990s, Philip Morris responded by developing an early warning system and rapid response "to decrease the amount of time between identification of inaccuracies/bias and finalization of response." By 1997, the budget for this "Media Fairness Program" had grown to $250,000 a year. "We do not expect the media's endorsement," read the plan for that year, "we are simply asking for the chance to give the facts and arguments."[19]

Soundly Attacking Science

Although the tobacco industry public relations campaign continued to stress objectivity, fairness, and balance in its communications with reporters and editors, the industry's strategy made a profound shift in the 1980s. When "secondhand smoke" became a cause of concern, following the 1981 publication of a study showing that nonsmoking wives of smokers were more likely to get lung cancer the more their husbands smoked, the battleground shifted, not just scientifically but ideologically. Exposure to the risks of smoking was no longer just personal and voluntary. Smoking affected nonsmokers involuntarily. The industry's argument began to shift over time from defending the rights of smokers to a full-blown attack on science.

Chris Cory came to Philip Morris eager to mount a campaign that would "raise public skepticism about science reporting" and "help us and the industry make common cause with companies in other fields like chemicals and drugs, and with parts of the foundation and scientific establishment which also are critical of science reporting." In 1990, Philip Morris budgeted $2.5 million for an ETS (environmental tobacco smoke) Communication Plan to "maintain the controversy and correct misinformation about tobacco smoke in public and scientific forums," including media briefings, a science journalists conference, and publishing reports around the world on sick-building syndrome. A year later, another plan to "generate a more balanced media presentation of ETS issues" was budgeted at $450,000 and included sponsoring educational programs for journalists "regarding the flaws in the risk assessment process and the way to accurately report on these issues," and identifying journalists and publications "opposed to government regulations that are based on inaccurate science."[20]

Often these journalists worked for conservative and libertarian publications, such as *Reason*, and their skeptical reporting could be used then to feed a media food chain consisting of conservative think tanks, campaigns such as the Advancement of Sound Science Coalition, columnists, and editorial pages. This campaign was augmented with a nationwide network of public relations consultants who monitored the press and coordinated the publication of letters to the editor and op-eds in response to reporting on any attempts to regulate indoor smoking. Through these public relations tactics, the tobacco industry was able simultaneously to maintain a semblance of balance in mainstream journalism while reinforcing its anti-regulatory campaign among conservative and libertarian media. This was crucial for maintaining its base among smokers, industrial allies, conservative politicians, and other industries opposed to regulation, and it allowed the industry to survive and maintain its base of strength up to and through the settlements that it reached with the state attorneys general in 1998.

No News Is Good News, Again

In the run-up to the settlement, a draft memo on "resolution & reconciliation strategy" by a strategic planning group at Philip Morris called this a "New Day" that would require defining what makes "a responsible marketer and manufacturer of [a] risky product."[21] Ironically, this brought the tobacco industry public relations campaign back to square one, except now the cigarette companies could proceed with marketing a risky product without worrying about scientific debates over its effects in an era in which the risk was no longer news. The settlement itself was news, of course, but it settled the controversy and ended the debate and with that much of what drives journalism.

In the fall of 2005, a study was published showing that viewing smoking in movies was the primary variable affecting whether teenagers smoked, but journalists could dismiss it as not news. Reports that did appear were short, buried deep in the newspapers, and bore no response from the tobacco industry. This final stage suggests another kind of agnogenesis is now at work different from the active construction of ignorance that the industry was engaged in earlier through deception, distraction, and demanding balance. The industry is now benefiting from what psychologists call habituation or desensitization, a response to something so constant and omnipresent that it is ignored. What everyone knows is no longer noteworthy. It may be one of the most useful and ultimately powerful forms of agnogenesis available.

HOW TO WIN THE WAR, AFTER LOSING EVERY BATTLE

When the tobacco industry conspiracy campaign began on December 11, 1953—the day tobacco company executives first met and agreed to schedule a meeting four days later with Hill and Knowlton—the conspirators let their positivism get them into something of a pickle. At John W. Hill's insistence, they made a commitment to science. They may have been cynical, or they may have sincerely believed that science would vindicate their product. Looking back, their sincerity seems doubtful. Even before doubt was acknowledged as their product, they began selling doubt. By the early 1960s, their cynicism was beyond doubt. It was then that their commitment to science became a commitment to lie about particular facts in the name of doubt, while touting the truth of abstract principles as their message. Their own scientists were telling them they had problems. Still they continued to fight science with science. After the 1964 Surgeon General's report, however, doubt, rather than science, became the industry's primary ideological weapon.[22] There was no longer reasonable hope of scientific vindication or that the industry could create a safe cigarette. Sowing doubt was steadily transformed from the dirty business of attacking particular scientists and studies and touting others into a wholesale attack on the science on which public health depends, which reached a crescendo in the battles over secondhand smoke in the 1980s and early 1990s. When that campaign succumbed to the wave of regulation of smoking in public places that is still sweeping the country, and the industry negotiated a settlement with state attorneys general, the public relations machine entered a new phase, the present phase, in which no news is good news, and the best news is no news at all.

In the end, the conspirators of December 1953 got exactly what they wanted: long life for their companies and their products, if not for their customers. Tobacco companies have won settlements that keep them alive, and they have rendered the widespread knowledge that they are marketing deadly products not news. It is hard to imagine a better outcome for cigarette companies. Ironically, they would win by losing. The industry public relations effort would succeed in managing this permanent crisis by first arguing that there was no controversy, then by keeping the controversy alive, and finally by returning to the position that there is no controversy.

Some observers of this history have argued that journalists have played a role in this case of agnogenesis because they have not adhered strongly enough to journalistic standards of fairness, balance, objectivity, and facts. They believe that journalistic ethics must be more strictly enforced to prevent journalists from reporting the tobacco industry's line.[23] On the contrary, I would argue that this half-century public relations war has proven that these journalistic standards render journalism constitutionally unfit, in general, to deal effectively with this kind of strategic manipulation of journalistic standards in the service of agnogenesis.

In order to not be accomplices in the social construction of ignorance, journalists must be more confident of what they know and how they know it. Investigative journalism provides a model and a long-standing, successful alternative that employs an engaged conscience, empiricism and verification, and the morality of the narrative form as powerful counterweights to the principles of objectivity, balance, and fairness.[24] Much of the best journalism on tobacco has been investigative journalism. Unfortunately, the business of journalism is not geared for regularly producing investigative journalism. Investigative journalism is the exception rather than the rule, but investigative journalism is not the only alternative.

In 1984, a *Newsday* article headlined "Steering young people to a smoke-free future" provided an example of a moral narrative in a story that was not investigative. It ended with a quote from Larry Hagman, the star of the hit TV show "Dallas." Hagman had enlisted in a campaign—the "Non-Smoking Generation"—to persuade kids that smoking was not cool. "When I was a kid, all the role models smoked," Hagman said. "Humphrey Bogart, John Wayne, Clark Gable. They smoked, so we smoked." The *Newsday* reporter Michael Unger added his own kicker: "All heavy smokers, John Wayne and Humphrey Bogart died of lung cancer, and Clark Gable died of heart attack." Somewhere inside a tobacco company, a diligent watchdog scrawled on a clipping of the story: "We should tell media: if you're going to fight, fight fair." [25] Industry insiders knew that tobacco companies could always survive in a fair fight, even while their customers continued to die.

NOTES

This chapter is based largely on documents found in online tobacco industry archives. The Bates number refers to a unique code for retrieving the specific document from online archives. Thanks to Lisa Bero of the University of California, San Francisco, for documents collected in searches conducted by Joshua Dunsby for materials related to journalism and science writing in the archives.

1. "April 9, 1962 Memorandum to C. C. Little from J. M. Brady, Subject: TIRC Program," L. Zahn Exhibit 4, in Deposition of Leonard Zahn, in *Commonwealth of Massachusetts v. Philip Morris Inc. et al.* (5/28/98), 91–92, Bates 70000662.

2. An internal document on a public relations campaign for the cigarette company Brown and Williamson stated: "Doubt is our product since it is the best means of competing with the 'body of fact' that exists in the mind of the general public. It is also the means

of establishing a controversy. Within the business we recognize that a controversy exists. However, with the general public the consensus is that cigarettes are in some way harmful to the health. If we are successful at establishing a controversy at the public level, then there is an opportunity to put across the real facts about smoking and health. Doubt is also the limit of our 'product.' Unfortunately, we cannot take a position directly opposing the anti-cigarette forces and say that cigarettes are a contributor to good health. No information that we have supports such a claim. Truth is our message because of its power to withstand a conflict and sustain a controversy. If in our pro-cigarette efforts we stick to well-documented fact, we can dominate a controversy and operate with the confidence of justifiable self-interest." "Smoking and Health Proposal," in *The Cigarette Papers*, ed. Stanton A. Glantz, John Slade, Lisa A. Bero, Peter Hanauer, Debora E. Barnes (Berkeley: University of California Press, 1996), 190–191. This passage is in itself worthy of an extended interpretation. For now, suffice it to say that the slippery terrain between selling doubt as a product and using truth as a message, is an apt marker of the transition underway in the industry's strategy at this time. The "keep controversy alive" quote comes from a handwritten note from industry files headed "Sterling" and dated 7/23/73, in author's files, Bates number illegible.

3. David Greenberg, Vic Han, Ellis Woodward, Jim Pontarelli, Rick Daniels, Peggy Kasza, "Draft memorandum on 'Resolution & Reconciliation Strategy'" (3/17/98), Bates 2063532497.

4. "'Smoking, Health and Statistics: The Story of the Tobacco Accounts,' Script of Presentation of T.I.R.C. and T.I. For 'Inside H&K'" (2/26/62), Bates 98721519.

5. Jennifer Howard, "Verbatim" (Interview with Steven R. Knowlton), *The Chronicle of Higher Education* (8/12/05), A14; David T. Z. Mindich, *Just the Facts: How "Objectivity" Came to Define American Journalism* (New York: New York University Press, 1998), 12–13. See also Jeffrey L. Pasley, *The Tyranny of Printers: Newspaper Politics in the Early American Republic* (Charlottesville: University of Virginia Press, 2001); Bill Kovach and Tom Rosensteil, *The Elements of Journalism: What Newspeople Should Know and the Public Should Expect* (New York: Three Rivers, 2001); Dan Schiller, *Objectivity and the News: The Public and the Rise of Commercial Journalism* (Philadelphia: University of Pennsylvania Press, 1981); Leonard W. Levy, *Emergence of a Free Press* (New York: Oxford University Press, 1985); Michael Schudson, *Discovering the News: A Social History of American Newspapers* (New York: Basic Books, 1978); Stephen J. A. Ward, *The Invention of Journalism Ethics: The Path to Objectivity and Beyond* (Montreal: McGill–Queen's University Press, 2004); Charles E. Rosenberg, *The Cholera Years: The United States in 1832, 1849, and 1866* (Chicago: University of Chicago Press, 1987).

6. Mindich, *Just the Facts*, 13–14, 95–112.

7. Hill and Knowlton, "Forwarding Memorandum to Members of the Planning Committee" (1953), 7, 3, http://www.ttlaonline.com/HKWIS/0375.pdf.

8. "Smoking, Health and Statistics," Bates 987215346.

9. Hill and Knowlton, "Forwarding Memorandum to Members of the Planning Committee," 2.

10. Hill and Knowlton, "Background Material on the Cigarette Industry Client" (12/15/53), http://www.ttlaonline.com/HKWIS/0295.pdf; Karen K. Jasa, "Confidential/ Attorney Work Product to Allen R. Purvis, Re: Summary of Important Documents in John W. Hill Collection" (5/7/90), Bates 680704707.

11. Hill and Knowlton, Inc., "To: T. V. Hartnett, Chairman, Tobacco Industry Research

Committee. From: Hill and Knowlton, Inc. Subject: Report of Activities through July 31, 1954," Bates 82106821.

12. "John W. Hill II, Health and Morality—Tobacco's Counter Campaign," Bates 2022849014.

13. "John W. Hill II, Health and Morality," Bates 2022849014–9015, 2022849018A; Hill and Knowlton, Inc., "To: T. V. Hartnett," Bates 82106838.

14. "Smoking, Health and Statistics," 7, Bates 98721520; Jasa, "Confidential/Attorney Work Product," Bates 680704712.

15. "Smoking, Health and Statistics," Bates 98721531–1532.

16. David Zimmerman, "Exposé 'Journalist' Conned Colleagues for 35 Years as Spy for Tobacco," *Probe Newsletter* (4/99); David Kalson, "Science Writers and Premier" (12/5/88), Bates 515280990; "Key Medical Reporters Individual Analysis of Coverage," Bates 506122355/2358.

17. Hill and Knowlton, Inc., "Confidential Public Relations Report on the Tobacco Industry Research Committee, Tuesday, October 9, 1956," Bates 501941613–1614.

18. Philip Morris USA Corporate Affairs Department, "Strategy and Tactics Combating Smoking Issues" (c. 1985), 7, 13, Bates 2021502332; "Draft LTE to Newport Daily News," Bates 2047009030-9031; "To Richard Brady, Editor, Milwaukee Sentinel" (10/4/89), Bates 2047009065.

19. "Media Accuracy and Fairness," Bates 2078323747; Beverly Tolbert, "Media Fairness" (8/20/97), Bates 2073830679B; "Media Fairness Program," Bates 2047726092.

20. Chris Cory, "Better Science Reporting" (8/15/85), Bates 2021273536; "ETS Communication/Merchandising," Bates 2023856040–6041; "Goal: Generate a More Balanced Media Presentation of ETS Issue" (c. 1991), Bates 2023281664.

21. Greenberg et al., "Draft memorandum on 'Resolution & Reconciliation Strategy,'" Bates 2065297762.

22. After reviewing internal documents from the tobacco industry, C. Everett Koop, the Surgeon General from 1981 to 1989, concluded "that the tobacco industry was demoralized and in disarray in the mid-1960s, but the public voluntary health agencies and others did not take the kind of decisive action against the industry that some inside the industry expected and feared." C. Everett Koop, "Foreword," in *The Cigarette Papers*, ed. Glantz et al., xiv. In fact, it seems rather that the industry learned and adapted in what became a major turning point, first by withholding scientific information from the surgeon general, then by weathering the warning label, and finally by recognizing that doubt was its product in the realm of smoking and health.

23. See, for example, Monique E. Muggli, Richard D. Hurt, and Lee B. Becker, "Turning Free Speech into Corporate Speech," *Preventive Medicine* 39 (2004), 576–577.

24. James S. Ettema and Theodore L. Glasser, *Custodians of Conscience: Investigative Journalism and Public Virtue* (New York: Columbia University Press, 1998).

25. Michael Unger, "Steering Young People to Smoke-Free Future," *Newsday* (August 8, 1984), with handwritten note, Bates 2023650553.

Contributors

JON CHRISTENSEN was a full-time environmental reporter and science writer for twenty years before deciding to return to Stanford University to work on a PhD in history, after visiting for a year on a John S. Knight Fellowship, a midcareer sabbatical for professional journalists. His work has appeared in the *New York Times Science Times*, *High Country News*, *San Francisco Chronicle Book Review*, and other newspapers, magazines, and journals, including *Nature*, *Conservation in Practice*, and *Environmental History*.

ERIK M. CONWAY is a historian of science and technology at the Jet Propulsion Laboratory, California Institute of Technology, Pasadena, California. He has published two books, *High-Speed Dreams: NASA and the Technopolitics of Supersonic Transportation, 1945–1999* (Johns Hopkins University Press, 2005) and *Blind Landings: Low-Visibility Operations in American Aviation, 1918–1958* (Johns Hopkins University Press, 2006), examining the intersection of aviation technologies and the natural environment, and has recently completed a history of atmospheric science at NASA under contract to the National Aeronautics and Space Administration. His contributions to this volume are drawn from this work.

PETER GALISON is the Joseph Pellegrino University Professor at Harvard University. His books include *How Experiments End* (University of Chicago Press, 1987), *Image and Logic: A Material Culture of Microphysics* (University of Chicago Press Press, 1997), *Einstein's Clocks, Poincaré's Maps: Empires of Time* (W. W. Norton, 2003), and *Objectivity* (with Lorraine Daston, Zone Books, 2007); he has coedited volumes on the relations between science, art, architecture, and authorship. Over the last years he coproduced a documentary film on the politics of science, *Ultimate Weapon: The H-Bomb Dilemma* (2000), and in 2008, with Robb Moss, completed a second, *Secrecy*, about the architecture and dynamics of state secrecy.

DAVID MAGNUS, PHD, is director of Stanford University's Center for Biomedical Ethics, where he is associate professor of pediatrics. His research focuses on the history and philosophy of biology and bioethics, including issues in genetics, stem cell research, and biotechnology. He is the principal editor of a collection of essays entitled *Who Owns Life?* (Prometheus, 2002) and he is coeditor of the *American Journal of Bioethics*. He served on the Secretary of Agriculture's Advisory Committee on Biotechnology and 21st Century Agriculture and on the National Research Council Ad Hoc Committee on Bioconfinement of Genetically Engineered Organisms. He currently serves on the California Human Stem Cell Research Advisory Committee.

ADRIENNE MAYOR is an independent scholar of folklore and the history of science, and a Visiting Fellow in Classics, and the History and Philosophy of Science, at Stanford University. She is the author of *The First Fossil Hunters: Paleontology in Greek and Roman Times* (Princeton University Press, 2000), *Greek Fire, Poison Arrows & Scorpion Bombs: Biological and Chemical Warfare in the Ancient World* (Overlook Duckworth, 2003), *Fossil Legends of the First Americans* (Princeton University Press, 2005), and numerous scholarly and popular articles on classical and indigenous natural knowledge.

DAVID MICHAELS is research professor and director of the Project on Scientific Knowledge and Public Policy at the George Washington University School of Public Health and Health Services. From 1998 to 2001, he served as the U.S. Department of Energy's Assistant Secretary for Environment, Safety and Health, where he had responsibility for protecting the health and safety of workers, the neighboring communities, and the environment surrounding the nation's nuclear weapons complex. He is the author of *Doubt Is Their Product: How Industry's Assault on Science Threatens Your Health* (Oxford University Press, 2008). Many of his publications, including *Manufacturing Uncertainty: Contested Science and the Protection of the Public's Health and Environment* (American Journal of Public Health, 2005), can be found at http://www.DefendingScience.org.

CHARLES W. MILLS is John Evans Professor of Moral and Intellectual Philosophy at Northwestern University. He works in the general area of oppositional political theory, and is the author of four books: *The Racial Contract* (Cornell University Press, 1997), *Blackness Visible: Essays on Philosophy and Race* (Cornell University Press, 1998), *From Class to Race: Essays in White Marxism and Black Radicalism* (Rowman & Littlefield, 2003), and, with Carole Pateman, *Contract and Domination* (Polity, 2007).

NAOMI ORESKES is professor of history and science studies at the University of California, San Diego, and studies the historical development of scientific knowledge, methods, and practices in the earth and environmental sciences. Her 2004 essay "The Scientific Consensus on Climate Change" (*Science* 306: 1686) led to op-ed pieces in the *Washington Post*, *Los Angeles Times*, and *San Francisco Chronicle*, and has been widely cited, including in the *New Yorker*, *USA Today*, the Royal Society's publication, "A Guide to Facts and Fictions about Climate Change," and the documentary film, *An Inconvenient Truth*. In 2006, she testified in the U.S. Senate on the history of climate science, and she will soon appear in "Sizzle," a comedy about global warming.

ROBERT N. PROCTOR is professor of the history of science at Stanford University and the author of *Racial Hygiene* (Harvard University Press, 1988), *Value-Free Science?* (Harvard University Press, 1991), *Cancer Wars* (Basic Books, 1995), and *The Nazi War on Cancer* (Princeton University Press, 1999). He has held positions as Senior Scholar in Residence at the U.S. Holocaust Memorial Museum in Washington, DC (1994) and as Visiting Fellow at the Max-Planck-Institute for the History of Science in Berlin (1999–2000); he is also a member of the American Academy of Arts and Sciences. He is now working on human origins (especially changing interpretations of the oldest tools), a book titled *Darwin in the History of Life*, a book on gemstone aesthetics ("Agate Eyes"), and a book on how and when tobacco hazards came to be recognized (and denied). He was the first historian to testify as an expert witness against the tobacco industry, and continues to testify as a witness in cases where "who knew what when" is in question.

LONDA SCHIEBINGER is the John L. Hinds Professor of History of Science and the Barbara D. Finberg Director of the Clayman Institute for

Gender Research at Stanford University. Her books include *The Mind Has No Sex? Women in the Origins of Modern Science* (Harvard University Press, 1989), the prize-winning *Nature's Body: Gender in the Making of Modern Science* (Beacon, 1993/Rutgers University Press, 2004), *Has Feminism Changed Science?* (Harvard University Press, 1999), the prize-winning *Plants and Empire: Colonial Bioprospecting in the Atlantic World* (Harvard University Press, 2004), and *Gendered Innovations in Science and Engineering* (Stanford University Press, 2008). Schiebinger is the recipient of numerous awards, including the prestigious Alexander von Humboldt Research Prize.

MICHAEL J. SMITHSON is a professor in the School of Psychology at The Australian National University in Canberra. He is the author of *Confidence Intervals* (Sage, 2003), *Statistics with Confidence* (Sage, 2000), *Ignorance and Uncertainty* (Springer Verlag, 1989), and *Fuzzy Set Analysis for the Behavioral and Social Sciences* (Springer Verlag, 1987); coauthor of *Fuzzy Set Theory: Applications in the Social Sciences* (Sage, 2006); and coeditor of *Resolving Social Dilemmas: Dynamic, Structural, and Intergroup Aspects* (Psychology Press, 1999) and *Uncertainty and Risk: Multidisciplinary Perspectives* (Earthscan, 2008). His primary research interests are in judgment and decision making under ignorance and uncertainty, social dilemmas, applications of fuzzy logic, and statistical methods.

NANCY TUANA is the DuPont/Class of 1949 Professor of Philosophy, Science, Technology, and Society and Women's Studies and director of the Rock Ethics Institute at the Pennsylvania State University. Her research and teaching specialties include feminist science studies, with particular attention to the intersection of ethical and epistemological issues in science, feminist theory, philosophy and sexuality, and environmental ethics. Her books include *Engendering Rationalities* (Indiana University Press, 2001), *Feminism and Science* (Indiana University Press, 1989), *The Less Noble Sex: Scientific, Religious, and Philosophical Conceptions of Woman's Nature* (Indiana University Press, 1993), *Revealing Male Bodies* (Indiana University Press, 2002), *Race and the Epistemologies of Ignorance* (SUNY Press, 2007), and *Women and the History of Philosophy* (Continuum/Paragon House, 1992). She is series editor of the Penn State Press series *ReReading the Canon*, and coeditor of the *Stanford Encyclopedia*'s entries on feminist philosophy.

ALISON WYLIE, professor of philosophy at the University of Washington, is a philosopher of science who focuses on issues raised by archaeological practice and by feminist philosophy of science. Her publications include *Thinking from Things: Essays in the Philosophy of Archaeology* (University of California Press, 2002), *Value-Free Science? Ideals and Illusions* (coeditor, Oxford University Press, 2007), *Doing Archaeology as a Feminist* (coeditor, *JAMT* 14.3, 2007), *Epistemic Diversity and Dissent* (editor, *Episteme* 3.1, 2006), and essays that appear in *Embedding Ethics* (Berg, 2005), *Science and Other Cultures* (Routledge, 2003), *Feminism in Twentieth-Century Science* (University of Chicago Press, 2001), and *The Cambridge Companion to Feminism in Philosophy* (Cambridge University Press, 2000).

Index

CPSIA information can be obtained
at www.ICGtesting.com
Printed in the USA
LVHW111042130123
737110LV00004B/36

9 780804 759014